Computer Privacy
ANNOYANCES™

How to Avoid the Most ANNOYING Invasions
of Your Personal and Online Privacy

Dan Tynan

O'REILLY®

Beijing · Cambridge · Farnham · Köln · Paris · Sebastopol · Taipei · Tokyo

Computer Privacy Annoyances™
How to Avoid the Most Annoying Invasions of Your Personal and Online Privacy

by Dan Tynan

Copyright © 2005 O'Reilly Media, Inc. All rights reserved.
Printed in the United States of America.

Illustrations © 2005 Hal Mayforth c/o theispot.com.

Published by O'Reilly Media, Inc., 1005 Gravenstein Highway North,
Sebastopol, CA 95472.

O'Reilly books may be purchased for educational, business, or sales promotional
use. Online editions are also available for most titles *(safari.oreilly.com)*. For more
information, contact our corporate/institutional sales department: 800-998-9938 or
corporate@oreilly.com.

Print History:		**Editor:**	Robert Luhn
July 2005:	First Edition.	**Production Editor:**	Philip Dangler
		Art Director:	Michele Wetherbee
		Cover Concept:	Volume Design, Inc.
		Cover Designer:	Ellie Volckhausen
		Interior Designer:	Patti Capaldi

RepKover™ This book uses RepKover™, a durable and flexible lay-flat binding.

0-596-00775-2
[C]

Contents

Introduction   vii

① PRIVACY AT RISK

2   The Spy on Your Desk
2   Dawn of the Undead PC
4   Working for the Man
5   The Information Explosion
6   The Data Industrial Complex
8   Location, Location, Location

② PRIVACY AT HOME

12 My Data, Myself
12   One Computer, Many Eyeballs
13   Foil Hard Disk Snoops
15   No Vault Insurance
15   Hide in Plain Sight
16   Complete Delete
16   Watch Your Backups
19   Microsoft Confidential
20   Cleaning up for Charity

21 Home Sweet Networks
21   Stop WiFi Drive Bys
21   Share and Unshare Alike

23 Cell Phones
23   Spam to Go
24   Cell Phone Candid Camera
24   Moblog Rules
26   Wireless Wiretaps?

26 Telemarketing, Junk Mail, and Faxes
26   Don't Ask, Don't Telemarket
26   Do Not Call Does Not Work
27   Block that Scam
28   Just the Fax, Ma'am
29   Junking Junk Mail
29   Flag Mag Nags
30   Pick Your Mail

30 Identity Theft
30   Foil Mailbox Miscreants
31   Check Your Reports
32   Stop, ID Thief!

③ PRIVACY ON THE NET

34 Browsing Around
34   Erase Your Browser's Footprints, Part 1
35   Erase Your Browser's Footprints, Part Deux
36   Make Web Forms Shoot Blanks
36   Rewrite Netscape's History
36   Maximum Privacy, Maximum Headaches
39   Tell People Finders to Get Lost
40   Fend off Cyber Stalkers
41   Make Ad Weasels Go Pop
41   Spies You Should Despise
42   Die Spy Die!
43   Change Browsers and Dance
44   Shoot the Messenger

45 Email

45 Spam Bam, No Thank You Ma'am

45 Whose Address Is It, Anyway?

46 Nix Those Nasty Pix

47 Declare War on Spam, Part I

47 Declare War on Spam, Part Deux

49 There Oughta Be a Law. Wait, There Is a Law!

49 Fight Fire with Water

50 Don't Bank on It

52 Watching the (Digital) Detectives

52 Swat Web Bugs

52 Enquiring Minds Don't Really Want to Know

52 Free Web Mail, Free Spam

53 Hackers, Viruses, and Worms—Oh My!

53 Attack of the Data-Eating Zombies

55 Don't Get Too Attached

55 Friends Don't Let Friends Open Attachments

56 Antivirus Software Is Not Enough

57 Stop Spreading the News

57 Make Updates Automatic

58 Online Shopping

58 Give Credit Where Credit is Due...

58 ...But Don't Take Undue Credit

60 They Know When You've Been Shopping

60 You Are What You Buy

61 Would You Like Spam with That?

62 99.44% Hacker Safe

63 Online File Swapping

63 I Share the Songs That Make the Whole World Sing...

64 The Sue Me, Sue You Blues

64 Avoid P2P Vermin

65 Kids and the Net

65 Let Internet Explorer Play Web Cop

66 Hire a Nanny

67 Thanks for Not Sharing

68 I H8 IM

70 Privacy @ Large

70 Whois Stalking Me?

71 Antidotes for Domain Poisoning

71 Bloggers are from Mars, Lawyers are from Venus

72 Usenet or Lose It

4 PRIVACY AT WORK

74 The Internet at Work

74 Surfing on Company Time

76 Visit NasteePix.com, Get Fired?

77 Out of the Office, But Not Out of Sight

78 Whose Email is it, Anyway?

79 Beware of IT Spies

79 Chewing the Fat on Chat

80 Do Your Hunting From Home

81 Applying for Work

81 This is Your Job on Drugs

82 The Background on Background Checks

84 Bury the Dirt

84 Avoid Questionable Questions

86 HR/Personnel Records

86 When Personnel Gets Personal

87 Avoid Bad PR from HR

88 Beware Employee ID Theft

89 Miscellaneous Work Issues

89 Dish the Dirt, Lose Your Job?

91 Medical Records May Be Hazardous to Your Job

92 Cameras, Cameras, Everywhere

92 The Searchers

5 PRIVACY IN PUBLIC

94 At the Store
94 Don't Get Cashiered
96 Your Loyalty Is Not Rewarded
98 My Soft Drink Is Spying on Me!
100 My Identity Has Been Swiped!
101 Be Anti-Social
103 Improving Your Rental Health

104 Libraries and Schools
104 Beware Public Net Terminals
105 Your Reading Habits Are Private ...
105 ...Except When the Feds Step In
107 So What's Your Major?
108 Apply With Care
110 High School Confidential

111 On the Road
111 Grounded By No-Fly Lists
112 My Bag Has Been Flagged
113 Your Life Is an Open Bag
114 High-Risk Frisks
115 The EZ Way to Track Your Movements
116 We Know Where You Drove Last Summer

119 At the Doctor's Office
119 Testing Can Be Hazardous to Your Health Insurance
121 Keep Your Hospital Stay Private
121 Medical Marketing Migraines
123 Report Privacy Gaffes
123 Be Careful What You Tell Your Doctor

124 At the Bank
124 All Offshore That's Going Offshore?
125 Tell Insurers to Drop Your SSN
126 Safety in Boxes?

128 Miscellaneous
128 Keep Those Cards at Home
128 Get Debt Collectors Off Your Back
129 Hello, My Name Is Brad, and I'll Be Your Thief This Evening
129 Get Ready for Your Close-Up

6 PRIVACY AND UNCLE SAM

134 Public Agencies and You
134 Private Lives, Public Information
135 Keep the USPS From Selling Your Address
138 Take Leave of Your Census
139 Taking License with Your License
139 The Taxman Cometh

141 Political Privacy
141 Vote Yes on Privacy
142 Voters for Sale
143 Retail Politics

144 Local Law Enforcement
144 Your Papers, Please
147 You're Under Arrest—Forever
147 Escaping the Long Arm of the Law
148 Pull Over and Show Me Your DNA

150 Spooks and Snoops
150 G-Man Spam
150 Are the Feds Tapping Your Phone?
154 What's in Your Files?

7 PRIVACY IN THE FUTURE

158   Slamming Spam

159   Assuring Authentication

160   Regarding Reputation

160   Foiling Phishers

162   Rating Risks

162   Insulating Identity

165   Whither Washington?

167   Privacy Power

Index   168

Introduction

A funny thing happened to me on my way to writing this book. My privacy was invaded, numerous times and in various ways. Worse, I was an involuntary participant in the destruction of other people's privacy. Here are just a few examples:

- One day last spring our home fax machine started spewing out pages of someone else's medical history. We had long lists of symptoms, doctor's notes, and copies of EKG printouts for some 64-year-old woman we'd never met. Turns out that a nearby heart clinic was trying to send this information to a local specialist but had our fax number instead of his. We tossed the pages and called the clinic, which told us they'd correct the problem. Two weeks later it happened again, with a different patient.

- Every morning at 6 a.m. that same fax machine spewed out ads for Caribbean cruises, cheap health care plans, worthless stock offers, and so on—despite a 13-year-old Federal law banning such junk faxes. When I called the companies advertising these services to complain, they hung up on me.

- Our tax accountant decided to go electronic last year. So he created a web page where each of his clients could enter their financial information. The site was secure, he assured us, because he had assigned us all a password to access it. But the passwords he chose were our Social Security numbers! He'd given no thought to what might happen to those numbers en route from his clients' keyboards to his unencrypted site. Needless to say, we didn't use it.

- On April 15, this same accountant emailed us a copy of our tax return. Only it wasn't our return, it was for one of his other clients, complete with her SSN, address, and taxable income—all the information we'd need to steal her identity and completely ruin her life. Lord knows who saw a copy of *our* return. (He is now our *former* tax accountant.)

- My computer got infected with a tenacious piece of spyware—malicious code that secretly installed itself on my PC and generated browser pop-up ads for, among other things, spyware removal software. I tried a dozen anti-spyware packages before I found one able to nuke the nasty bugger (see Chapter 3 for tips on spyware removal).

- For six months I was a magnet for telemarketing investment scams. I got calls asking me to invest $25,000 in movies, oil wells, rare coins, emu farms, you name it. When I began to interrupt the sales pitch to ask pointed questions—like who was behind these investment schemes and how they might be contacted—the callers invariably got belligerent and hung up. But I ultimately discovered how these sleazoids got my number, and got the calls to stop.

- I arrived home from a business trip and discovered that my office WiFi network had been hacked. In fact, an apparently benevolent intruder had gone so far as to change the name of my network to "Wide Open—Hack Me!" without doing any other damage. Since then, I've fixed the problem (see Chapter 2 for tips on securing your own WiFi net).

- On my way home from a privacy conference last spring, I opened my suitcase to find a calling card from the Transportation Security Administration (TSA). The card said my bag had been opened at random and searched in accordance with new airport security rules. (A few months later my wife got an identical notice in her bag.) Good thing I'm an upright law-abiding citizen, or I might be writing this book from Guantanamo.

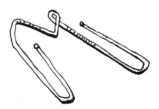

I won't even go into the volume and types of spam I receive, or offers for low-interest credit cards, or the times I've been asked for my Social Security Number by someone who didn't really need it. None of these problems is particularly unique or onerous. In fact, as a journalist who has covered privacy and technology for more than a decade, I'm probably better off than most.

Privacy Is Personal

So when my editor at O'Reilly approached me to write *Computer Privacy Annoyances*, I practically leapt at the chance. I realized I had a lot to say—and a lot to learn.

One thing I learned is that privacy is, well, personal. Everyone has their own definition of what's an acceptable level of privacy and when that limit has been exceeded. My wife, for example, loves to get catalogs in the mail, so our house is littered with slick publications from The Company Store, J. Jill, L.L.Bean, Pottery Barn, Sundance, Victoria's Secret, Williams-Sonoma, and more. Every time we order something from one of them, it seems like two new catalogs show up. She will also happily hand over her email address or apply for a store credit card if it means getting a 10 or 20 percent discount.

Not me. I loathe credit cards and hate catalogs (with the possible exception of Victoria's Secret). If it were up to me, I'd cut up all our plastic and remove our address permanently from mailing lists. Then again, divorces can be messy—and extremely detrimental to one's privacy—so I restrain myself.

I also learned that too much privacy can hurt you in other ways. While writing this book, I heard from an old friend from junior high school. He found me on a whim by typing my name into Google. Had I removed my traces from the Web (you'll find out how in Chapter 3) I would never have reconnected with him.

There are other, more literal costs. If you tell your bank to stop sharing your data (see Chapter 2), you'll get fewer offers for low-cost credit cards, so you may end up paying more in interest. If you refuse to hand over your Social Security number to a prospective landlord, she may not be able to run a credit check on you, which means someone else may get the apartment you want.

My point is that many of these things are in your control. Sometimes the law works against you or (more often) there are no restrictions on what corporations or the government can do with your data. But in many situations you can choose exactly how private you want to be. This book will show you how.

Who Should Read This Book?

Everyone—and I'm not saying that just to boost sales (though if you want to buy copies for your friends and loved ones, I won't object). You don't need to be a paranoid nut job holed up in a windowless cabin in Montana to be concerned about the loss of your privacy. Every person above the age of zero has an interest in protecting his or her personal information, whether they know it or not. In fact, most people don't care much about their privacy, although with the boom in identity theft crimes, that's rapidly changing.

From the moment you're born, you enter the data stream—from birth certificates to inoculation records through school, work, marriage, and the great beyond. This data can easily end up in the hands of stalkers or identity thieves, nosy neighbors or snooping spouses, eavesdropping employers, divorce attorneys, business rivals—the list is almost endless. Unless you know what data is available about you and how to protect it, you're a sitting duck.

Luckily, you don't have to be a computer geek to use this book. True, the majority of the material relates to computing and your privacy, and how you can protect yourself. But you can also hand this book to your technology-challenged grandmother and she'll still get plenty out of it—like how to free herself from telemarketers and junk faxers, how to protect her medical and financial information, and how to find out what her favorite grocery store knows about her and who they're telling.

Most important, this book is just a beginning. Privacy is a complex topic impossible to cover in a mere 170 pages—or even a book five times that long. Think of *Computer Privacy Annoyances* as a gateway to other sources—the first stop on your journey toward a more private life.

How This Book Is Organized

There are a lot of ways to tackle the topic of privacy. For simplicity's sake, I organized this book based on where an intrusion is likely to occur, whether in your home, online, at work, or in public. To wit:

Chapter 1, *Privacy at Risk.* What's the big deal about privacy? Well, for starters, your computer is leaking your personal information all over the Internet, data brokers are selling your vital records to anyone who asks, and the Feds want to know what toothpaste you buy. In this chapter I lay out the growing risks to personal privacy, why the privacy protections we have are ineffectual, and what the future may hold.

Chapter 2, *Privacy at Home.* Your phone rings at dinner time—it's yet another telemarketer. Your fax machine is spewing out ads for cheap vacations and discount health insurance. Unwanted catalogs and credit card offers are spilling out of your mailbox. Your home computer is a data thief's playground—everything from your personal finances and correspondence to the web sites you visit is available to anyone with an interest and a few minutes alone with your stuff. This chapter shows you how to fight back against aggressive marketers and identity thieves, along with step-by-step instructions on how to secure your PC or a Mac, make your wireless home network hack-proof, and more.

Chapter 3, *Privacy on the Net.* Spammers, scammers, and hackers, oh my! In the age of the Internet, data thieves don't need to enter your living room to unlock your secrets. In this chapter I discuss the essential software that every Netizen needs, and offer advice on reducing junk email, removing spyware, recognizing "phisher" emails that try to steal your personal information, and keeping digital delinquents from taking over your machine. You'll also find out how to fend off cyber-stalkers, stop viruses from spreading, and shop safely online.

Chapter 4, *Privacy at Work.* Your boss would never spy on you, right? Don't be so sure. During the last decade employee surveillance has steadily risen, especially when it comes to electronic communications. More than two-thirds of all firms watch where their employees go on the Web, and around half scan employee email. In some cases employers are legally required to record all of your communications, though some go well beyond the letter of the law. This chapter will help you find out what your boss is doing, and then work out rules and guidelines you both can live with.

Chapter 5, *Privacy in Public.* What does your supermarket know about you? Who gets to look at your library or school records? What happens to your personal information when you visit the doctor or go to the bank? Is your soft drink spying on you? In this chapter I tackle what happens to your personal information when you enter the world at large. You'll learn how to keep your shopping history from being shared, to identify and remove radio frequency identification (RFID) tags hidden inside packaging, and what an airport security screener can and can't do when you pass through a checkpoint. I talk about the uses and abuses of private commercial databases, electronic toll payment systems, public video cameras, and more.

Chapter 6, *Privacy and Your Uncle.* Nobody knows you like your Uncle Sam, or collects more data. This chapter reveals what kind of dirt local, state, and federal entities gather about you and whom they're sharing it with. Along the way I discuss the differences between public and private information, how you can seal your court records, gain access to your FBI files, and avoid (or at least survive) a tax audit. You'll also read about the growth in DNA databases, the growing momentum toward a national ID card requirement, and the impact of laws like the Patriot Act on our civil liberties.

Chapter 7, *Privacy in the Future.* Don't fret. While you sit there worrying about who may be stealing your data, smart people are working on solutions to problems like spam, phishing, spyware, identity theft, and the abuse of commercial and public data. Here I'll explore the possible cures for our worst privacy ills.

Tips...and a Whole Lot More

As with every volume in this series, annoyances and fixes are the heart of this book. But each chapter features more than just gripes and solutions. You'll find sidebars listing the essential things you should do to protect your privacy, software packages you need, the ways your boss (or the government) can spy on you, and web sites you can visit to learn about your rights. You'll find tables and charts detailing the kind of information that's collected, and which states do a better job of protecting you. Sprinkled liberally through the book are "Privacy in Peril" sidebars—brief, cautionary dispatches from the frontlines of the data wars, taken from published accounts. Finally, Chapters 2 through 6 end with a quick numerical look at how our privacy is evaporating, which I've called (with no originality whatsoever) "Privacy by the Numbers."

Accuracy and Timeliness

Privacy threats and technology both move at a dizzying pace. It seems like every week a new privacy law is passed or rejected, or a new court decision is announced that changes how an existing law is interpreted. New threats constantly emerge, as well as new responses to these threats. While I've made every effort to keep this book timely and accurate, some items will surely be out of date by the time you read this.

I am also not an attorney. And while I consulted with many, many attorneys during the writing of this book, it's entirely likely that in my efforts to summarize complex topics I bludgeoned some of the finer legal points. So I'm just going to apologize now and get it over with. Any readers who notice errors of fact or judgment on my part should please contact me at *annoyances@oreilly.com*. I promise to read every comment and make necessary corrections to future editions of this book.

Conventions Used in This Book

Italic is used for filenames, pathnames, URLs, email addresses, and emphasis.

`Constant width` is used for keywords, and other items that should be typed verbatim.

Menu sequences are separated by arrows, such as Data→List→Create List. Tabs, radio buttons, buttons, checkboxes, and the like are identified by name—for example, "click the Options tab and check the 'Always show full menus' box."

O'Reilly Would Like to Hear From You

Please address comments and questions concerning this book to the publisher:

O'Reilly Media, Inc.
1005 Gravenstein Highway North
Sebastopol, CA 95472
(800) 998-9938 (in the United States or Canada)
(707) 829-0515 (international or local)
(707) 829-0104 (fax)

There is a web page for this book, where you'll find errata and additional information. You can access this page via:

http://annoyances.oreilly.com

To comment or ask technical questions about this book, send email to:

bookquestions@oreilly.com

For more information about our books, conferences, Resource Centers, and the O'Reilly Network, go to:

http://www.oreilly.com

About the Author

Dan Tynan has been writing and editing stories about technology and its discontents for nearly 20 years. During that time he's been an editor in chief and an executive editor, written for more than 40 publications, and taken home a closet full of awards.

As Executive Editor for *PC World,* Tynan edited a series of articles on Internet privacy that became a finalist for a National Magazine Award in 1999. (They lost to a *Good Housekeeping* series on colon cancer featuring Katie Couric.) In 2002, he wrote a feature for *Popular Science* on the future of airport security, part of a 9/11 anniversary issue that was nominated for Best Single Issue. (*Scientific American* won that one.)

Tynan earned consecutive Maggies from the Western Publications Association for his CNET.com column, Inside @ccess. He's won several Jesse H. Neal National Business Journalism Awards for investigative journalism and privacy-related articles. He's also shared in awards from the American Society of Business Publication Editors, Computer Press Association, and others he can no longer recall.

Tynan has appeared on CNN, CBS, NPR, and a raft of local TV and radio stations, and has been quoted on technology issues in the *Wall Street Journal* and the *New York Times.* His work has appeared in *Cargo*, CNET.com, *Family Circle*, *InfoWorld*, *Men's Fitness*, *Newsweek*, Playboy.com, *Wired*, and a small flotilla of magazines with "PC" or "Computer" in the title. He currently writes the Gadget Freak column for *PC World* and TechSmart for *Attache* magazine.

Yet he remains a humble scribe, working for relative peanuts and the fleeting adoration of the book-buying public.

Everything else about him is private.

Acknowledgments

First, I must thank my editor at O'Reilly, Robert Luhn, who pummeled me with information about the latest privacy breaches several times a day for nearly a year. Robert displayed a deft editorial hand and infinite patience as this manuscript grew increasingly late. I owe him a debt of gratitude. My thanks go as well to Derek Di Matteo for his fastidious (but not fussy) copyedit.

No reporter can do his job without the help of many others. I relied on many privacy wonks for the information in this book, many of whom are quoted in the following pages. The list includes Parry Aftab, Steven Aftergood, Katherine Albrecht, Kim Alexander, Jim Aspinwall, Lisa Bennett, Naftali Bennett, Bill Brown, Stephen Buckner, Dr. Nancy Canning, Jason Catlett, Christina Clearwater, Ray Everett Church, Frederick W. Daily, Will Doherty, Fred Felman, Angela Fulcher, Tena Friery, Robert Gellman, Steve Gibson, Beth Givens, Michelle Greenberg, Chris Griffin, Rod Griffin, Jim Harper, Bill Harris, Don Harris, Edward Hasbrouck, Chris Hoofnagle, Alfred Huger, Lisa Hurst, Dan Kahn, Rachel Keener, Ken Klingenstein, Jim Kuhn, Frederick S. Lane, Kraig Lane, Dan Larkin, Denise Lieberman, Felix Lin, Steve Linford, Erin Long, Lewis Maltby, Jennifer Martin, David McGuinn, Barmack Nassirian, Larry Noble, Michael Ostrolenk, John Pescatore, Ed Petersen, James Plummer, Larry Ponemon, James C. Pyles, Mark Roberti, April Robertson, Mark Rowe, Marcus Sachs, Mark Sunner, Bill Scannell, Dr. Phyllis Schneck, Bruce Schneier, Scott Silverman, Brooke Singer, Richard Smith, Robert Ellis Smith, Te Smith, Lisa Sotto, Shelby Stanfield, Kirk Steers, Chris Stimmel, Razvan Stoica, Deborah Stone, Peter Swire, Linus Upson, Sam Walker, John Walls, Peter Wayner, Lauren Weinstein, Pete Wellborn, Tom Werner, Susan Wilson, Don Wright, Amit Yoran, and David Zumwalt. (My apologies if I left anybody out.)

A special nod of the cap goes to O'Reilly authors Steve Bass (*PC Annoyances*), Preston Galla (*Internet Annoyances*), and Scott Granneman (*Don't Click on the Blue E!*) for their help in reading parts of this manuscript and/or answering my many pesky questions.

There are a handful of reporters who cover the privacy beat with great acumen. They were an enormous help to me, even if they weren't aware of it. Of particular note are CNET's Declan McCullough, *PC World*'s Andy Brandt and Tom Spring, and Wired News' Ryan Singel and Kim Zetter.

During my research I also leaned rather heavily on several Web sites, among them those for the American Civil Liberties Union (*http://www.aclu.org*), the Electronic Privacy Information Center (*http://www.epic.org*), and the Privacy Rights Clearinghouse (*http://www.privacyrights.org*). A more complete list of essential web sites appears in Chapter 5.

Finally, I must acknowledge my adoring wife and children, whom I embarrassed on more than one occasion by refusing to provide information to and/or interrogating store personnel while my family was just trying to shop. Thanks for your patience and support.

Privacy at Risk

It's an unwritten law that you can't write a book about personal privacy without quoting Sun Microsystems CEO Scott McNealy's infamous 1999 statement: "You have zero privacy anyway. Get over it."

There, I've done my duty. But before we move on, let's examine his statement a little more closely.

Fact is, McNealy was wrong. Although privacy protections in this country are not exactly plentiful, this isn't *1984* or *The Trial*—at least, not yet. There's no video camera trained on you in your home, recording your every moment. (Or if there is, it's a webcam and you probably put it there.) You enjoy relative freedom of movement, though you may be frisked or required to show your ID to board an airplane.

Your bank account, medical records, and school transcripts are all more or less protected by Federal and state law; there's even a law that keeps nosy people from obtaining the names of the videos you rent. Though there are few limits on how corporations can use your data, the courts are starting to force them to follow the policies laid out in their own privacy statements. And while FBI agents can theoretically demand your library records or bookstore receipts if they decide you pose a terrorist threat, odds are pretty good that no one else knows you're reading this book right now.

The trouble is, there's just not enough privacy. There are huge gaps in our legal protections, and the laws we do have are generally half measures at best. (And unlike many European countries, we lack anything resembling a federal Privacy Commissioner.) The privacy that remains is rapidly being eroded by technology, commercial interests, and increasing government surveillance.

In this chapter, I'll outline the threats to your privacy and how we've gotten in this mess. The rest of this book is devoted to what you can do about it. It all starts with a big noisy machine that's probably sitting on or near your desk right now.

THE SPY ON YOUR DESK

Once upon a time, when you needed to deposit money in your checking account, you visited the bank. If you were hungry for something new to read, you went to the bookstore. When you purchased music or rented a movie it came home on a shiny silver disc. Had a medical question? You called your doctor or pulled a book off a shelf. When you wanted to have a private conversation with a friend, you called them on the phone or sent a letter.

Today, you may be doing all of the above online. It's incredibly convenient and often cheaper. But the threat to your privacy increases exponentially.

All of a sudden, your personal finances, the books you bought at Amazon, the music and video files you downloaded, the medical web sites you visited, the search terms you typed into Google or Yahoo, your email and instant message conversations—all are concentrated in a single point of entry: your computer.

A computer is a secretary who jots everything down, takes perfect notes, and never forgets a thing until you tell it to (or the hard disk crashes). Unless you've taken steps to protect yourself—and most people don't—anyone with rudimentary computer skills can sit at your keyboard and learn everything about you in just a few minutes. They can look at your browser history or your cookie files, scan your document folders, peek inside your personal finance software, and so on. They can build a highly detailed dossier of your hobbies and interests, your physical ailments, your fiscal health, and any naughtiness you may have been up to. No hacking required.

This also includes any law enforcement agencies, divorce attorneys, and possibly your boss—anyone with an adversarial interest and/or the legal right to impound your computer can see what you've been up to.

Oh, and those files you deleted? They're still there (see Figure 1-1). Unless you're very careful and know precisely what to do, anything that's been "deleted" can be retrieved fairly easily. (For tips on how to secure your PC, see Chapter 2.)

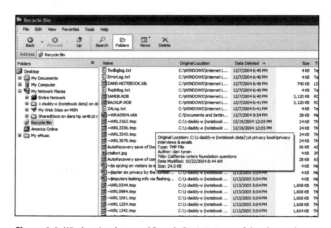

Figure 1-1. Windows' aptly named Recycle Bin is just one of the places where "deleted" files may be lurking—and can be revived with a few clicks.

DAWN OF THE UNDEAD PC

But that's not the scary problem. The scary problem is what happens out there in the depths of cyberspace.

In the last two years, we've seen wave upon wave of email worms sent with a single purpose: to take control of our computers. They rummage through your address book and send themselves to all your friends and associates, so the email looks like it's coming from someone you know and trust.

Many worms come in the guise of what looks like a harmless file attachment. But when the file is opened, it can unleash any number of e-plagues. For example, it might install a *keylogger*—software that captures everything you type and secretly transmits the data back to the sociopaths who sent you the worm. Some keyloggers are clever enough to wait until you visit your bank's web site, then capture your account information and password and shoot it off to cyber criminals halfway around the world.

Alternately, the attachment may install "malware" that lets someone take complete control of your machine, turning it into a "zombie" that can be used to send more worms, spew spam, launch attacks against web sites, or steal your personal information. The number of zombie PCs increased by 1500 percent in the first six months of 2004, according to a report issued by security vendor Symantec. There are probably millions of remotely controlled PCs in the wild. Nobody knows the exact number—especially not the owners of the zombies.

Even if you're savvy enough to avoid worms, keyloggers, and malware, your privacy can be compromised in myriad other ways. Visit the wrong web site or download the wrong "free" software, and your computer could end up with a spyware infection (see Figure 1-2). Spyware can not only pop up obnoxious ads every time you surf the Web, it can also record the address of every page you look at and "phone home" with the information. Anti-spyware vendor PC Pitstop says at least one out of five PCs tested on its web site (*http://www.pcpitstop.com/spycheck/default.asp*) report some kind of spyware infection.

You could also be duped by a "phisher" email that pretends to be from your bank. But the link inside the email message leads not to your bank's web site but to a cleverly designed fake. Once you're on the fake site, it captures the account information and password you enter into the bogus page. Some phishers are even cleverer—the link brings you to the bank's actual site, and then pops up a new browser window where you enter your data. Needless to say, that data never makes it to the bank. Nearly 2 million Americans got hooked by phishers in 2003, according to a report by the Gartner research group, with losses to financial institutions estimated at $1.2 billion (see Table 1-1).

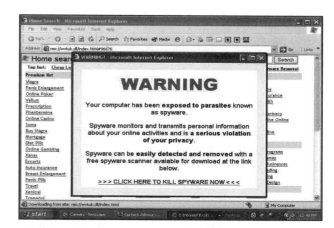

Figure 1-2. Particularly nasty spyware can hijack your browser's home page to a directory of advertisers and pop up scary advertisements for, among other things, anti-spyware tools. (In case you're wondering, those tools don't really work.)

Table 1-1. Hooked by phishers.

The scams	The math
Americans who received phisher email in 2003.	57 million
Consumers who clicked links inside phisher emails	11 million
Consumers who provided account and other sensitive information to phisher sites.	1.8 million
Percentage of phisher emails spoofing banks and other financial institutions	85 percent[a]
Average monthly growth in phishing scams from July to December 2004	38 percent
Odds that a phisher will end up being caught	>700 to 1

* December, 2004.
  Sources: Gartner Group, Anti-Phishing.org

But wait, we're not done. Any unprotected computer sitting on the Internet is easy pickings for hackers, who scan thousands of Internet addresses each minute, probing for insecure machines. In tests conducted in November 2004 by *USA Today*, an unprotected Windows XP system was attacked within 4 minutes of hooking up to the Net.

Once inside, hackers can snoop around as if they were sitting at your keyboard, check your email, scan your Quicken data, install software to control your machine, delete everything on your hard drive—pretty much do anything they want. And unless they nuke all your files, you'll probably never find out.

For these and other reasons, we are in the throes of an identity theft epidemic. With identify theft, someone can use your information to open up bank accounts, run up credit card bills, apply for jobs, buy cars and houses, and commit crimes in your name. They don't need very much information; sometimes your username and password are enough. The more information the thief has—especially sensitive data like your credit card number, date of birth, Social Security Number, or mother's maiden name—the more damage he can do.

By all accounts, recovering from identity theft is a nightmare. On average, it takes 600 hours and $1,400 for consumers to straighten out their records and clear their name, according to the Identity Theft Resource Center (*http://www.idtheft-center.org/index.shtml*).

The Federal Trade Commission estimates that nearly 10 million Americans suffered some form of identity theft in 2003, with total losses to businesses and consumers in excess of $50 billion. So far only about 1 in 10 of those thefts happen over the Net, but that percentage is likely to grow dramatically as phishers proliferate and more consumers move their finances online.

The good news? You don't have to be a victim of online snoops or identity thieves, as long as you're aware and prepared. (For information on how to keep your PC safe from online intruders, see Chapter 3.)

WORKING FOR THE MAN

Of course, somebody might already be reading your email and logging what web sites you frequent. He may be listening to your phone conversations and secretly photographing you. He could be talking to your friends and associates about you and tracking your movements. He might be examining the content of your bloodstream and the depths of your psyche. And he'd be doing all of it without breaking a single law.

That somebody would be your boss.

By nearly every measure, employer surveillance is on the rise. According to surveys by the American Management Association, around two-thirds of employers monitor Web use on the job and half scan your email. More than a third poke around your hard drive, and one out of five admits to using software that keeps a running record of everything an employee does on his or her computer.

The spying goes well beyond your desktop. More and more firms are relying on pre-employment background checks, notes Beth Givens, Director of the Privacy Rights Clearinghouse. According to The Society for Human Resource Management (*http://www.shrm.org*), 80 percent of large employers conduct background screens on job applicants, nearly twice as many as eight years ago (see Figure 1-3). While employee drug testing has declined in recent years, 2 out of 3 companies continue to test job applicants. And your personnel files may be an open book to nosy employees looking to steal your information. According to a study by Michigan State University, employee records are the single largest resource for identity thieves. In most cases, the courts have ruled that you give up nearly all expectations of privacy when you join a corporation. (The rules for government employees are better, but only slightly.) Even so, you aren't entirely without rights at work. Recent changes to credit reporting laws give you access

Figure 1-3. With thousands of low-rent web sites hawking background checks on the cheap, even small businesses can afford to check up on their employees (or business associates, spouses, neighbors, etc).

to your personnel files, including information such as your driving or criminal record and interviews with friends and neighbors obtained about you during a background check. Courts have established limits on the kinds of information a company can collect on you and how they can do it.

Over the years many employers have been caught red-handed illegally collecting or misusing data. For example, Hilton Hotels was sued by a former sales manager who was fired because a background check indicated he'd done time in prison—inaccurately, as it turned out. A trucking firm in California got nailed for installing video cameras in employee bathrooms. Wal-Mart was fined nearly $7 million by the Equal Employment Opportunity Commission for asking questions that violated the Americans with Disabilities Act. Burlington Northern Santa Fe Corporation paid more than $2 million in fines to the EEOC for secretly performing genetic testing on employees who'd filed health claims against the railroad. An appliance rental firm had to pay a $2.2 million settlement for using a pre-employment questionnaire that asked about applicants' sexual proclivities.

How did these firms get nabbed? Because employees knew their privacy rights were being violated (see Table 1-2), and did something about it. (For more on how to protect your privacy on the job, see Chapter 4.)

Table 1-2. Do you know your privacy rights at work? Answers are at the end of this chapter.

Pop Quiz	True	False
1. My boss can require me to take a lie detector test		
2. My boss can search my office, desk, or bag		
3. My boss can ask me to submit to genetic testing to determine if I'm an insurance risk.		
4. My boss can fire me because of something he found during a background check.		
5. My boss can ask about my criminal history during my job interview		
6. My boss can ask about my mental health history during my job interview		

THE INFORMATION EXPLOSION

Even with the dangers posed by digital delinquents and eavesdropping employers, the biggest threat to your personal privacy is your own bad self. But who can blame you? We've all been trained to fork over our personal information since kindergarten, filling out form after form in school, doctor's offices, work, and for an ever-expanding number of governmental entities.

The problem is that in the USA, once you give up your personal information it no longer belongs to you. In a 1976 decision (*Miller vs. U.S.*), the U.S. Supreme Court ruled that Americans do not have a reasonable expectation of privacy for information they voluntarily provide to others. In other words, if you tell someone something they're free to tell anyone else, unless there's a specific law that forbids sharing this info or you make someone sign a legal document that says they won't disclose it.

(Of course, if you don't give up your data you can't get a job, or a credit card, or insurance, or medical care, and so on. So the notion that we "volunteer" this information is questionable. But I digress.)

In the past, keeping this data private wasn't an issue. When you filled out at a form at the doctor's office, that's where it stayed. Some of that information might go to your insurer or to your employer, where it would sit in an equally musty drawer until a clerk pulled your file. Even as records began to find their way onto computers in the '60s and '70s, the information was generally stored on mainframes sitting in the basement, accessible only to a few chosen geeks. Thus you were protected by what's known as "security through obscurity."

But the personal computer, and later the Internet, changed all that. Suddenly your files were accessible to anyone with a PC and a connection. With just a few clicks your data could be easily acquired and combined with other files. And outside of a few very limited legal restrictions, it could be sold and resold almost endlessly. The result: a boom in massive commercial databases and a multi-billion dollar data mining industry.

Every time you use your credit card, book an airline ticket, file a claim with your insurance company, mail back a product warranty, order something from a catalog, or buy toothpaste with your supermarket loyalty card, that information is entered into a commercial database (see Figure 1-4). Aside from credit bureaus, the companies that gather and sell this information are almost entirely unregulated.

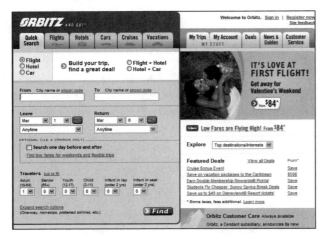

Figure 1-4. Web sites like Orbitz, Travelocity, and Expedia all hook into the four big computerized reservation systems, some of the largest commercial databases on the planet.

Adding to the data glut are public records laws, which require that certain information about you—like the property you own, the lawsuits you've suffered, or your criminal record—be available for public inspection. In the pre-Internet days, a snoop would have to totter down to the county seat and paw through paper records. Although these records were nominally public, getting at them and making copies was a royal pain, making this data essentially private. As state and local governments discovered the Internet, they began to put many of these records online, where virtually anyone could get to them at any time.

The exponential growth of commercial databases and easy access to public records combined to create an information explosion. And when information blows up, privacy is almost always a casualty. (For tips on how to avoid having your personal information sucked up by commercial databases, see Chapter 5.)

THE DATA INDUSTRIAL COMPLEX

What happens to all this data? It gets vacuumed up by huge data mining companies like Acxiom and ChoicePoint, who merge public and private data, then slice and dice it based on where you live, the products you buy, the magazines you read, how much money you make, and so on. This information is then resold to marketers, insurers, potential employers, and law enforcement agencies.

This data is used in myriad ways. For example, ChoicePoint's 19 billion records are used for employer background checks, drug screening, criminal records searches, locating deadbeat dads, preventing mortgage or insurance fraud, biometric screening, analyzing DNA samples, verifying applicants for public assistance programs, and making sure banks comply with the guidelines of the USA Patriot Act (see Figure 1-5). ChoicePoint records have been used to locate 822 missing children, and to scrub the names of alleged felons from the rolls of Florida voters in 2000. The company is a particular favorite of Uncle Sam. According to a 2001 report in the *Wall Street Journal*, ChoicePoint has contracts with 35 Federal agencies; on its web site, the company boasts of its contracts with the Department of Homeland Security.

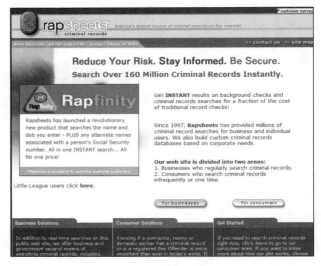

Figure 1-5. ChoicePoint owns Rapsheets.com, a national criminal records database, and Vital Chek Network, which maintains birth records of all babies born in the U.S.

FAIR INFORMATION PRACTICE PRINCIPLES

Collecting data on consumers isn't necessarily a bad thing; it's what the data collector *does* with your information afterward that counts. Over the years, a generally agreed upon set of principles have developed that apply to organizations that gather data on individuals, be they a government agency or a mom-and-pop web site. Here's how a by-the-book data collector should operate—and what most of them actually do.

Notice: At minimum, anyone collecting data should tell you what kinds of information they're gathering and how they're planning to use it. If they're sharing the data, they should tell you who will have access to it. In most cases this information is buried inside a web site's privacy policy, hidden in a software license splash screen, or printed in tiny text on what looks like a piece of junk mail.

Consent: Ideally the data collector asks permission before sharing your data with third parties. In most cases, though, it's the opposite—you must tell the data collector to stop sharing your data, assuming they even give you that option.

(In Europe, Canada, and much of Asia, a data collector can't share your information without your explicit permission.)

Access: You should be able to view your data and correct any mistakes. For example, the Fair Credit Reporting Act makes it possible to view your credit report and challenge erroneous information—a good thing, given that most credit reports are rife with errors.

Security: The data collector must make efforts to limit access to your information and keep it secure. They might even tell you, in general terms, how they keep the information safe. Of course, this doesn't mean squat if the company gets hacked or an employee steals your information.

Enforcement: If the company has to comply with laws regulating data collection, they should tell you. In some cases, they might have to answer to the FTC, FCC, or the state attorneys general; in other cases, private citizens may be able to sue companies that fail to follow the rules. But most data collectors are self-regulated—so it's strictly buyer beware.

Acxiom, which maintains records on 169 million consumers, is another grateful recipient of your tax dollars. The firm's consumer data was used in the controversial Computer Assisted Passenger Pre-screening System II (CAPPS II), which attempted to identify potential terrorists by analyzing their purchase histories and other data. The project was pronounced dead in July 2004 by then-DHS chief Tom Ridge, though aspects of it have re-emerged in the department's new Secure Flight program.

The Federal government's increasing reliance on commercial databases has been spurred largely by the war on terror. According to documents obtained by the Electronic Privacy Information Center (EPIC), the FBI requested and received more than 300 million passenger records from major U.S. airlines after 9/11. Virtually everyone who flew, booked a rental car, or checked into a hotel between June 2001 and January 2002 is now on file at the FBI.

But it's not limited to just the Feds fighting terrorism. Grocery store loyalty programs and electronic toll booth records have been used for routine criminal investigations by local law enforcement.

The use of commercial databases by government agencies has privacy advocates deeply concerned. Unlike public records, commercial databases operate with little or no legal oversight, and mistakes are common. A US Public Interest Research Group study in June 2004 found that 4 out of 5 credit reports contain errors. It's one thing to have your credit denied because of a mistake in a database; it's quite another to find yourself fired or arrested for a crime you didn't commit. And even accurate data can be misinterpreted.

Case in point: In August 2004, Philip Scott Lyons was arrested for attempting to burn down his own house while his wife and child were inside. Law enforcement agents thought they'd obtained an important clue when they accessed Lyons' Safeway Club Card shopping records and discovered he'd purchased a fire-starter similar to the one used to ignite his house. Lyons, a 25-year veteran of the Tukwila, Washington fire department, was relieved of his duties until someone else confessed to the crime five months later.

"The ugly scenario is that information from a commercial database, which is subject to few accountability rules, may be used for government decision making," says Chris Hoofnagle, Associate Director of EPIC. "Someone might use it to screen you, arrest you, or question you every time you fly. A whole series of governmental powers could be triggered by data collected by the private sector."

Unfortunately, you may never find out what the government thinks it knows about you. In the current political climate, privacy has taken a back seat to concerns over security—if it's even in the vehicle at all. (For the 411 on what data Uncle Sam collects and what you can do about it, see Chapter 6.)

LOCATION, LOCATION, LOCATION

Scared? In the next few years privacy advocates foresee far more Orwellian scenarios. For several years, thanks to Global Positioning Systems (GPS), someone could track your location anywhere on the globe, cheaply and relatively easily. Now surveillance is being supersized; the authorities may soon have the ability to track everyone, everywhere. They may even be able to track the vehicles you drive and the products you buy.

In fact, you probably already have a tracking device in your pocket. By law, new "E911 capable" cell phones must have tracking technology built-in so emergency services can locate you when you call 911 on your mobile phone. (Whether this service actually works depends on where you live; it has yet to be implemented nationwide, due to problems upgrading antiquated emergency dispatch systems.)

But the same technology that brings the paramedics to your rescue may also let the police locate you at other times, or request a record of your 'sightings' from your wireless company. A divorce or civil attorney could subpoena your location

records for use in a trial. Don't forget the capitalist angle. Depending on the agreement you sign, your wireless company could sell your location information to advertisers—so when you're driving by McDonald's, your cell phone might receive a coupon for a free Healthee Burger. Revenues for location-based services are expected to reach anywhere from $15 billion to $40 billion by 2007.

The National Transportation Safety Board has called for all cars to be outfitted with event data recorders—a "black box" that records how far and fast you've driven, and whether you slammed on the brakes or were wearing your seatbelt. Ostensibly designed to help investigators determine the cause of accidents and improve safety, EDRs could also be used to monitor your driving, issue tickets, assess mileage taxes, or boost your insurance rates. Progressive Insurance of Minneapolis has started a pilot program offering discounts to drivers who agree to upload their EDR data. Approximately two-thirds of 2004 model cars have some kind of EDR installed, according to the U.S. National Highway Traffic Safety Administration.

"Telematics" systems from companies such as OnStar or ATX Technologies provide instant-on cellular connections when your car has been in an accident, and a GPS transponder to help emergency workers locate you. But these same systems could be used to spy on you. Rental car agencies have already used vehicle GPS systems to fine customers who exceeded speed limits or crossed state lines in violation of their rental agreements (although public outcry has made them largely back down). Courts have ruled that police may attach a GPS device to a car without a warrant. FBI agents have used telematics systems to eavesdrop on suspects traveling in a car—a practice the courts ruled illegal because the tap interfered with the car owner's ability to use the system to call for help, not because of privacy concerns.

Electronic passes that let you avoid long toll booth lines have been used in hundreds of criminal and civil lawsuits to document people's comings and goings. These passes come with Radio Frequency Identification chips inside that broadcast a unique number when scanned. Any time you pass within range of an RFID scanner—which can be hidden inside a doorway or a wall—the tag transmits your information. RFID tags are being built into all kinds of products, from car tires and hand guns to the packaging of consumer goods. (See "All RFID, All the Time" in Chapter 5.) The little snooping chips may find their way into passports and driver's licenses, and some people are (voluntarily, so far) inserting them under

THERE'S GOLD IN THEM THAR DATA MINES

The billions of records maintained by data mining companies aren't just attractive to Corporate America and Uncle Sam—they're also a tempting prize for hackers. For example, Acxiom was hacked multiple times over the past four years and the company never knew it.

Between April 2002 and August 2003, Acxiom's file servers were compromised 137 times by hackers, who made off with 8.2 gigabytes of customer data. Scott Levine, an alleged spammer based in Florida, has been charged with what the U.S. Department of Justice termed the "largest illegal invasion and theft of personal data to date." Authorities discovered the data loss while investigating a completely unrelated incident in which Acxiom was hacked. In December 2003, 25-year-old hacker Daniel Baas pleaded guilty to a single count of "exceeding authorized access" to the company's file servers. Baas, who was working for one of Acxiom's subcontractors at the time, accessed millions of customer records the company maintains for its corporate clientele—including major U.S. banks, insurance, and phone companies.

Baas's crime was also discovered accidentally when investigators in Hamilton County, Ohio, impounded another hacker's computer and discovered a chat session between the two in which Baas admitted to having some of the Acxiom data. As far as investigators can determine, Baas copied the data to CDs but didn't do anything else with it.

Acxiom wasn't the only data mining giant to have its records pilfered. Over the course of 2004, ChoicePoint was victimized by a ring of identity thieves who posed as legitimate businesses to set up fraudulent accounts. After they signed on with ChoicePoint, they trolled the company's databases and scooped up names, addresses, Social Security Numbers, and other personal information. Credit card accounts for approximately 750 people were used to purchase jewelry, electronics, and other consumer goods, according to a statement by the company. At press time, ChoicePoint plans to notify up to 145,000 people that their personal data may have been stolen.

Since the break-ins became public, both companies say they've tightened up their security procedures. One can only hope.

---

their own skin. In the future, when you walk into a room, it could know who you are and where you've been. MIT's Auto-ID Center predicts that some 500 billion RFID tags may be in use by 2010.

Is personal privacy a dead duck? Only if you believe Scott "Get over it" McNealy. Technologies like GPS and RFID are not inherently bad, but history shows time and again that data collected for a helpful purpose invariably ends up being used for another, less benign one.

History also shows that when citizens raise hell and actively oppose privacy intrusions, the intruders back down or are forced to implement safeguards to keep data from being misused or abused. Not always, but often enough to make it a fight worth waging. The first step is securing your personal privacy at home. The next chapter shows you how.

PRIVACY AND THE LAW

In most of the industrialized world, your personal information is largely in your control, at least when it comes to its commercial use. Not in the USA. Instead, we have a patchwork quilt of Federal and state laws addressing various aspects of privacy. Most are essentially "buyer beware" laws—they tell you how your privacy is being violated, but it's up to you to make it stop. Here are some of the important Federal privacy protections for consumers.

- *Privacy Act of 1974.* This seminal piece of legislation prohibits the Federal government from creating secret databases on individuals and limits how agencies can share information. It also gives you the right to request your information and to sue the government for failing to follow the Act. For more details (and limitations), see EPIC's summary at *http://www.epic.org/privacy/1974act/*.

- *Fair Credit Reporting Act.* The FCRA lets you access your credit bureau records and correct inaccuracies. The more recent Fair and Accurate Credit Transaction Act (FACTA) allows you to obtain a free credit report every year.

- *Telephone Consumer Protection Act of 1991.* Though it provides little actual protection against telemarketing calls, the TCPA made it illegal to send unsolicited fax advertisements, allowing citizens to sue junk faxers for $500 per violation.

- *Family Educational Rights and Privacy Act.* FERPA limits sharing of student data to "directory information" (name, address, and so on) and lets you opt out of directories, too.

- *Gramm-Leach-Bliley Act.* The GLBA's main purpose was to allow banks, insurance companies, and brokerages to merge, but it also lets you tell your bank to stop sharing your information with third parties. (See Chapter 5, "Financial Privacy? Don't Bank on It..")

- *Health Insurance Portability and Privacy Act.* Passed in 1996 and still being implemented, HIPPA gives you access to your medical records and limits the disclosure of medical information by health care providers. (See Chapter 5, "Getting Hip to HIPAA.")

Table 1-3. Answers to the quiz on page 5.

True or False?	Correct Response
1. My boss can require me to take a lie detector test.	False. A federal law prohibits using polygraphs in hiring, though certain professions (e.g., security guard) are exempt. Employees accused of a crime can also be asked to take the test.
2. My boss can search my office, desk, or bag.	True. Private employers can search your office or desk with relative impunity; they may also be able to search your bag, if such searches are standard procedure in your workplace or you're suspected of theft.
3. My boss can ask me to submit to genetic testing to determine if I'm an insurance risk.	Unclear. In February 2005 the Senate unanimously passed the Genetic Information Nondiscrimination Act (S. 306), which would prohibit employers from using genetic test results to deny insurance or employment. At press time, the bill was being considered in the House.
4. My boss can fire me because of something he found during a background check.	True. Your boss can fire you for virtually any reason, as long as it's not violating your civil rights or related to criminal activity.
5. My boss can ask about my criminal history during my job interview.	True. In most states your criminal history, if you have one, is public information that's accessible to employers. Any arrests without convictions in the past seven years are also fair game.
6. My boss can ask about my mental health history during my job interview.	False. Under the Americans with Disabilities Act, employers are forbidden to ask questions that might reveal a physical or mental handicap.

Privacy at Home

2

Like charity, privacy begins at home. The threats are almost too numerous to name. Your privacy can be accidentally or deliberately violated by your spouse, your kids, roommates, house guests, or simply by your own carelessness.

Many privacy threats involve the treasure trove of data you store on your home PC. Inquisitive types could glean reams of information about you just by glancing at your screen or examining your browser history. Strangers driving by your house could tap into your wireless home network. Hackers could secretly install software that logs your keystrokes in order to steal passwords and personal information. (To learn how to prevent such threats, see Chapter 3.) The list goes on.

But computers are hardly the only places where your privacy is at risk Privacy annoyances abound thanks to your telephone (telemarketers and tele-stalkers), your mailbox (junk mail and thieves), fax machine (low-rent advertisers), cell phone (eavesdroppers and text spammers), and so on. Perhaps worst of all, poor privacy practices could lead to the theft of your personal identity—and a world of hurt for your reputation and credit rating. Feeling paranoid yet? Read on and take action!

MY DATA, MYSELF

One Computer, Many Eyeballs

The Annoyance: I keep sensitive files on my home desktop machine—my banking records, old love letters, the chapters from my unfinished best-selling novel—that are nobody else's business, damn it. How do I keep Nosy Nellies from walking up to my computer while I'm not there and rummaging around on it?

The Fix: One way is to use a password-protected logon so that only you can gain access to your desktop's...er, desktop. If you're sharing the computer, you'll need to set up multiple logons, each with a unique password (see Figure 2-1).

To set up different identities in Windows XP, open the Control Panel, double-click User Accounts, click "Create a new account," supply a username and click Next. Under "Pick an account type" select Limited and click the Create Account button. XP will add the username to the group of accounts on your system. Select the new account in the subsequent screen by clicking its icon. Select "Create a password," then enter a password for the account. Do this for everyone who's likely to use your system.

If you want to be able to quickly switch between users without having to close all your documents and programs, make sure Fast User Switching is turned on. From the main User Accounts Window, select "Change the way users log on and off" and check the Use Fast User Switching box. Click the Apply Options button and close the User Accounts window.

> When you first set up Windows XP, create a limited user account for your everyday use in addition to your administrative account. A limited account can't create passwords, install software, or perform other system chores; if bad guys hijack your system when you're logged on as a limited user, they won't be able to do as much damage.

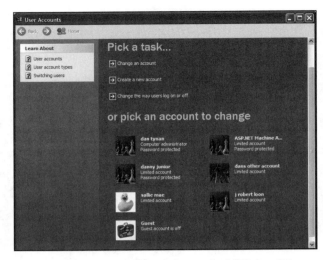

Figure 2-1. Sharing your computer with the entire family? Windows XP lets you create accounts for multiple users and assign different rights and passwords to each. That way, junior or sis can still muck about on your machine without messing with your private stuff.

Wait, you're not done yet. If you wander off while you're logged on to your PC, anyone can walk up to your machine and have their way with it. You have two options: you can "lock" your computer every time you get up, or you can set up a password-protected screensaver that will thwart the little sneaks.

To lock your computer, simply press the Windows Logo key (it looks like a tiny flag) and the letter L; Windows will display a blank desktop. Press the logo key and L again to get to a Welcome screen where you must log back in with a password. If your keyboard lacks a Windows key, you can force the logon screen to appear by clicking the Start button and selecting Log Off→Switch User (or→Log Off Administrator→Switch User). When you log back in, your computer will be just as you left it.

To password protect your screensaver, open the Display control panel. (If you're using Control Panel's Categories view, you'll find it under Appearance and Themes.) Select the Screen Saver tab, select a screensaver, set the delay, and check the "On resume, display Welcome screen" box. Anyone attempting to slip onto your machine while you're away will have to cough up a password.

If you use Mac OS X, this process is even simpler (naturally). Click the System Preferences icon (it looks like a light switch) on the Mac's toolbar; under "System" select Accounts. To add a new account, click the plus symbol (+) below Login Options, and enter the name and password for each new user. When you're done, click the padlock at the bottom of the Accounts window and close it to keep anyone else from changing your settings. Relaunch System Preferences and under "Personal" select Security; make sure the "Require password to wake this computer from sleep or screensaver" box is checked, then close the Security window. That's it.

Remember, the security of either scheme depends entirely on how tough a password you pick. (For sage advice on creating a password, see the sidebar "Pick a Peck of Passwords.")

Foil Hard Disk Snoops

The Annoyance: What's to keep these busybodies from snooping around my files once they've logged on?

The Fix: Not much—unless you take a few more steps to cover yourself. For example, XP lets you make your files and folders private, so other folks who log onto your computer or home network can't open them. However, this feature only works if your hard drive uses the New Technology File System (NTFS).

To figure out what file system you're using, open Windows Explorer, select the drive where you store the files you want to protect, right click the drive letter, and select Properties. On the General tab you'll find an entry for "File system." If it says NTFS, you're golden; if you see FAT or FAT32, then you'll need to convert the drive to NTFS (for instructions on how, see the tip in the next column).

Once you're sure you're using NTFS, open Windows Explorer, right-click the folder you want to make private, and select Sharing and Security. On the Sharing tab, check the "Make this folder private" box and click OK. (If you haven't already set up a password for your user logon, you'll be prompted to do so now). XP will then make this folder and any subfolders private; when other users log on they'll see the name of the folder you've protected but won't be able to peer inside it. Files you drag inside the folder later will also be invisible to others.

The New Technology File System (NTFS) is more secure and efficient than Window's older File Allocation Table (FAT) system, which is why new Windows XP PCs ship with NTFS in place. If you've got an older system you can covert it from FAT to NTFS. The process is quite easy—and not to worry, XP will keep your programs and data intact. To convert a drive, select Start→Run and type "cmd" in the Open box to bring up a DOS prompt. At the prompt type convert x: /fs:ntfs (where x: is the letter of the drive you want to convert), then press Enter. If files on the drive are in use (and if the drive holds the OS, they will be) you'll need to tell XP to convert the drive the next time you restart. Once you have an NTFS drive, you'll be able to make folders private, encrypt data, and do other neat tricks.

With Mac OS X, file sharing is turned off by default. To make sure, open System Preferences from the toolbar, click the Sharing icon (it's under Internet & Network), and select Services. If Personal File Sharing is selected, you can turn it off by clicking the Stop button.

TEN ESSENTIAL PRIVACY PRACTICES

Want more control over your personal privacy? If you ignore all of the other advice in this book but follow these 10 steps, you'll gain more privacy than 90 percent of your fellow Americans. (Of course, to get that last 9.99 percent, read the rest of the book!)

Be stingy with your data. In particular, don't share information like your Social Security Number, date of birth, mother's maiden name, or driver's license number with anyone who doesn't really need it. (And most folks really don't need it.) As a general rule, only a handful of government authorities and financial institutions legally require this kind of information.

Check your rep. At least once a year, order a credit report from the major credit reporting agencies (Equifax, Experian, Innovis, TransUnion). Check it for errors and anything else that doesn't look right. Thanks to the recently passed Fair and Accurate Credit Transactions Act, you can get a free report once a year. If someone's mucking with your credit or your reputation, this is where it will show up.

Write a blank check. Don't put your home address, phone number, or driver's license number on your printed checks. If they're stolen, you may have handed the thief the keys to your personal kingdom.

Use a private mailbox. Getting a Post Office box or private mail drop is a little more hassle, but you won't have to worry about marketers having your home address or your Social Security checks being stolen by mailbox looters.

Delist yourself. Remove your name—or at least, your street address—from phonebooks, online directories, and search engines. The lack of an address makes you less attractive to marketers (and harder for stalkers, collection agents, or ex-spouses to find).

Be smart about the Internet. It's a big bad World Wide Web out there, and no sane person goes online without some kind of protection. (For more on the tools you need, see Chapter 3.)

Opt out early and often. If a web site, email advertisement, or telemarketer asks if you'd like them to contact you again, just say no. If you really want their stuff, you'll know where to find them. When you sign up for a new site or service, ask the company to not share your personal information.

Control access to your PC. You've got a lot of personal information on that little box, and it's nobody business but yours (unless, of course, you're served with a court order).

Avoid surveys, contests, and sweepstakes. These are cheap ways to suck personal information from you for a one-in-a-million shot at winning. "You may have already won"? Maybe—but you've definitely lost your privacy.

Know your rights. U.S. privacy laws leave a lot to be desired, but some (like the Fair Credit Reporting Act) can be lifesavers in the right circumstances. Don't expect other people, companies, or agencies to defend your rights for you. (For more on key Federal protections, see the sidebar "Privacy and the Law" in Chapter 1.)

No Vault Insurance

The Annoyance: I've got seriously sensitive work materials I need to protect, so simply making files private ain't gonna cut it.

The Fix: Encrypting your data folders can help. (Encryption is an especially good idea if you need to protect notebook data. See "A Note About Notebooks.") If someone manages to circumvent your logon security and copy your files, they won't be able to read them. Windows XP Professional comes with an Encrypting File System (EFS) tool built in, though it only works on NTFS hard drives. To encrypt a folder using XP Pro, launch Windows Explorer, right-click the folder you want to protect, select Properties and click the Advanced button. Check the "Encrypt contents to secure data" box and click OK, followed by Apply. In the Confirm Attribute Changes dialog, choose whether you wish to apply the changes only to that folder or all subfolders and files within it, then click OK. You'll have to wait a bit while the attributes are applied. (If you use XP Home and/or want to protect just a single file on your computer, see the tip below.)

However, XP Pro shipped with relatively weak 40-bit encryption. (In general, the more bits used to generate the encryption key that scrambles your data, the harder it is to break. Researchers have broken 40-bit keys in about three hours using high-speed computers.) If you need to secure your files from crooks, hackers, or other serious threats, you'll want 128-bit encryption at a minimum, and that means turning to off-the-shelf encryption software for the PC and Mac, such as PGP Desktop Home ($69, *http://www.pgp.com*). PGP supports a wide range of different encryption methods, up to 4096-bit RSA, which means you could have a roomful of NSA agents with keyboards and supercomputers and they still wouldn't be able to crack it.

Mac OS X aficionados can employ the built-in 128-bit File-Vault to encrypt files and password-protect data. Click the System Preferences icon—that light switch on the Mac's toolbar—and select Personal→Security. Click "Turn on FileVault," enter your system password (if you have one), then click "Turn on FileVault" again. The Mac will shut down any open data files while it's encrypting your Home folder.

Windows doesn't provide an obvious way to protect individual files in XP Home (thanks, Microsoft), but here's a workaround that will do the trick: put the file inside a compressed folder, then assign it a password. Open Windows Explorer or My Computer and right-click the file you want to protect. Select Send To→Compressed (zipped) Folder. Windows will create a zipped folder (with a little zipper icon next to it) inside the same folder where your file is stored. Double-click the zipped folder to open it in a new Explorer window. Pull down the File menu inside the new window and select Add a Password. (On some systems, you may need to select Options→Password.) Type your password (twice), click OK, and close the new window. When you want to open the file, double-click the zipped folder, then double-click the filename. You'll be prompted to supply a password. But remember to delete the original (uncompressed and unprotected) version of the file, or all your skullduggery will be for naught.

Hide in Plain Sight

The Annoyance: I don't want to make a second career out of securing my hard drive; I just have a few files that I want to keep private. Isn't there a simpler way?

The Fix: There is. Windows lets you hide any file or even entire folders so they won't show up in My Computer or Windows Explorer.

First, store your sensitive files in a subfolder and pick a boring name for it (like "spreadsheets" or "work"). (You don't have to do this, but it will make your files harder to find and appear less interesting to snoops.) In Windows Explorer, right-click that new folder, and select Properties. In the Attributes section check the Hidden box, then click the Apply button, then OK. Then select Tools→Folder Options and click the View tab.

Scroll down to the item that reads Hidden Files and Folders and select the "Do not show" option and click OK. Close Explorer and reopen it. Your folder will not be visible until you go back into your Folder Options menu and select "Show hidden files and folders" (see Figure 2-2).

You can do the same thing with individual files: Just right-click on the file, select Properties, check the Hidden box on the General tab, then click OK.

Remember, while this technique works fairly well to stop folks from accidentally stumbling upon your private stuff, it won't stop a savvy spy (or determined spouse) who knows what to look for.

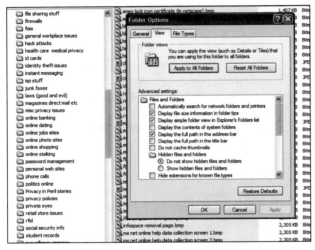

Figure 2-2. To keep snoops out of your files, mark them as hidden.

Complete Delete

The Annoyance: I used to be a bad person, but I've reformed. I've also deleted every file on my computer that could get me in trouble with the law, my spouse, or the Recording Industry Association of America. But I hear that deleted files never really go away. Is that true? How can I make sure the stuff that I deleted stays deleted?

The Fix: When you click "delete," the files stay in your Recycle Bin until you empty it. Even then they can be restored fairly easily using file recovery software such as Executive Software's Undelete ($30, *http://www.executivesoftware. com*). That's because the data isn't actually deleted; Windows just lops off part of the filename so your hard drive's filing

system can't locate it. Eventually, an application will overwrite the file with new data, but that could take months. Meanwhile, the data is accessible to anyone with decent computer forensics skills.

The cheapskate's way of purging files? Erase the files, empty the Recycle Bin, and defrag the hard disk. This can overwrite erased files, making their secrets unavailable to snoops. To run the defragger, select Start→All Programs→Accessories→ System Tools→Disk Defragmenter. Then go do your laundry or crack open a good book, because it's likely to take a while.

But to be sure the data is really gone, you'll need an electronic file shredder such as CyberScrub Privacy Suite ($50, *http://www.cyberscrub.com*) that can overwrite deleted files multiple times so that nobody—not even the spooks at the NSA—can recover them. WinGuides' Privacy Guardian 3.0 ($30, *http://www.winguides.com*) can also wipe your Recycle Bin and shred individual files so they'll never be seen again. Both products can also wipe out data lurking in temp files, document histories, and much more. Best of all, you can tell them to clean out your old stuff on an hourly, daily, or weekly basis, so you never have to think about it again.

To make deleted files unrecoverable on Mac OS X systems, just open the Trash Can, click Finder, and select Secure Empty Trash. But to evict any file fragments or temp files still loitering on your hard drive, you'll need a tool like Jiiva's Auto-Scrubber ($60, *http://www.jiiva.com*).

Watch Your Backups

The Annoyance: I am a backup fanatic—I've got Zip discs full of backup copies of every file that's ever been on my computer. But that means my Quicken data and personal correspondence are also on these discs. How do I keep somebody from stealing my financial info by taking the discs?

The Fix: You can turn your PC into a digital Fort Knox but still get burned by an errant floppy. You've got to protect your data everywhere it resides, but especially on your backup discs, since they're easier to steal and you may never notice they're missing.

WinBackUp ($50, *http://www.liutilities.com/products/winbackup/*) automates data backups, protects data using strong 256-bit encryption, and lets you assign passwords to backup data sets so only you can open them. If you're doing manual backups, you can also use PKWare's PKZIP ($29, *http://www.*

pkware.com) or SecureZIP ($100) to compress and encrypt your data files, no matter where they reside. But PKZip encyption is fairly weak—you can find free software on the Net that helps you crack it—so SecureZIP is a better call for scrambling sensitive data.

The next issue: where do you plan to store the backups? A locked drawer in your desk may be fine if you're just stashing old love letters and other personal correspondence. But if you want to store tax or financial information, work-related documents, or anything else whose loss would keep you awake at night, you'll want to keep backups in a secure off-site location. Otherwise, any natural disaster (fire, flood, locusts) that takes out your home computer could also wipe out your backups. Smart thieves might also leave the heavy computer and take the highly portable discs, since they can make a lot more money by stealing your identity.

A safe deposit box at your bank is a reasonable storage option, though it can be a bit of a hassle going to the bank every time you make a backup set. (See Chapter 5, "Safety in Boxes?") Another option is online backup.

ISPs such as Earthlink (*http://www.earthlink.net*) and Microsoft Network (*http://www.msn.com*) and web services such as Yahoo (*http://www.yahoo.com*) offer some online storage space with each account—enough for quick-and-dirty backups of data files. But you'll have to copy your files manually, and the data isn't protected as it passes from your PC to their servers. If you're running a small business or need to store sensitive stuff, get a dedicated online backup service that encrypts the data so hackers and other snoops can't get at it, and automates the process so you can set it up and forget about it.

Connected's DataProtector service (*http://connected.com/solution/DataProtector.asp*) offers backup plans ranging from $80 a year (for 250MB) to $800 (30GB), with a 30-day free trial. @Backup (*http://www.backup.com*) offers a similar service starting at $50 (50MB). Both make it simple to set up and schedule backups, and both provide enterprise-level security and redundant copies of your data, in case there's a problem with their servers. The downside? If your Net connection goes down, you can't get at your backups.

PICK A PECK OF PASSWORDS

For better or worse, the main form of privacy protection for most people is the password. It's also one of the weakest, but it's better than nothing. You can make it stronger by picking a good one. In general, the longer and more obscure the password, the less risk someone will guess it and go to town with your data.

You don't need to create unique passwords for every web site, file, or account, just the important ones—your online bank account, sensitive files on your hard drive, and so on. For less vital stuff you can get away with reusing the same password.

The obvious advice? Don't be obvious. Avoid using your name, your dog's name, your Social Security Number, birthdates, or any other information that others can readily obtain about you. Avoid words normally found in the dictionary, and use a mix of letters and numbers, upper and lower case. For example: "Password" is a bad choice, "pAssWoRD" is slightly better, and "2P@$$w0rd468" is better still.

If you can, choose a pass phrase—such as "I used to be disgusted but now I try to be amused"—instead of a single word. But remember this could backfire if you choose something others might be able to guess (like if a snoop knows you're a longtime Elvis Costello fan).

Write your passwords down and keep them in a secure place away from your computer (not in your wallet or purse, either). Better yet, use a free program like Any Password (*http://www.anypassword.com*), which can generate random passwords and store them in an encrypted file so you don't have to remember them (though you will need to remember the password to get your Any Password files).

IS YOUR TV SPYING ON YOU?

While you sit in that comfy chair watching the tube, your TV could be watching you. Sound far-fetched? If you use a personal video recorder (PVR) such as a TiVo, it may not be.

Around 3 million people use TiVo to pre-record their favorite programs and fast-forward through commercials. But every time you record something, that information is sent back to TiVo. By default, TiVo collects only anonymous viewing information, which it shares with advertisers and third parties such as Nielsen Media Research. In other words, TiVo might know that 987 people in your ZIP code recorded The Quilting Channel, but it wouldn't know that you were one of them.

However, if you buy something through TiVo service, such as a pay-per-view event, or you request information from one of its advertising partners, TiVo knows who you are and what you bought, and so do its partners. (They have to know who you are so they can bill you for it.) If you use TiVo's Online Scheduling feature to program your DVR via the Internet, TiVo captures who you are and what you plan to record.

According to TiVo's privacy policy, the service can also "use anonymous viewing information to develop inferences that people who watch show X also watch show Y," which suggests that it could be technically possible to match your viewing history with your ID. (TiVo officials were not available for comment.)

What do they do with this information? TiVo may use it to promote more products to you, and so might the third-party. (In fact, once another company has your information, they can do whatever they want with it, as long as it's legal and within the limits of their privacy policy). But if you're caught in a legal tussle where your viewing habits become relevant—say, you're in a custody battle and your spouse's attorney wants to know how much time you spend recording the Spice Channel—your viewing habits could come back to bite you.

In 2002, a group of studios and broadcasters sued SonicBlue, maker of the ReplayTV device, and convinced a judge to make SonicBlue hand over information about who owned the machines and what they watched. But the ReplayTV boxes weren't set up to record this information, and SonicBlue got a U.S. District Court judge to overturn the order. (In April 2003 SonicBlue filed for bankruptcy; its assets were purchased by Japan's D&M Holdings.)

If you don't want TiVo to know who you are, don't buy anything from them, or use their Online Schedule features selectively. You can tell TiVo to stop tracking your anonymous viewing habits. Call them at (877)367-8486, or send a letter to:

TiVo, Inc.
ATTN: Privacy Policy
2160 Gold Street
P.O. Box 2160
Alviso, CA 95002-2160

But that's just TiVo. Many cable and satellite companies offer their own brand of DVR, and their privacy polices may vary. (And, of course, if you record programs using a Windows Media Center PC or other PC-based DVR, then anyone can find out what you've recorded simply by looking on your PC.) Examine their privacy policies to find out what information they collect and what they do with it—and stay tuned in case their policies change.

Microsoft Confidential

The Annoyance: There are only a handful of Office files that are really for my eyes only—I don't want to invest a lot of time and money in encryption products.

The Fix: Microsoft Office 2000, 2002, and 2003 let you password protect—and with 2002 and 2003, heavily encrypt—individual files (see Figure 2-3). In Microsoft Word 2002 and 2003, open the file you want to protect, select File→Save As, click the Tools menu in the upper right corner of the dialog box, select Security Options, and then enter passwords in the "Password to open" and "Password to modify" boxes, and click OK. (In Word 2000, select Tools→General Options.) For corporate-level security that's hard to hack, in Word 2002 and 2003, click the Advanced button in the Security tab and select a more robust encryption scheme (such as 128-bit Microsoft Enhanced RSA), and click OK twice. In Excel, the commands are slightly different (File→Save As→Tools→ General Options) but the effect is the same.

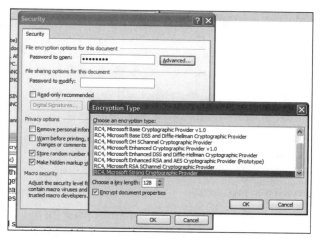

Figure 2-3. Microsoft Office 2003 gives you loads of options for encrypting individual files so that nobody can unscramble them-including you, if you forget your password.

BEYOND PASSWORDS

Tired of remembering passwords? American Power Conversion's Biometric Password Manager can put dozens of logon names and passwords at your fingertips—literally. Just plug this $50 fingerprint scanner into your USB port. After you've trained it to recognize your fingerprint, you can use it to control access to Windows, the Web, or virtually any password-protected file on your PC. Whenever a dialog box prompts you for a password, just stick your finger on the pad—Windows loads, web sites grant you entry, and files open—no typing required. You can also use it to encrypt and decrypt folders and files on your hard drive. (Even if you unplug the device, APC's software will prompt you for a password before you can access the files.) That's a good way to keep your notebook data from walking off. *http://www.apc.com/products/family/index.cfm?id=246*; (800)877-4080.

Cleaning up for Charity

The Annoyance: I've got an old computer that's too slow to be used as anything but a doorstop. I was thinking of donating it to a local charity and getting the tax deduction, or maybe selling it as an antique on eBay. But it still has old financial records of mine. Should I worry?

The Fix: Old hard drives, even ones its owners think are clean, can be packed with sensitive information that's nobody else's business. In June 2004, Pointsec Mobile Technologies, a security firm based in Stockholm, purchased 100 old hard drives on eBay. Approximately 70 had data that could be recovered; one drive contained the customer records of a leading European financial services firm. (The cost of said drive? $10. The information? Priceless.)

If you don't need any of the data on the system, the best thing to do is reformat the entire hard drive (and, if you want to be truly nice, reinstall a clean copy of the original operating system). If you've still got the CDs that came with the machine, you should be able to find instructions on how to do this. If you've lost the CDs (or the system is so old it didn't come with CDs), you can manually reformat the disc. Here are the two basic ways to reformat a hard drive:

1. First, create a startup disk. After inserting a floppy disk into the drive, launch Windows Explorer and right click on the A: drive and select Format. In the next dialog box, check the "Create an MS-DOS startup disk" box and click the Start button. When Windows warns you that all data on the disk will be overwritten, click OK. Click OK when the "Format complete" window appears, then click the Close button.

A NOTE ABOUT NOTEBOOKS

Notebook PCs present an even bigger privacy challenge than desktops, since nogoodniks can simply walk off with them, taking your personal correspondence, address book, financial information, and more in the process. So you need to be careful (approaching paranoia) about keeping your laptop in reach of your lap.

Use an old bag. Nothing screams "steal me!" quite like a fancy leather laptop bag in an airport. When you travel, put your machine inside something less obvious, like a briefcase (the more worn out, the better) or a backpack. Be sure to add sufficient padding to avoid jostling the hard drive too much.

Take a number. Write down your machine's serial number and stick it a safe place (i.e., not in a Word doc on your laptop). This will come in handy later if the machine is recovered.

Let a password be your watchword. This almost goes without saying, but the logon precautions you use on a desktop are de rigueur for anything built to move. If you've got both a desktop and a laptop, choose a different password for each.

Encrypt your data. Even if a thief manages to circumvent your logon security, he or she won't be able to get at your data if it's encrypted and password protected. (See "No Vault Insurance").

Tell it to phone home. Software such as CyberAngel Security ($60 annually, *http://www.sentryinc.com*) and Computrace Personal ($99 for three years, *http://www.computrace.com*) can help you track down a stolen notebook by secretly sending you an alert if the thief logs onto the Internet with your machine.

Be alarmed. Make thieves think twice by adding an alarm to your notebook. The Targus PA480U DEFCOM MDP ($100, *http://www.targus.com*) plugs into your laptop's PC card slot and emits an 110db shriek if anyone tampers with or tries to abscond with your machine.

Lock it down. Even when you're not on the road, your notebook is at risk from burglars or light-fingered co-workers who prowl the cubicles looking for swag. Secure-It (*http://www.secure-it.com*) and Kensington (*http://www.kensington.com*) offer cables that plug into your laptop's security slot and lash the notebook to anything immovable, starting at just $30.

2. Second, use that startup disk to format the drive. With the floppy still inside the machine, restart Windows. It should boot up to a DOS prompt. At the A:> prompt type `format c: /s` (assuming that the C: drive contains your system files). When it warns you that your data will be lost , type Y to proceed.

If you get a "command not found" error, you may need to manually copy the ancient DOS program Format.com to the floppy. You should be able to find it in the \Windows\System32 folder.

If your drive is split into other logical partitions (D:, E:, and so on), you'll need to follow the same steps, but substituting the appropriate drive letter for C: and leaving off the /s switch (since those drives won't contain system files).

However, even a reformat isn't entirely bulletproof. If your old data is truly sensitive (e.g., secret plans for a missile defense system, Britney Spears' unlisted home number), you may want to wipe the disk first. One free alternative is Darik's Boot and Nuke, a program you can download at *http://dban. sourceforge.net/*. After you install it onto a floppy or CD, just insert the disk into the drive of the machine you want to wipe, reboot the machine, and follow the prompts.

If that's too geeky for you (and it probably will be), you can also pony up for a product such as CyberScrub or Privacy Guard (see "Complete Delete"), or Symantec's Norton SystemWorks 2005 ($70, *http://www.symantec.com*). These will all allow you to wipe your old system so that even the NSA wouldn't be able to reconstruct your data.

HOME SWEET NETWORKS

Stop WiFi Drive Bys

The Annoyance: My home wireless network has been acting funky and some of the settings seem to be changed. What's going on?

The Fix: You could be a victim of drive-by hacking. Freeloaders may be taking a joyride on your home network, accessing the Net via your wireless connection or worse, pawing through your system. Keep in mind that a WiFi setup uses radio signals to broadcast data up to 500 feet from the router, which means a network you set up in your home office can easily extend into the street outside your house. In fact, seeking out unprotected WiFi networks—called *wardriving*—

has become a favorite pastime of some geeks (see *http:// www.wardriving.com*). A recent survey of some 225,000 home WiFi networks by WorldWideWardrive.com found more than 60 percent were completely wide open. Talk about an entrée for freeloaders and hackers!

Aside from tightwad neighbors sucking up your Internet bandwidth, you could be a sitting duck for anyone who wants to troll your hard drive for juicy information. Even if your PC is protected with a firewall, somebody could use your LAN to send out malware-laden email or download kiddie porn—and it will be you the Feds are chasing, not the bad guys. To find out if your WiFi network is open, download the free Net Stumbler (*http://www.netstumbler.com*) and run a scan (see Figure 2-4). If your network is unprotected, it will be listed with a green light next to it. (Secure networks have green lights with locks inside). Odds are you're giving the neighbors a free ride. (For tips on how to secure your WiFi network, see the sidebar "WiFi Tiki Tavi.")

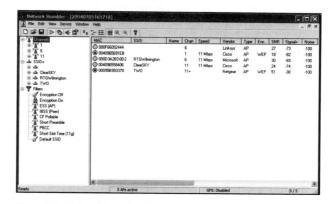

Figure 2-4. NetStumbler is a handy (and free) tool for finding WiFi networks in your vicinity—and seeing which ones are wide open and easy to access. (Make sure yours isn't one of them.)

Share and Unshare Alike

The Annoyance: I want to share some folders on my PC with other folks connected to my home network. But I definitely do not want to share all of them. How do I pick and choose?

The Fix: To its credit, Windows XP ships with file and folder sharing turned off by default. With sharing turned on, anyone connected to your network can peer inside your files. (This led to a huge privacy snafu for the first cable broadband users, who were essentially connected to a neighborhood-wide local area network, which made it easy for neighbors to snoop at will inside anyone's shared folders.)

XP makes it fairly easy to share document folders across your network. Open Windows Explorer or My Computer, right-click the folder you want to share, select Sharing and Security, and then check the "Share this folder on the network" box to allow other folks on your network to read (but not edit) documents inside that folder. To let people edit your stuff, check the "Allow network users to change my files" box. When you're done, click OK.

To share individual files, drag the file into your shared documents folder (usually called "My Shared Documents"), and then change the settings of the folder as outlined above to make it available on the network.

With Mac OS X, you can share files and folders by dragging them into your Public folder and turning on file sharing (open System Preferences, select Internet & Network→Sharing→ Services, put a checkmark next to Personal File Sharing, and click Start).

Remember, if you have a WiFi network, follow the security measures outlined in the "WiFi Tiki Tavi" sidebar, or you could be sharing files with any snoop who passes by. My advice? When in doubt, make sure file and folder sharing is turned off and make My Documents (or whatever folders you store data files in) private. (For tips on how to do this, see the "Foil Hard Disk Snoops" sidebar.)

WIFI TIKI TAVI

Your WiFi network doesn't have to be wide open. All WiFi routers—the boxes that connect your broadband modem to other devices in your home—can be made more secure, though instructions vary depending on the equipment. You'll need to load the CD (or visit the site) you used when you first installed the router, and find the Advanced settings. Once you get there, take these steps:

Change your logons. Most routers come with a default logon and password for administrators (something clever like "default" or "admin"). A hacker could log in as you and change all your network settings. Change the defaults to something that's easy for you to remember but hard for others to guess.

Name your network. When you set up your WiFi router, you're asked to supply a name for your network (known as the Service Set Identifier, or SSID). Anyone who wants to log on needs to know your SSID, so pick one that's hard to guess. (For example, the default name for Linksys routers out of the box is, duh, "Linksys"—something you'll want to change ASAP.) Don't forget to change the SSID settings for each computer on the network.

Interrupt this broadcast. Most wireless routers are set to broadcast your SSID to anyone that passes by. Disable this feature and it'll be much harder for strangers to find your network. Make sure you only disable SSID broadcasting; if you turn off anything akin to wireless networking in the router's setup screens, you might shut down your entire network.

Make yours scrambled. All WiFi routers come with encryption that scrambles data passing over the network so no one else can peek at it, but this option is usually turned off by default. You typically have two choices: Wireless Encryption Protocol (WEP) is considered weak encryption but probably fine for most home users; the stronger WiFi Protected Access (WPA) is harder to hack, but not all WiFi equipment supports it. Your wireless adapter(s) must support the encryption scheme offered by your router and provide the correct key (or password) for entry. If you're stuck using WEP, remember to regularly change the WEP key—and always choose the 128-bit encryption option.

Check your firmware. Before you fire up either WEP or WPA, download any firmware updates for your router and other WiFi hardware—these patches may offer enhanced security features.

Change channels. Another good scrambling trick is to regularly change the channel your router broadcasts over. Since your computers already know your new and improved SSID, all you have to do is reboot them after this change and they'll find your network without a hitch.

Pull over MAC. You can tell your router to let only specific devices log on and reject all others. The trick? Simply add the each machine's Media Access Control (MAC) address, a 12-digit number usually found on wireless network cards, to the router's list of allowed devices.

CELL PHONES

Spam to Go

The Annoyance: I just received a text ad for a cheap home mortgage on my cell phone. Not only am I receiving ads I don't want, I'm being forced to pay for them! What can I do to stop cell phone spam?

The Fix: Unsolicited ads sent via cell phone text messaging services has been an unpleasant fact of life in Japan and Europe for a few years, and it could become a big problem for the United States' 165 million cell phone owners. The CAN SPAM Act of 2003 authorized the FCC to look into methods for stopping phone spam; in February 2005, the agency published a list of wireless domains to which spammers were forbidden to send commercial text messages without a customer's permission. (For more info, see *http://ftp.fcc.gov/cgb/ policy/canspam.html*.) But given the miniscule impact CAN SPAM has had on our email inboxes, don't expect much relief from the FCC ruling.

The practical step is to call your wireless provider to register a complaint; many will simply take the spam messaging charges off your bill, says John Walls, VP of public affairs for the Cellular Telecommunications and Internet Association (CTIA). He adds that major wireless carriers are aware of the problem and actively filter out most spam messages before they reach customers. While you're at it, be sure to file a complaint with the FCC at *http://www.fcc.gov/cgb/complaints. html* or call them at (888)225-5322.

IS YOUR CELL PHONE STALKING YOU?

In the good old days, dialing 911 on your cell phone was about as effective as rolling down the window and shouting "Help!" Unlike traditional land line phones, emergency operators had no easy way to trace wireless calls back to their physical location. That began to change in 1996 when the Federal Communications Commission mandated that tracking technology, such as Global Positioning Satellite transponders, be built into every cell phone, which allows emergency responders to pinpoint their locations. Wireless carriers are required to implement "Enhanced 911" (E911) capabilities in their networks by December 31, 2005, but when this service will be available nationwide is anyone's guess, thanks to problems upgrading the country's antiquated emergency response equipment. (For the 411 on E911, see *http://www.fcc.gov/911/enhanced/*.)

But this GPS data may also be available for commercial use. In 2002, AT&T Wireless (now part of Cingular) rolled out a "Find Friends" service in 15 U.S. cities that let subscribers locate people via their cell phones, as well as seek out restaurants, ATMs, and so on, based on their location. In both cases, these services rely on GPS data to figure out where you (or your friends) are on the globe. This is just the beginning of a multi-billion-dollar "location-based services" market in which your cell phone becomes a playback device for advertisements based on where you happen to be. Walk by an Italian restaurant, for instance, and your cell phone might alert you it's just received a coupon for a free Coke with every purchase of a pepperoni pizza. And if the pizzeria can triangulate your location, what's to stop local law enforcement officials—or your spouse's divorce attorney—from tracking your movements? So far, not much. The courts have barely begun to address such issues, in part because such services are only starting to appear. Wireless industry groups say commercial GPS services will only be implemented with the customer's permission, though they've yet to define how such permission will be obtained. Moral of the story? The next time you're going out on a private errand or a discreet rendezvous, you may want to turn off your cell phone.

Cell Phone Candid Camera

The Annoyance: Somebody just snapped a picture of me in a compromising position with their cell phone camera. Can I have him killed?

The Fix: Not legally. But you may be able to have him fined and sent up the river for a year. Thanks to the recently enacted Video Voyeurism Prevention Act of 2004 (*http://thomas.loc. gov/cgi-bin/bdquery/z?d108:S.1301:*), covert cameras are banned in locker rooms, bedrooms, up or inside various bits of clothing—anywhere the involuntary photo subject had a "reasonable expectation of privacy." (So if someone captures you during a wardrobe malfunction at the Super Bowl, you're out of luck.) A more realistic solution: approach the shutterbug, remind him or her of the law, and politely ask that the photo be deleted (assuming, of course, he hasn't already emailed it to his blog—see "Moblog Rules").

Moblog Rules

The Annoyance: OK, I wasn't naked when they took the shot, but it wasn't pretty—and then they posted it on their mobile phone web blog, where various strangers have been commenting on it. How can I get it removed?

The Fix: The proprietors of mobile web logs (moblogs) take a dim view of people posting photos without the subject's consent—though with hundreds of thousands of such blogs sprouting up, enforcing this practice is next to impossible. If your picture appears on a moblog site such as TextAmerica or FotoLog and you don't want it there, contact the service and complain. Most moblogs list a contacts page (TextAmerica's is at *http://www.textamerica.com/contact.aspx;* to contact FotoLog send email to *admin@fotolog.com*). You will likely have to surrender some personal information, such as who you are and why you feel the photo invades your privacy. If your mug shot appears on a private web site and the owner refuses to remove it, contact their web hosting company or Internet Service Provider—most have similar rules about posting inappropriate or copyrighted material.

PRIVACY IN PERIL: VIRUSES ON THE MOVE

In June 2004, Russian security vendor Kaspersky Labs announced it had detected the first virus specifically targeting mobile phones. The virus, named Cabir, affects only Bluetooth phones using the Symbian operating system, which includes Series 60 phones made by Nokia.

Cabir spreads wirelessly from phone to phone using Bluetooth, and had been sighted in 17 countries at press time. According to Finnish anti-virus vendor F-Secure, Cabir-infected phones could be used for Bluejacking (inserting contacts or messages on someone else's phone), Bluesnarfing (data theft), Bluetracking (following the owner's movements) or Bluebugging (listening in on conversations by getting the phone to call you back). Mostly, however, the virus runs down cell phone batteries by constantly scanning for Bluetooth devices. F-Secure makes a patch that detects and neutralizes the virus (see *http://www. f-secure.com/estore/avmobile.shtml*).

F-Secure warns that before long we're likely to see Trojan Horses masquerading as games or screensavers that can falsify billing records and steal personal information from your phone. And as Microsoft moves aggressively into the mobile market, one can only imagine what virus writers will conjure up for Windows-based phones.

IS YOUR PHONE TAPPED?

You hear a strange clicking sound whenever you pick up the phone. Is it squirrels chewing on the wires, or are G-men camped out in a laundry truck outside your house tapping your line? Unless you're a drug lord, a Mafia don, or a suspected member of a worldwide terrorist conspiracy, it's probably the squirrels.

For starters, today's surveillance equipment is so sophisticated you'd never be able to tell if your line was bugged. For another, authorized wiretaps are exceedingly rare. According to the Administrative Office of the United States Courts, there were 1,442 Federal and state wiretaps in 2003, with nearly 4 out of 5 related to drug cases. (For the full report, see *http://www.uscourts.gov/wiretap03/2003WireTap.pdf*.) Add to that another 1,724 intercepts approved under the Foreign Intelligence Surveillance Act, and we're up to roughly 3,200 taps—still an infinitesimal fraction of the more than 300 million land and cell phones in the U.S.

If you get your phone service using a voice over Internet protocol (VoIP) hookup, your conversations could theoretically be open to hackers as well as the Feds. In August 2004, the FCC directed VoIP vendors to make their networks accessible to law enforcement. Security experts point to VoIP as a likely target for hackers and crackers looking to eavesdrop on conversations or flood your digital line with "voice spam."

Louis Mamakos, chief technology officer for VoIP vendor Vonage, acknowledges that hacking into an unencrypted VoIP stream is possible, though difficult. Hackers would have to intercept the calls near the source and pick through a stream of data to identify the voice packets. He says a bigger concern is simple fraud, where people steal your phone service for free.

Of course, a private party could be tapping your line, which is a federal crime. If you suspect someone's listening in on your calls, contact your phone company and ask them to check the line. If your suspicions prove true, the phone company will alert you and notify the authorities. But if you're the subject of an official wiretap, don't expect them to tell you—at least, until after the investigation is long over.

Your cordless phone could be transmitting your conversations to the world—or at least, nosy neighbors with a cheap radio receiver or even a baby monitor. The solution? Replace your old 46MHz or 900MHz unit with a spread-spectrum 2.4GHz or 5.8MHz digital phone that's harder to eavesdrop on. And use a wired, landline phone for making confidential calls.

If you're worried about the Feds snooping on you, it's better to contact the FTC by phone than by filling out a form online. According to Chris Hoofnagle, associate director of the Electronic Privacy Information Center, material submitted to the FTC can be disclosed to law enforcement with a court order. So if the FBI wants to match an email address to a phone number, they've got a handy list of 85 million Americans they can scan. When you call, they don't have your email address.

Wireless Wiretaps?

The Annoyance: Maybe I've been watching too many episodes of *The Sopranos*, but I'm wary of talking on my cell phone for fear someone else might be listening in. Can people tap my mobile calls?

The Fix: It depends on the type of phone you're using. Calls made with older analog cell phones could be heard using police radio scanners you could buy via mail order. (The sale of such spy gear is now illegal—as is private citizens tapping into other people's phone calls, of course.) Today's digital cell phone transmissions are much harder to tap into. You're more at risk from someone overhearing your conversation. (For more info, see *http://www.spybusters.com/cell_phone_privacy.html*.) The real question is why anyone would want to listen in; the answer probably depends on how much time you've been spending at the Bada Bing!

Are people you're talking to recording the conversation? They may be—and may have every right to do so, depending on where they live. In California, for example, recording is legal only if both parties consent. But in Texas only one party—the one capturing the call—needs to consent. In fact, 38 states have "one-party" rules. (*See http://www.pimall. com/nais/n.recordlaw.html* for more info.) Think about that the next time you call your paramour in the panhandle.

TELEMARKETING, JUNK MAIL, AND FAXES

Don't Ask, Don't Telemarket

The Annoyance: I get more calls from telemarketers—or their auto-dialer machines—than from people I know. I'm sick to death of it. How do I make it stop?

The Fix: Here's something that actually seems to work: sign up for the Federal Trade Commission's Do Not Call List. Since it launched in June 2003, more than 85 million Americans have signed up. You can add your name and number to the rolls by visiting *www.donotcall.gov* or calling (888) 382-1222. You'll have to wait three months before your request officially takes effect. Telemarketers that violate the Do Not Call rules can be fined up to $11,000 per incident (to file a complaint, visit *https://www.donotcall.gov/Complain/ComplainCheck.aspx*). As of June 2004, the FTC had received more than 550,000 complaints about companies violating the list, though it had taken action against only one telemarketing firm thus far.

Do Not Call Does Not Work

The Annoyance: OK, I signed up for the Do Not Call list (DNC). Yet I still get calls at my place of work from charitable organizations and other businesses. What gives?

The Fix: Unfortunately, the Feds also built in a number of exceptions to the DNC. For example, the list only covers home numbers, not businesses. Political or charitable organizations and people taking surveys are also exempt. You can try adding your business number to see if telemarketers will remove it anyway (seemed to work for me). You can also use the Direct Marketing Association's mail preference service, which is used by some charities as well as businesses, to take your name off calling lists (see *http://www.dmaconsumers.org/cgi/offtelephonedave*). Otherwise you'll have to ask each organization that calls you to put your name and number on its internal do-not-call list, which they're legally required to honor.

Block that Scam

The Annoyance: I've signed the DNC and opted out from various businesses that call me. Yet I'm still harangued by callers touting bogus investments, rare coins and stamps, offshore lotteries, and emu farms. How do I get these sleaze merchants out of my life?

The Fix: The bad news is that once you're on somebody's sucker list, it's hard to get off. Your name and number will get sold from one scammer to the next (and if you actually invest in any of these flimflams, you'll get even more calls). You can report these con artists to your local police and the FBI's Consumer Sentinel site (*http://www.consumer.gov/sentinel/*), but first you'll have to keep the scammers on the phone long enough to capture information (like a street address or call back number) that the Feds can use to nail them. The Junkbusters site offers a script (*http://www.junkbusters.com/script.html*) you can use the next time a scammer calls. Or you can download the free Enigma Anti-Telemarketing software (*http://www.kahl.net/reduce/telemarketing.html#Enigma*), which contains a similar script alongside relevant laws, and lets you keep a record of your conversations with these folks (see Figure 2-5).

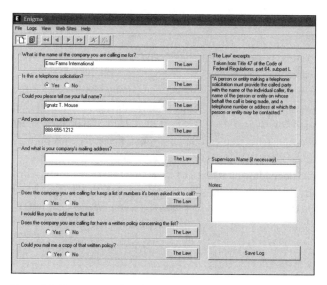

Figure 2-5. Want to see a telemarketer wrapped in an Enigma? This very simple PC and Mac program gives you an easy way to track and report unwanted telemarketing calls.

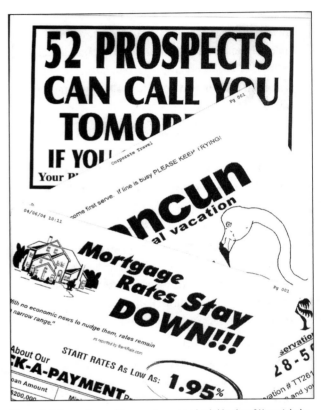

When you dial a toll-free number, your number is recorded by the company you're calling (hey, they're paying for it, so they get to see who's calling). Even if you've got Caller ID blocking turned on, the company may be able to see it using a system called Automatic Number Identification. Theoretically, they could add it to their lists and use it to call you at some later date. If you jealously guard your phone number, use a calling card or call from a different number, or dial the company's toll number.

Just the Fax, Ma'am

The Annoyance: Every morning at 6 a.m., my fax machine spews out another ad for cheap health insurance, stupid stock tips, or low-rent cruise vacations. Isn't there a law against this? What can I do to stop it?

The Fix: Yes, there's a law all right. The Telephone Consumer Protection Act of 1991 specifically prohibits the involuntary use of your fax machine as an advertising medium (see Figure 2-6). But that hasn't stopped companies like Fax.com from spewing out tens of millions of unwanted ads—or from being sued for *trillions* (yes, trillions) of dollars in damages under the Act. What you can do about junk faxes depends on how much time you want to devote to the topic. The simplest method? Most junk faxes come with a toll-free opt out number you can call to unsubscribe. In my experience, about half the time the number doesn't work. But I have seen a reduction in junk faxes since I called (your mileage may vary).

If you're in a fighting mood, you can demand money (from $500 to $1,500 per fax) from the fax broadcasters and/or the companies that use them. The Junkfax.org site details a dozen different ways to fight back, from sending demand letters to suing in small claims court, along with ways to figure out just who's sending you all this crap and lists of attorneys who specialize in such cases. Just be sure to hang onto the faxes; you'll need them when you have your day in court.

Figure 2-6. Is your fax machine spewing out junk ads like these? You might be able to sue the pants off the folks who send it (though collecting on the suit is another matter).

Junking Junk Mail

The Annoyance: My mailbox is groaning under the weight of catalogs, mailers, brochures, and "You may have already won!" offers. I want to get letters from only people I know.

The Fix: You're not alone. According to the Privacy Rights Clearinghouse, the average American receives around 30 pounds of junk mail per year—about four trees' worth. You'll never totally eliminate junk mail, but you can reduce the level of deforestation slightly. First, use the Direct Marketing Association's Mail Preference Service to get your name off national mailing lists. If you're willing to pony up $5 for the privilege, you can sign up online (*http://www.dmaconsumers. org/cgi/offmailinglist*). You can also send your request via snail mail to:

> Mail Preference Service
> Direct Marketing Association
> PO Box 643
> Carmel, NY 10512

Naturally, there are some caveats. You'll wait at least three months before you'll see any effect; many direct marketers don't adhere to the DMA's mail preferences, so they'll continue to send you junk; and this request only covers mail sent to a home, not a business. But that's just the beginning. The Privacy Rights Clearinghouse site has excellent, highly detailed instructions on how to get off other mailing lists (see *http://www.privacyrights.org/fs/fs4-junk.htm*).

Be careful when tossing your junk mail; companies (particularly financial institutions) have been known to send privacy disclosure information in packages that look suspiciously like unsolicited advertisements. So look before you feed everything to the shredder.

Direct the Junk Elsewhere

Want to reduce your junk mail, but still want long-lost friends and relatives to find you? Call the phone company and change your directory entry so it only lists your name and number, not your address. If there's no street address or ZIP code, marketers will be less interested in you.

Flag Mag Nags

The Annoyance: I get a lot of catalogs and other junk I don't want, and I'm convinced that the magazines I subscribe to are selling my name to these merchants. How do I get them to stop? How do I know who they're selling it to? Is there a one-stop place to opt out?

The Fix: When it comes to generating unwanted marketing dreck, magazines are some of the biggest culprits (and I know, because I've worked for a bunch of them). They rent their subscriber lists to advertisers, catalog merchants, and anyone willing to pony up a few pennies per name. The classic trick for tracking who's renting your name is to sign up for subscriptions using a slightly different name for each publication—so if you signed up for *The New Yorker*, you might use Bob NYer Smith. Then track how much junk mail comes addressed to Bob NYer. To simply stop them from renting your name, check the magazine masthead—you'll usually find an address or phone number you can use to opt out.

Pick Your Mail

The Annoyance: I don't want to stop all mail advertisements. I'm in the market for a retirement home, so I want to receive any offers related to retirement communities and resorts. How do I attract the mail I want without getting buried by stuff I detest?

The Fix: Laser-like precision in this realm isn't likely. Still, you may be able to winnow a bit by using Junkbuster's handy Declarations Form (*http://www.junkbusters.com/jdu.html*). This form lets you state exactly what kinds of solicitations you will or won't accept, and from what kinds of companies (charities, magazines, financial services, etc). You can then send the declaration to direct mailers, post it on your web site, or ask Junkbusters to send the form to you. Marketers may ignore your request, but at least you've tried.

IDENTITY THEFT

Foil Mailbox Miscreants

The Annoyance: My mailbox is bursting with offers for pre-approved credit cards and home equity loans. I'm worried somebody might get to my mail before I do and steal these offers.

The Fix: You should be. Your mailbox is a prime target for identity thieves, and any mail containing sensitive information—like credit card offers, bills, receipts—could be used by a thief to create new accounts in your name.

The first step is to tell the big credit reporting agencies (Equifax, Experian, Innovis, and TransUnion) to stop selling your information for use in pre-approved credit card offers. Simply call (888) 567-8688 and provide your home phone number, full name, address, zip code, Social Security Number, and date of birth. You can choose to have information suppressed for five years or permanently. You can also fill out a form online at *http://www.optoutprescreen.com* (see Figure 2-7).

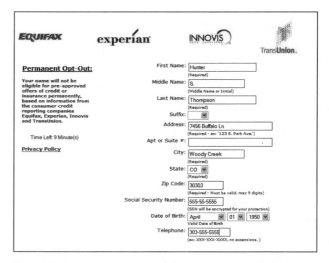

Figure 2-7. You can opt out permanently from pre-approved card offers at optoutprescreen.com, but do it quickly-if you don't fill out the form within 10 minutes it turns into a pumpkin.

But you might still get credit offers from banks that get your name from other sources, as well as other offers that contain information ID thieves would love to get their hands on. Worse, anyone going through your trash could easily find the stuff you thought you'd tossed. To foil dumpster divers, buy a good crosscut paper shredder. You can find one that will even chew up your old credit cards for around $70 at an office supply store. To limit strangers' access to your mail, get a locked mailbox that lets your mail carrier feed everything through a slot (prices start at around $150), or direct all your commercial mail to a Post Office box or private mailbox.

Check Your Reports

The Annoyance: Someone broke into my home and stole my wallet. They took all my credit cards, my driver's license, various shopping affinity cards, and club membership IDs. What could happen to me? Can someone steal my identity?

The Fix: Absolutely. In fact, the loss (or borrowing) of your identity is a far greater problem than losing the cash and the cards. Identity thieves can run up bills, take out loans, and skip bail—all in your name. Left unchecked, they can seriously impair your ability to obtain a loan, medical insurance, student aid, housing, or employment. You could also end up being arrested for crimes you didn't commit. According to the FTC, there were nearly 10 million victims of identity theft in 2003. In most cases, the theft wasn't committed electronically but the old fashioned way—from stolen wallets, credit card receipts, unopened or misdirected mail, or eavesdropping.

Obviously, if your wallet is gone you'll want to call and cancel all your cards (you did write your credit issuer's phone numbers down, didn't you?). The best way to find out if someone is running amok with your identity is to check your bank account online (once a week is probably sufficient) and order credit reports from the major credit reporting agencies (see Figure 2-8). Here's how to find them:

Equifax Information Services, LLC
Disclosure Department
P.O. Box 740241
Atlanta, GA 30374 (800) 685-1111
http://www.equifax.com

Experian
National Consumer Assistance
Box 2104
Allen, TX 75013-2104
(888) 397-3742
http://www.experian.com

Innovis Consumer Assistance
P.O. Box 1358
Columbus, OH 43216-1358
(800) 540-2505
http://www.innovis.com

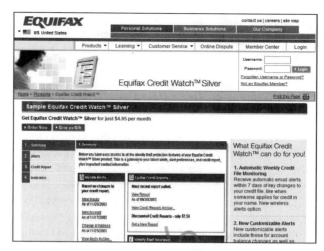

Figure 2-8. Identity theft has been good to one group at least: the credit reporting agencies. Each offers a suite of services for consumers afraid of having their identities stolen, for fees ranging up to $120 a year.

TransUnion LLC
Consumer Disclosure Center
P.O. Box 1000
Chester, PA 19022
(800) 888-4213
http://www.transunion.com

All but Innovis let you order instant reports online, though to get them you'll have to surrender your Social Security Number, date of birth, and mother's maiden name, as well as your credit card info. The web entry form is on an encrypted page, but if that makes you nervous you can order your report by phone or mail instead. In most cases, reports cost $10 for one or $30 to $35 for a consolidated report from all three agencies. All are also happy to sell you services that alert you to new activity on your credit report for a cost of $5 to $10 a month.

A new law, the Fair and Accurate Credit Transaction Act, lets all U.S. consumers order a free credit report each year, though this service won't be available in all regions of the country until Fall 2005. To find out if it's available where you live, visit the site at *http://www.annualcreditreport.com*. You can also get a free report if you've recently been turned down for credit, you're unemployed, or you live in states that require the agencies to provide a free report.

Stop, ID Thief!

The Annoyance: Yep, it's happened to me. I checked my credit reports and there's another person out there pretending to be me, opening new accounts, and ruining my credit rating. Help!

The Fix: If you've been a victim of ID theft, you've got your work cut out. According to a survey conducted by the Identity Theft Resource Center (*http://www.idtheftcenter.org*), it takes 600 hours on average for victims to correct the damage brought on by the pilfering of their IDs, along with more than $1,400 in out-of-pocket expenses. Here are the most important things to do if you believe your identity has been nabbed, courtesy of the FTC, identitytheft.org, and the Privacy Rights Clearinghouse:

- Close any accounts you think may have been affected. This can include accounts at department stores and utility companies as well as banks. Get new accounts with different numbers. If any accounts have been opened by the thief in your name, ask that they be permanently removed from your record.

- Contact at least one of the major credit reporting agencies and place a "fraud alert" on your file. (See "Check Your Reports" for contact information.) If you contact one agency, it's required to contact the others. This will tell the bureaus to look for and flag any unusual activity, such as the opening of new accounts under your name. Request they keep the alert live for seven years.

- The agencies should send you a copy of your credit report after you issue the fraud alert. Go over it in minute detail, to find out when the thieves began usurping your identity. Dispute any charges that look suspicious, and close down any new accounts that you did not open.

- Report the incident to the police and insist they file a report, even if the chances of catching the thief are slim. Make copies of the police report.

- Send letters via certified mail, with return receipt requested, to all of the agencies and credit card accounts, detailing the incident. Include a copy of the police report with each letter. This will help if you need to dispute charges later.

- Instruct your state DMV, Social Security Administration, and U.S. State Department to be on the lookout for anyone applying for identification in your name.

- Keep a journal of whom you contacted and when, along with copies of all correspondence and receipts.

For more detailed instructions on the appropriate steps to take, see the Privacy Rights Clearinghouse's fact sheet on recovering from ID theft (*http://www.privacyrights.org/fs/ fs17a.htm*). You'll also want to visit the Identity Theft site *http://identitytheft.org* created by ID theft victim and book author Mari Frank, which offers a wealth of information and comfort to those similarly afflicted.

PRIVACY BY THE NUMBERS

27.3 Million
U.S. victims of identity theft, 1998 to 2003

$5 Billion
Money lost by ID theft victims in that period

1 in 4
Odds that your credit report contains an error serious enough to deny you credit or employment

62%
US wireless home networks that are vulnerable to drive-by hackers

$5.4 Million
Fine levied by the FCC against Fax.com for flouting anti-junk fax laws

$2.2 Trillion
Amount of private class action suits brought against Fax.com

130,000
Number of telemarketers that have allegedly violated FTC's Do Not Call rules

1
Number of telemarketers pursued by FTC as of February 2005

Sources: FTC, Public Research Interest Group, The Washington Post, worldwidewardrive.com, junkfax.org.

3

Privacy on the Net

Seemingly overnight, the World Wide Web has turned into the Big Bad Net. You can't open a newspaper (or dial up a newspaper's web site) without reading about another privacy threat traveling over the wires or across our WiFi networks.

More and more it seems like we're engaged in a cyber war, and the bad guys are winning. Spammers overwhelm our inboxes with sleazy come-ons, and no one seems able to stop them. Every few days a new email worm appears, more virulent than the last. Trojan Horses and spyware infect our PCs and steal our data, or turn our machines into tools for digital delinquents to launch attacks. If online stalkers don't track us down, identity thieves surely will, ruining credit ratings and reputations in the process. You say you live to swap MP3s? You may live to regret it when a record industry subpoena lands on your doorstep.

Meanwhile, your browser holds a veritable cornucopia of personal information about you and your habits, which rapacious e-marketers will capture and sell to the highest bidder. And no one, not even a child, is safe.

Is life on the Net really that bad? No. But it can be, if you don't take sufficient precautions. Here are some real-world ways to protect yourself in cyberspace.

BROWSING AROUND

Erase Your Browser's Footprints, Part 1

The Annoyance: I surf the Web every day and never give a thought to online threats. But what about the information on my surfing stored on my PC? Can anyone simply walk up to my computer and see where I've been and what I've been up to?

The Fix: You bet. A web browser like Internet Explorer can build an amazing dossier on you and your interests, available to anyone who sits at your keyboard while you're away. (Of course, first they have to get at your browser—see Chapter 2, "One Computer, Many Eyeballs," for information on how to limit access to your machine.) They can see the pages you've looked at, the places you've shopped, the terms you've searched for, and much more. Fortunately, there are ways to cover your tracks and keep your browsing habits private. As with most of life's odious chores you can either do the job yourself or hire someone else—in this case a software utility—to do your dirty work. Here's the DIY route.

Step 1: Forget Your History. By default, Internet Explorer 6.x and Mozilla Firefox 1.0 maintain nearly three weeks worth of browsing history (Netscape 7.x and 8.x store a mere 9 days by default). That can be handy for those senior moments when you know you saw a fascinating web page last week but can't remember when or where; unfortunately, it's also like having a digital gumshoe on your trail. To erase your history in IE 6.0, go to Tools→Internet Options, click the General tab, click the Clear History button, and then OK. Now you're back to square one. To keep IE from recording your future wanderings, in the same dialog box set the "Days to keep pages in history" to 0. (But if you have another senior moment, you're on your own.)

In Netscape 7.x, you'd select Edit→Preferences, double-click Navigator in the left-hand pane and select History, then click Clear History. In the same window you can also set the number of days you want Netscape to remember your web travels. Then click OK.

In Netscape 8.0, you'd select Tools→Options→Privacy, then click the Clear button next to the Page History item. Click the + sign next to Page History and tell Netscape how many days you want it to remember your web travels. To have Netscape erase its memory when you're done surfing, check the "Clear Page History on browser exit" box and click OK.

In Firefox the steps are virtually identical (not surprising, since both browsers are based on the same open-source code). Choose Tools→Options→Privacy, and then click the Clear button next to the History window. Click the + sign next to History, and you can tell Firefox how good you want its memory to be. You can use this same window to clean out your cookies, file cache, and other traces of your surfing past (see "Make Web Forms Shoot Blanks").

Step 2: Dunk Your Cookies. Nearly every site likes to leave a little snack behind in your cookies folder. Some are temporary and may get deleted when you close the browser; others can linger for years. At the very least, a cookie contains the address of a web site you viewed—even if it was only an ad placed by another site. To erase the temporary cookies in IE 6.0, go to Tools Internet Options, click the General tab, then click the Delete Cookies button. You'll still have your permanent cookies—the ones that help you automatically log onto sites where you've registered or remember your preferences for a particular site. If you want to lose those as well, you must manually delete them from your cookies directory; on an XP system, they're typically in \Documents and Settings\ *yourname*\Cookies. Select them all and press Delete.

To crush cookies in Netscape 7.x, go to Tools→Cookie Manager→Manage Stored Cookies. In the next dialog box you can select which cookies to delete or simply click Remove All Cookies and then Close to nuke them en masse. Just remember, this last step will also delete permanent cookies you might want to keep.

To crush cookies in Netscape 8.0, go to Tools→Options→Privacy, and click the + sign next to Cookies. To remove some but not all cookies, click the View Cookies button, select the web sites whose cookies you don't want to keep, and click Remove Cookie. To crumble all the cookies at once, click Remove All Cookies.

Step 3: Clear out your files. IE may download graphics and other content from sites to speed up page displays. These files can give away where you've been. So open up the familiar Tools→Internet Options box and click the Delete Files button; in the ensuing dialog box, check the "Delete all offline content" box, then click OK. This will nuke any images or other content stored on your hard drive. (It will also make frequently visited web sites a little slower to load at first.)

To accomplish the same trick in Netscape 7.x, select Edit→ Preferences, and double-click Advanced in the left-hand pane. Select Cache, then click the Clear Cache button. If you don't want Navigator to cache web content in the future, set the Cache setting to 0MB. Then click OK.

In Netscape 8.0 the steps are slightly different. Select Tools→ Options→Privacy, and click the Clear button next to Cache. If you don't want Navigator to cache web content in the future, click the + sign next to Cache, and check the "Clear Cache on browser exit" box. When you're done customizing Netscape's privacy settings, click OK.

Step 4: Fire those temps. IE squirrels even more files away in temp folders, whose contents you'll have to delete manually. Windows XP users will generally find them in the \Documents and Settings*yourname*\Local Settings\Temp and \Temporary Internet Files folders. (Netscape buries its Cache folder even deeper—in a subfolder under \Documents and Settings*yourname*\Application Data\Mozilla\Profiles*yourname*) You may need to go in and periodically clear them out to fully cover your tracks.

Netscape 8.0 gives you a quick-n-easy way to privatize all of your browsing. Select Tools→Options→Privacy, and check the "Clear My Tracks on Exit" box. That will obliterate virtually all traces of your activity when you close down Netscape.

Erase Your Browser's Footprints, Part Deux

The Annoyance: Oy! Do I really have to do all this every time I use Internet Explorer or Netscape? Surely there's an easier way.

The Fix: There is, but it'll cost ya. For wall to wall protection, WinGuide's Privacy Guardian for Windows ($30, limited-feature free trial available, *http://www.winguides.com*) can automatically clear histories and tons of other incriminating data for IE, Netscape, Firefox, and the Opera browser, as well as Windows and Microsoft Office apps. You can schedule it to run at startup or have it clean house several times a day; you can even tell it to "bleach" free disk space so that any lingering traces of data are unrecoverable even by the CIA. And it's truly a snap to use. Though a smidge more expensive and trickier to use, CyberScrub Privacy Suite Professional 4.0 ($50, 15-day free trial, *http://www.cyberscrub. com*) offers slightly broader protection, such as cleaning out the traces left behind by dozens of apps, including AOL 9.0's browser.

Even after you clear out Netscape 7.x's history and cache, the browser's Download Manager still maintains a list of every file you've downloaded off the Net. To purge this list, select Tools→ Download Manager, highlight the listed items, and select Remove from List. To do the same in Netscape 8, select Tools→Options→Privacy, click the Clear button next to Downloads Manager History. To tell Netscape to not remember your downloads, click the + sign and put a checkmark next to "Clear Download Manager History on browser exit."

Make Web Forms Shoot Blanks

The Annoyance: Every time I start to fill in the blanks on a web form, my browser pops open a little window showing me stuff I've typed before that's similar to it—including my address, phone numbers, and sometimes even my credit card numbers. Can anyone who uses my computer also get this information simply by typing a few keys at random?

The Fix: Yes, they can. But this is another situation where you must balance privacy and convenience. It's a pain in the carpals to continually retype your shipping address or phone number on each web site. Fortunately, the major browsers give you some control over the information they store.

In IE 6.0, select Tools→Internet Options, click the Content tab, then click the AutoComplete button. To make IE forget what you've filled out, click the Clear Forms button, and then click OK to confirm. You can also do the same for your passwords by clicking Clear Passwords and OK. Of course, IE will then start remembering your keystrokes all over again. To tell IE to forget what you've typed into the browser's address window, online forms, and login screens, uncheck the boxes next to each item in the AutoComplete Settings dialog box, then click OK twice.

Netscape 7.x gives you a lot more control. Select Tools→Form Manager→Edit Form Info. Here you can provide your shipping and billing addresses, phone numbers, even your credit card and Social Security info (if you dare). Personally, I'd recommend filling in your credit card info manually on sites you trust, and not sharing your SSN online *anywhere* if you can avoid it. If you later decide Netscape should not be so free and easy with your data, select Remove All Saved Data and start over with a blank slate.

In Firefox, select Tools→Options→Privacy. Here you can erase your browser history, form information, passwords, downloads, cookies and cache files by clicking the Clear button next to each category; to nuke everything at once click Clear All (see Figure 3-1). If you don't want Firefox to remember what you've filled in, click the + sign next to Saved Form Information and uncheck the "Save information I enter into web page forms and the Search bar" box. When you're done, click OK.

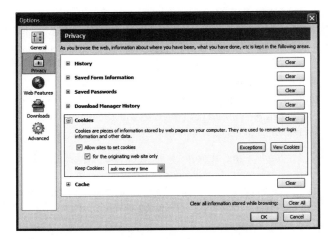

Figure 3-1. Among its many other benefits, Firefox provides an easy way to clear out cookies, file cache, and other evidence of your web surfing history

Rewrite Netscape's History

The Annoyance: I've cleared my history in Netscape, but the names of some web sites still show up when I click the down arrow in the address bar.

The Fix: You've discovered one of the chinks in Netscape 7.x's armor. Unlike IE, Navigator doesn't automatically clear out the names of web sites you've typed into the address bar. To wipe these out, go into Edit→Preferences→History and click the Clear Location Bar button. (This problem is solved in the Netscape 8.0.)

Maximum Privacy, Maximum Headaches

The Annoyance: I set my browser's privacy to its highest possible setting. But now I can't log onto any of my favorite web sites. What gives?

The Fix: At its highest privacy setting, IE 6 blocks all cookies, including those already planted on your hard disk. Unfortunately, many sites—including the *New York Times* web site and sites like Hotmail that require Microsoft .NET passports to log in—say 'no cookie, no entry.' Nice, eh? You'll need to crank down IE's privacy settings in order to access these sites.

So open the ever-popular Tools→Internet Options, click the Privacy tab, and move the slider bar to Medium High (see Figure 3-2). That setting allows some sites to plant cookies but not others. You can also customize IE's automated cookie settings. In the Privacy tab window click the Advanced button and check the "Override automatic cookie handling" box. Now you can tell IE to accept all first-party cookies (those set by the site you're visiting) and block third-party cookies (those set by another site, such as a banner advertiser), or to prompt you each time so you can make decisions on the fly. (For more information on which cookies to accept, see "How the Cookies Crumble.".)

In Netscape 7.x, use Edit→Preferences→Privacy and Security→Cookies, then select "Enable cookies for the originating web site only." This allows, say, *nytimes.com* to set cookies on your hard drive (so you can log in), but forbids banner ads on the Times site from feeding you cookies.

Firefox fans should select Tools→Options→Privacy, click the + sign next to Cookies, then check the boxes next to "Allow sites to set cookies" and "for the originating site only." In the drop-down menu under Keep Cookies, select "Until they expire." That way, you can keep the helpful cookies—like the ones that contain your login information and site preferences—while rejecting the nosy ones.

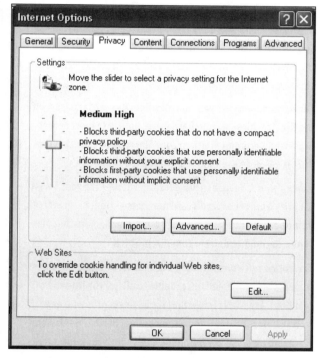

Figure 3-2. Hang 'em high. Well, medium high. IE 6.0 lets you adjust your browser's privacy settings higher than many sites (including Microsoft's) can tolerate. Medium High is usually the best compromise, allowing some sites to place their cookies on your PC while crumbling those delivered by other sites.

> **t i p**
>
> Security guru Steve Gibson (see his site at *http://grc.com*) has another approach to browser safety. He leaves his browser on its highest possible security setting, then creates exceptions for web sites he trusts and uses on a regular basis (such as Amazon or CNN). To do this in IE 6.0, select Tools→ Internet Options, click the Privacy tab, and move the slider all the way up so it reads "Block All Cookies." Then go to the Security tab, click the Trusted sites icon, click the Sites button, and type in the names of sites whose cookies you're willing to accept. Click the Add button and then OK twice.

TEN ESSENTIAL PRIVACY TOOLS

Hackers, viruses, spam, spyware—it's just not safe to go on the Net unarmed. Here's a quick guide to essential tools for safeguarding your privacy; most cost from $20 to $40, and many are available for free or a nominal license fee.

My recommendation? Get a security suite that combines several tools in one. Suites are both easier to use (only one interface to master) and significantly cheaper than buying each piece separately. For my money ZoneLabs' ZoneAlarm Security Suite ($40 annually, *http://www.zonelabs.com*) offers the widest range of tools and is the easiest to use.

Firewall: This software is like a bouncer at a nightclub—nobody gets in or out until your firewall gives the thumbs up. The best firewalls make your PC invisible to hackers trolling the Net and alert you if a program tries to do something it shouldn't (e.g., send data across the Net without your permission). Recommendation: ZoneLabs Suite. Cheapskates might check out ZoneLabs' free download (*http://www.zonelabs. com/store/content/company/products/znalm/freeDownload. jsp*), which provides basic firewall protection.

Anti-virus package: Prowls your computer's hard disk, memory, and email/IM traffic looking for malicious software to neutralize, using a constantly updated list of viral signatures to identify them. The best A/V programs automatically update their signature lists several times a week and make it easy to scan individual files or your entire disk. Recommendation: ZoneLabs Security Suite or Norton AntiVirus 2005 ($50, *http:// www.symantec.com*).

Spam filter: Scans your incoming email and shunts suspect messages into a penalty box so you can get to your legitimate mail. If your inbox looks like a junkyard, these filters can be a real time saver. The best ones, such as MailFrontier Desktop ($30, *http://www.mailfrontier.com*), install automatically inside Outlook or Outlook Express. Recommendation: ZoneLabs Suite comes with MailFrontier built in; a good standalone alternative is Qurb ($30, *http://www.qurb.com*).

Phish detector: Keeps your spam filter from being fooled by a "phisher" email—a message that lures you to a fake web site so scammers can steal your account information. (Qurb and MailFrontier both feature special tools for identifying phisher mail—another good reason to use them.) Recommendation:

EarthLink's free IE Toolbar can keep you from reaching fake sites set up by phishers; toolbars for Firefox and other browsers are due out later this year. (See "Don't Bank on It.")

Adware/spyware blocker: Scans your system for secretly installed programs that can barrage you with pop up ads (or worse, report on your web movements), and eradicates them. Recommendation: Sunbelt Software's CounterSpy ($20 annually, *http://www.sunbelt-software.com*) or WebRoot's Spy Sweeper ($30 annually, *http://www.webroot.com*).

Pop-up blocker: Stops annoying advertisements that can install spyware or other malicious software on your computer. Firefox, IE (with Service Pack 2), and Netscape all come with pop-up blockers, but none is foolproof. Recommendation: if your browser isn't doing the trick, STOPZilla ($30 annually, *http://www.stopzilla.com*) surely will; it can also eradicate spyware.

Cookie manager: Lets you control what sites can leave identifying files (cookies) on your hard drive; built into most recent browsers. Recommendation: ZoneAlarm Suite's cookie manager is easier to use than IE's, Firefox's, or Netscape's.

Privacy guard: Keeps sensitive information—like your Social Security Number or credit card numbers—from inadvertently being sent over the Net via web forms, email, or Instant Messages. Recommendation: ZoneAlarm Suite.

Encryption software: Scrambles data so no one else can access it, or makes your email unreadable to all but the intended recipient. Especially important for business pros who need to transmit sensitive information online. Recommendation: HushMail (*http://www.hushmail.com*), which comes in a free web-only version. The $30 paid version gives you more storage, comes with tech support, and can work inside Outlook.

Web monitor: Blocks web sites with objectionable content, used widely in schools and households with small children. The apps can be helpful but only with regular parental input. ZoneLabs' Suite has a web monitor, but you can't tweak the settings to block only certain sites in a category (e.g., Online Games or Shopping) while allowing others. Recommendation: NetNanny ($40, *http://www.netnanny.com*) gives you more features and flexibility.

HOW THE COOKIES CRUMBLE

Despite the tasty-sounding name, some folks find cookies a little hard to swallow. These tiny text files, deposited by web sites on your computer's hard drive, usually contain nothing more than the site's address and a series of letters and numbers that look like gibberish. But when you revisit a web site, it can read the cookie, use that information to locate you in the site's database, and then customize the page to, say, display a personal greeting or access your account information. However, some types of cookies are used for less benign purposes—such as tracking your movements across the Web—which is why there's such a hullaballoo about them.

The different flavors:

First-party cookies. Set by the site you're visiting, these cookies usually contain information to help the site verify your identity and customize pages to your liking. If you've registered for the site, the cookie may contain personally identifiable information such as your name and email address.

Third-party cookies. These cookies are deposited by web sites other than the one you're visiting—for instance, banner ad networks. These cookies tell advertisers how many people saw the ad and what page they saw it on. That's useful for them, but since they can record the site you've visited, such cookies could be used to track your movements from site to site. Adware and spyware programs use such tracking cookies to pummel you with pop-up ads.

Temporary (or session) cookies. These cookies disappear once you close your browser. Some browsers (such as Netscape) can be set to accept session cookies only from certain sites.

Permanent (or persistent) cookies. These cookies live on your hard drive long after your browser session has ended, providing irrefutable evidence that you've been visiting *http://www.senatorspanking.com*.

Managing cookies is confusing, which is why the major browsers do their best to automate the process for you. When in doubt, only accept cookies from sites you trust, and only first-party cookies at that (see "Maximum Privacy, Maximum Headaches"). A good anti-spyware program will also help you separate the good cookies from the evil ones.

Tell People Finders to Get Lost

The Annoyance: I just typed my phone number into Google and boy did I get a shock—it had my name, phone number, address, even a map to my house. It's like The Complete Stalker's Toolkit. How do I "un-Google" myself?

The Fix: I've got some bad news; it's not just Google. You may well be listed in any number of online directories, such as AnyWho, Whitepages.com, Switchboard.com, and so on (see Table 3-1). Online directories buy this information from data brokers, who get their data from phone directories and other public and private sources. Some—like InfoSpace, Switchboard.com, and Yahoo People Search—obtain their listings from Acxiom, a major U.S. data vendor. You can ask Acxiom to remove your data by sending email to *optout@acxiom.com* or calling 1-877-774-2094; either way,

they'll mail you an opt-out form to send back. But you'll still need to visit each directory and remove yourself, because your data can linger for months and even years. (See Table 3-1 for ways to get removed from major online directories.) In some cases, you may have to call, send a letter, or respond to an email to confirm the deletion.

You should also remember to unlist your phone number with your local phone company, otherwise this information will end up in the white pages, and thence online, and you'll have to start all over again. But remember: delisting yourself will make it harder for old college roommates or ex-spouses to look you up (which may be a good thing).

Table 3-1. Directory assistance.

Directory	Removal page
AnyWho	*http://www.anywho.com/help/ privacy_list.html*
Google	*http://www.google.com/help/ pbremoval.html*
Lycos WhoWhere	*http://help.lycos.com/peoplesearch/ ps_help_form.asp*
Switchboard.com	*http://www.switchboard.com/bin/cgiqa. dll?LNK=24:3&MEM=1&FUNC=DELETE and click the Add/Remove Listing link.*
Whitepages.com	*http://www.whitepages.com/0000/ cust_serv/removal_form*
Yahoo people search	*http://help.yahoo.com/help/us/yps/ yps-03.html*

Fend off Cyber Stalkers

The Annoyance: Virtually every online directory is full of ads hawking background searches, criminal record checks, even photos of my house! Can they really do this?

The Fix: You'd be shocked by how much information anyone can get about you for a few dollars. For about $20 to $60, you can order a background check from sites such as Intelius (*http://intelius.com*), US Search (*http://ussearch.com*), or KnowX (*http://www.knowx.com*) and get a list of former addresses, past and current neighbors, marriages, bankruptcies, tax liens, and more. Drop another $30 to $60 and you can look up someone's criminal record, while $5 to $15 buys a grainy satellite photo of someone's house from PeopleData. com (useful if you're planning an aerial attack, I suppose). See Figure 3-3.

Figure 3-3. "Pilot to bombardier, we have acquired the target." Along with names, address, and various other bits of personal info, PeopleData will sell you a grainy satellite photo of virtually any building you specify.

Most of this information is available for free in phonebooks, county courthouses, and public records databases; you can even get free aerial photos from MSN's TerraServer (*http:// terraserver.homeadvisor.msn.com/default.aspx*). Online data brokers just collate it and make it accessible to anyone willing to pay for it—like stalkers, disgruntled former employees, identity thieves, or anyone else who has it in for you. Nice, eh?

The good news is that, if you ask nicely, some brokers will remove your information from their databases, though they can't remove it from the original data sources, since it's in the public record and can't be deleted. The bad news is the process is tedious, time consuming, and—surprise!—could compromise your privacy by requiring you to send sensitive information through the U.S. mail.

t i p

Don't touch that pop-up. It may look inviting, but clicking certain pop-ups can send a signal to a distant server to install spyware or other nasty bits of code on your machine. In fact, if you're using IE and you haven't installed the current security patches, you don't even have to click—a malicious pop-up ad can infect your computer simply by loading into your browser. The rule: look but don't touch (better yet, don't even look), and patch your OS pronto.

First, run a search on your name and number to find out if your info is even in the site's database. If it is, you'll have to contact each site individually and ask to be removed. You'll usually find this information in the site's Privacy Policy (see the "How to Read a Privacy Policy" sidebar). To opt out of PeopleData, for example, you send an email to *customerservice@peopledata. com*, listing your name, address, phone number, and date of birth. To remove yourself from some (but not all) searches on US Search, you'll need to mail a letter to:

US SEARCH
Opt-Out Program
600 Corporate Pointe, Suite 220
Culver City, CA 90230

US Search asks you to supply your name, email address, current and former street addresses, date of birth, Social Security Number, and any aliases you might be using. (Then just hope nobody steals the letter out of your mailbox.) Intelius's web site says it does not honor opt-out requests, but Ed Petersen, the company's vice president for consumer affairs, says you can remove your name by calling Intelius's customer service line at (425) 974-6100.

Make Ad Weasels Go Pop

The Annoyance: I hate it when ads pop up in front of me when I'm trying to read something on a web page. What can I do to nuke these annoying things?

The Fix: Get yourself a pop-up blocker—or better yet, switch to a browser that has one built in. Netscape 7.x, Firefox, Opera (*http://www.opera.com*), and Mozilla (*http://www. mozilla.org/products/mozilla1.x/*) all come with their own pop-up blockers; Windows XP's Service Pack 2 adds one to IE 6 (see "Making the Move to Service Pack 2" sidebar). Earthlink, Google, and Yahoo also offer free pop-up stopping toolbars that install inside IE. For reliable popup stoppage at a price, the $30 STOPZilla (*http://www.stopzilla.com*) is my personal favorite; it can also clean out IE's browser history and block adware.

But no pop-up blocker works perfectly, and many ads still manage to get around these blockers. With more sites using pop-up windows to deliver useful information—like printer-friendly versions of articles—you'll also spend a fair amount of time creating exceptions for your favorite sites.

Spies You Should Despise

The Annoyance: OK, I installed a pop-up blocker. But I'm still getting swarmed by browser windows filled with sleazy ads. Help!

The Fix: It sounds like your problem isn't pop-up ads, but adware or spyware—probably delivered when you downloaded a file-sharing or animated cursor app. Typical adware apps just track your movements on the Web and serve up advertisements, but some spyware apps can hijack your browser, steal your personal information, or let a remote hacker take control of your system. (For the deep dish on spyware and adware, visit Counterexploitation at *http://cexx.org/adware. htm*.)

Here are five ways to detect a spy in your midst:

1. Some cocky programs will tell you that you're about to install ad-serving software along with the app. They may notify you via a pop-up box during install, or bury this information inside the End User Licensing Agreement. The easiest way to read a EULA is to select all the text inside the EULA dialog during install, then copy and paste it into a document—before you click the "I Accept" button. (In Windows, press Ctrl-A to select all the text, Ctrl-C to copy it, and Ctrl-V to paste it.) If the EULA says a condition of using the software is accepting adware or spyware, don't install it. There's almost always a spyware-free program available that does the same thing. (For more on sneaky license agreements, see "EULA Be Sorry You Did.")

2. Few spyware apps are this up-front, so look for clues. For example, if your browser's home page has suddenly changed, strange items appear in your browser menus or your bookmarks, or your system's performance suddenly sucks, there's a good chance you've been infiltrated. (See "Die Spy Die!" for advice on how to remove it.)

3. Spyware often loads at startup and runs continuously thereafter. Close all your applications so it's just you and your desktop. Launch the Windows Task Manager by pressing Ctrl-Alt-Del (just once, please), then select the Processes tab. Note the name of any processes that look suspicious—for example, the User Name is blank or says "unknown"—and type the name of the file in the "Search

the spyware database" field at SpywareGuide (*http:// spyware-guide.com*). If it's not in the site's spyware list, type the name into Google and see what comes back; it may be an obscure Windows applet.

4. Look at what Windows loads at startup. Select Start→ Run, type msconfig in the Run box, click OK, and select the Startup tab. Scroll down the list of items and look for any checked items that reside in an unfamiliar folder or don't seem to be associated with anything you've installed. Check with SpywareGuide and run Google searches on these files as well.

5. Finally, run a spyware scanner. Earthlink (*http://www. earthlink.net/software/nmfree/spyaudit/*) and PestScan online Spyware Detector (*http://www.pestscan.com*) both offer free downloadable applets that scan your system and report on infestations. But neither tool can solve your problem. For that, you'll have to buy a dedicated anti-spyware utility.

Die Spy Die!

The Annoyance: Ok, I've caught a spy lurking on my system. Now what?

The Fix: Spyware is notoriously hard to remove by yourself. Even if you can delete the pest, it may resintall itself the next time you start your computer. So the best solution is to get a tool that removes it for you and stops future spyware apps from slipping through.

First, try out one of the free anti-spy tools available on the Internet. Spybot Search and Destroy (*http://www.safer-networking.org/*) is a comprehensive shareware application that can hunt down ad cookies, keyloggers, auto-dialers, and Trojan horses in addition to spies, but it may be a little daunting for newbies. Lavasoft's immensely popular Ad-Aware (*http://www.lavasoftusa.com*) is more limited but easier to use. The free version can scan your system and assassinate any spies it finds, while the SE Plus ($27) and SE Professional ($40) versions can prevent spyware infestations in realtime and block other malicious nogoodniks from compromising your system.

EULA BE SORRY YOU DID

So you download some free file-swapping software and decide to read the end user license agreement (EULA) before installing it. Sixty-three pages later you're still reading. Welcome to Claria's Gator Advertising Information Network, perhaps the most notorious piece of adware on the planet.

Gator is found inside free applications such as Kazaa, eWallet, WeatherScope, DivX Pro, and Date Manager, among others. If you've ever clicked a web ad and found yourself suddenly installing software, you may have Gator on your system. Once installed, the software serves up pop-up advertisements (often for other Gator-bundled products) as you surf.

As privacy advocate Ben Edelman points out on his web site (*http://www.benedelman.org/news/112904-1.html*), Claria's 63-page, 5,936-word agreement is chock full of hidden gems. For example, the Gator license prohibits you from using anti-spyware apps to remove it (not that they can do much to stop you). The agreement forbids the use of devices (such as

network sniffers) that can detect what kind of data Gator is sending back about you. And the program is devilishly difficult to evict, especially if you've installed more than one Gator-bearing applet.

In October 2003, security software vendor PC Pitstop surveyed owners of more than 7,000 PCs containing the Gator software. Three-quarters of them did not remember installing Gator. No big surprise—only about 1 percent had taken more than 15 minutes to read the license agreement. For more information, including tips on how to remove Gator and recommendations for software that's similar to Kazaa et al but without the hidden adware, visit PC Pitstop's Gator Information Center at *http://www.pcpitstop.com/gator/default.asp*.

And if you find yourself about to install free software that comes with an enormous EULA (or one that's impossible to read), resist the temptation. There's undoubtedly something in there you don't really want.

If you're lucky, one of those programs can terminate the spy with prejudice. If not, you may need to call in reinforcements. You'll want a program that runs seamlessly in the background while you work, alerts you to any suspicious behavior, and updates itself on a near-daily basis. Webroot's Spy Sweeper ($30, *http://www.webroot.com*) and Sunbelt Software's CounterSpy ($20, *http://www.sunbelt-software.com*) both fit the bill nicely. Microsoft Windows AntiSpyware also looks promising, though it was still in beta at press time. You may need to try out several packages before you find one that purges all the spies from your machine.

Change Browsers and Dance

The Annoyance: I've tried everything to get rid of spyware, but no matter what I do it keeps coming back. Is it possible to surf in peace, or do I have to give up the Internet altogether?

The Fix: Some spyware programs are like in-laws—impossible to get rid of without a painful, messy procedure (like divorce or reformatting your hard drive). For example, there's one particularly virulent piece of spyware called Cool Web Search that hijacks your browser and then delivers an unremitting stream of sleazy pop-up ads. When you try to remove it, CWS simply reinstalls itself in dozens of new places on your computer.

Although no browser is immune to spyware infestations, the one most often targeted is Microsoft's Internet Explorer. If IE has been overrun with spies, you may be able to use another browser—such as Netscape, Firefox, Opera, or Safari for the Mac—without launching a spyware attack. Just remember that some sites won't display correctly in non-Microsoft browsers, and that some services—such as Microsoft's Windows Update (*http://windowsupdate.microsoft.com*)—need IE or they simply won't work. Depending on what malware has wormed its way onto your system, the spyware may be browser-independent and launch itself anyway, even if you don't use IE. So the best plan is to switch browsers *before* you're infected. (See "Should You Dump Internet Explorer?.")

But just using another browser isn't enough. You want to change your default browser, so every time you click a web link you don't launch IE and end up back in spyware hell. For this tip to work, Windows XP Service Pack 1 or later must be installed, and you must be logged on as the computer's administrator.

Open the Add or Remove Programs control panel, and then click the Set Program Access and Defaults button in the left column (see Figure 3-4). Select Custom and click the down arrow to the right. Select an alternate browser that you've installed, such as Firefox. (Don't worry if the "Enable access to this program" box appears to be grayed out—your new browser will still work.) You can also choose different default programs for email, media player, and instant messaging from this same screen, or disable access to programs you no longer want to use (such as Internet Explorer). Click OK. The next time you click a hyperlink, your new browser should launch—free of spies, at least for the time being.

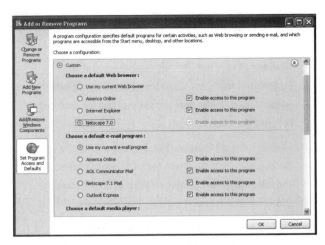

Figure 3-4. Microsoft may automatically makes its browser, email software, and media player your defaults, but you don't have to take it. The Set Program Access and Defaults dialog lets you pick your own default tools-Redmond be damned.

Shoot the Messenger

The Annoyance: The other day a message popped up over my Windows system tray asking "Want sex?" (Sure I do, but I prefer to have mine with humans, not computers.) I wasn't surfing the Web and haven't downloaded anything to my hard disk. What the heck happened?

The Fix: You've been had by a spammer exploiting a flaw (or, if you like, a feature) in Windows Messenger Service. Though easily confused with MSN Messenger, Microsoft's online chat software, Windows Messenger Service was designed to let network administrators communicate with folks over their corporate networks. These days, it's used by a handful of noxious spammers to spread ads for porn sites and other charming services. Fortunately the fix is easy. Simply download and install Gibson Research's free Shoot The Messenger applet at *http://www.grc.com/stm/shootthemessenger. htm*. Click the Disable Messenger button, and then Exit. Simplicity itself. Or, better yet, download Windows XP Service Pack 2, which turns WMS off by default (see the sidebar, "Making the Move to Service Pack 2").

SHOULD YOU DUMP INTERNET EXPLORER?

It's no secret that the world's number one browser has a big bull's-eye on its back. Even the U.S. Computer Emergency Readiness Team—the country's top computer security wonks—says IE is way too vulnerable to attacks. In an advisory issued in June 2004, US-CERT said users should abandon IE for a more secure alternative (for the nitty-gritty, geeky details seek out *http://www. kb.cert.org/vuls/id/713878*).

This advisory followed the discovery of malicious code—known as download.ject or Scob—that could be used to infect web sites and capture the keystrokes of any users who visit them. The site responsible for distributing Scob was shut down shortly after being discovered, and Microsoft says it was "unaware of any widespread customer impact" due to the code. (Then again, how would they know?)

Since then, some 50 million users have downloaded and installed Firefox (*http://www.getfirefox.com*), a free open-source browser that gives web sites far less latitude to muck with people's computers. That doesn't mean Firefox is flawless. In its March 2005 Internet Security Threat Report, Symantec reported that Firefox had more vulnerabilities than IE, but IE's security holes were more serious.

In summer 2005, Microsoft plans to release a beta of Internet Explorer 7, its first new browser release in years. According to Microsoft, the new IE will provide "stronger defenses against phishing, malicious software and spyware," though the company has yet to describe what those defenses will look like.

Bottom line? No piece of software is 100 percent secure. But when you're in a shooting war, it's always a smart idea to choose the smaller target.

EMAIL

Spam Bam, No Thank You Ma'am

The Annoyance: Spam spam egg sausage and spam—that's all I get in my inbox. How did these spammers get my email address?

The Fix: Spammers can grab your email address in any number of ways. If you posted your address in an online forum, newsgroup, or on a web page, it was probably harvested by a spambot—special software that scours the web looking for "@" signs, then collects the addresses surrounding them. You may have signed up for an online sweepstakes at a site like jackpot.com or grouplotto.com and agreed to receive the junk, even if you're not aware you agreed to it. (See the "How to Read a Privacy Policy" sidebar in this chapter.) Or a friend might have signed you up at one of these sites (friends like this you don't need). More likely you were the victim of a "dictionary" or "brute force" attack, where a spammer overwhelms your ISP's email server with messages sent to random combinations of letters (like *bob-aaa@yoursisp.com*, *bob-aab@yourisp.com*, etc); those that don't bounce back are added to the spammers' collection and then sold—over and over and over. So, in other words, you could do absolutely nothing on the Net and some spammer could *still* find your email address and start filling your inbox with junk.

For a detailed discussion of the many ways spammers harvest email addresses, see *http://www.private.org.il/harvest.html*. For a good general discussion of Spam, read the FAQ provided by the Coalition Against Unsolicited Commercial Email (*http://www.cauce.org/about/faq.shtml*).

Whose Address Is It, Anyway?

The Annoyance: I'm tired of being a magnet for electronic luncheon meat. What can I do to wrest my email address from the clutches of these evildoers?

The Fix: Sorry. Once a spammer has your address there isn't much you can do to get it back, short of abandoning your old address and starting from scratch with a new one. But you can limit exposing your new address using a few time-tested tricks. For a start, don't use your primary email address when you fill out web forms, especially for sites that offer something free in exchange for your information. Instead, set up a junk address on a free web mail service (such as Yahoo Mail) and use that one when you sign up. You may have to check that address periodically for legit mail, such as the confirmation messages you get when you sign up for some sites.

If you post information to newsgroups or online forums, you can subtly alter your real email address so it's easy for humans to decipher but impossible for spam bots to harvest. Something as simple as "Bob at yourisp dot com" will tell people you can be reached via *bob@yourisp.com*. If you're starting over, choose an email address that's harder for brute force attacks to guess, such as *bob1776smith@yourisp.com*. That may slow the attackers down a bit.

Finally, if you've got your heart set on putting your email address on your web site, do it by creating an image of your email address with a tool such as Windows Paint, or take a screenshot of your email address (that you've typed into a Word document) and save it as a GIF or JPEG file. Then plop the image onto your page like any other picture. Spambots can't read graphics.

Some ISPs and web services offer disposable email addresses you can use to fight spam. For example, Yahoo Mail Plus ($20 a year, *http://mail.yahoo.com*) lets you create up to 500 addresses you can use to register at sites or hand out in public. All the mail is funneled to your normal Yahoo inbox. When that address starts gathering spam, you can throw it away—essentially turn it off—so the spam no longer flows into your real inbox. ZoEmail ($12 year, *http://www. zoemail.com*) offers a similar system for creating and managing temporary email addresses.

Nix Those Nasty Pix

The Annoyance: I don't mind deleting spam. Sometimes I even enjoy reading the stranger ones—it's like haiku for geeks. But the porn photos do intrude on my right to be let alone. How do I turn these images off?

The Fix: You need to tell your email client to stop displaying email formatted to look like a web page (i.e., written in HTML), and instead display it as plain text. To turn off HTML display in Outlook 2003, for example, you'd select Tools→ Options, click the Preferences tab, click the E-mail Options button, then check the "Read all standard mail in plain text" box (see Figure 3-5). Click OK twice and you're done. From now on, all your mail will be displayed as plain text, with links taking the place of images.

But remember, this change also applies to newsletters and other HTML-formatted mail whose pictures you would want to see. To get around this setting, open the email, right-click the bar across the top of the message that says "This message was converted to plain text," and select Display as HTML.

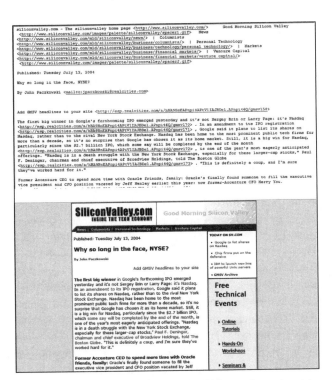

Figure 3-5. You can tell Outlook 2003 to display HTML pages (bottom) as plain text (top) and effectively turn off offensive images. When you get an email you want to see in all its HTML glory, you can restore its appearance with just a couple of clicks.

Some ISPs and web mail services likewise let you turn off pictures in email. In Yahoo Mail, click the Mail Options link, then Spam Protection, scroll down to the Image Blocking section, and decide whether you want to block all images or only those in messages marked as spam; then click the Save Changes button. (If this is the first time you're setting up spam protection, you'll first go through Step 1, Step 2, and Step 3 screens.) With Hotmail you select Mail→Options→Mail Display Settings, and then under Display Internet Images select "Remove images until messages are reviewed," followed by OK. If you're using AOL 9.0, select Settings→Mail Settings, and check the "Notify me before opening mail containing pictures" box and the "Hide images and disable links in mail from unknown senders" box, then click the Save button.

When you create email filters, include misspellings and junk characters—like "ci@lis, cia*lis, cialus," and so on—which spammers use to thwart anti-spam software.

Declare War on Spam, Part I

The Annoyance: Deleting spam takes forever. Isn't there some way to get rid of all the junk before it hits my inbox?

The Fix: Yes, but the solution will cost you time and/or money. The cheap fix is to set up filtering rules in your email client that look for obvious spam messages and route them to a special folder, where you can look them over. If you get only a handful of junk each day, this approach can be effective. If you're swimming in the stuff, you'll spend more time creating and tweaking the rules than you would simply deleting each spam that comes in.

Some email packages, such as Outlook 2003 or Eudora 6.0, already have spam filtering built in (see "Declare War on Spam, Part Deux"). Most other email clients let you build rules from scratch. For example, to set up a filter in Outlook Express 6.x, you'd select Tools→Message Rules→Mail, select the Mail Rules tab, then click the New button and select the conditions and actions for the rule. For example, to limit the number of Cialis ads you receive, check the "Where the subject line contains specific words" box, move down to the Rule Description area and click the "contains specified words" link. Type Cialis into the dialog box that appears, click the Add button and then OK. In the Select the Actions area, check the "Move it to specified folder" box and below in the Rule Description area, click the "specified folder" link. You'll see a list of your current email folders. Highlight Local Folders, click the New Folder button, and name the folder where you want to stash the spam, then click OK twice. At the bottom of the dialog in the "Name of the rule" area, type in a name for your rule (e.g., "No Cialis Spam Rule") and click OK twice.

Now all suspect mail with "Cialis" in the subject line will be shuttled to your spam folder where you can review the messages before deleting them, just in case your filter catches legit mail by mistake. When you create the rule, make sure the rule also searches the From field, message text, and so on. You'll also need to continually add new filters and tweak old ones as new spam pours in.

Declare War on Spam, Part Deux

The Annoyance: It sounds like creating and maintaining email is more work than just deleting the junk.

The Fix: You got that right. Fortunately, there are simpler solutions. You can use tools provided by your Internet or web mail service provider to block spam, provided they have any. You can buy a third-party spam filter that works with your existing email package (the best ones actually work *inside* your email program, which saves you some hassle). You can move up to an email package that has spam filtering built in. Or you can adopt a new email service that filters mail for you. Here's the skinny on each.

1. The biggest service providers—AOL, Microsoft Networks, EarthLink, Hotmail, and Yahoo—all stop millions of junk messages so the stuff never reaches your inbox. They also give you tools for filtering spam that manages to slip by. For example, AOL, MSN, and Yahoo let you provide feedback to the filters by telling them what is and isn't spam—which they use to improve the filters' performance. You can also tweak the settings to stop more spam; for example, you can choose to only receive email from people whose names are already in your address book (a so-called whitelist). This works pretty well for stopping junk, but this also means you'll never get email from new business contacts or your old high school girlfriend.

2. If you don't use one of these services or their spam filters suck eggs, buy a third-party spam filter. This software scans your email as it comes in, shuttles the likely spam into some safe place, and sends the rest of your email to your inbox. There are hundreds of such programs, all claiming to be the best. My personal favorites are Mail Frontier Desktop ($30, *http://www.mailfrontier.com*) and Qurb ($30, *http://www.qurb.com*). Both insert themselves directly into Outlook or Outlook Express, nail the junk, and automatically update themselves to keep up with the latest spammer tricks. But no spam filter is perfect, so you'll still have to delete some junk by hand. All such tools also flag some legitimate email by mistake—especially email newsletters formatted in HTML, which look like spam to most filters. You'll need to periodically scan the junk folders to make sure there aren't any ponies in all that manure.

SPAMOLOGY 101

Approved sender list (or whitelist). This is a list of the people you want to get email from. Many spam filters automatically generate this list by importing contacts from your address book and from mail you've already saved in folders. You can add or delete people from this list at will—depending on, say, how nice they are to you.

Blacklist or blocklist. The opposite of a whitelist; a blacklist consists of email addresses that have sent you spam. Filters will block all subsequent mail from these addresses, but that's small comfort, since spammers rarely use the same address twice. There are also regularly updated blacklists maintained by numerous web sites (such as Spamhaus.org or Spamcop. net) that contain Internet addresses of companies known to have sent unsolicited email. Some spam filters let you check incoming mail against these lists before accepting or rejecting the messages.

Challenge/response. A system where mail from anyone not on your approved sender list is blocked, until the sender can prove (by answering a question, usually via a web form) that they're human beings and not spambots. Very effective but may be off-putting for your correspondents.

False positive. A message your filter thinks is spam, but isn't. No spam filter is perfect, so you must be on the lookout for false positives or you could lose important correspondence.

Junk or quarantine folder. Where spam filters stash all those Viagra ads. You'll need to scan this folder regularly to look for false positives.

Phisher email. A phony message designed to lure you to a bogus web site so scammers can steal your personal information. Most phishers pretend to be from banks and other financial institutions, and may look genuine enough to fool your spam filter.

Spam. Everyone has their own definition. Mine is "commercial email you don't want from people you don't know." Yours might be 'damn near everything in my inbox.'

Spam threshold. Most spam filters let you control how strict they are when they mark messages as spam. The stricter the setting, the more messages—both spam and legit mail— they will block.

Unsubscribe. A link at the bottom of an email ad that theoretically takes you off the spammer's list. Legit businesses are required by law to honor your request. In the past, spammers were notorious for using unsubscribe requests to verify your email address (and thus send more spam). Today they might honor your request—but don't bet on it.

3. Switch to an email app that comes with anti-spam features built in, such as Outlook 2003 or Eudora 6.0. Generally, these filters work as well as the standalone programs, which means you'll still need to boot a few stragglers from your inbox and scan your spam folders for legit messages. But integrated filters can be harder to update than standalone anti-spam programs, so their effectiveness may degrade over time as spammers implement new tricks.

4. Web email services dedicated to blocking spam, such as Spam Arrest (*http://www.spamarrest.com*) and Earth-Link's spamBlocker, can stop 100 percent of the spam, but at a price. Each time someone new sends you mail they must answer a challenge—typically by visiting a web page where they answer a simple question—before their message can reach you. Only those you give the answer to can get through. Because most spam is sent by machines and not humans, challenges aren't answered and the nasty stuff is stopped in its tracks. It's the only type of spam blocker that's 100 percent effective, but impatient humans may ignore the challenge entirely, which means you'll never get their mail.

There Oughta Be a Law.
Wait, There Is a Law!

The Annoyance: I thought spamming was illegal. Why am I still getting this stuff?

The Fix: At last count, 36 states had rules on the books outlawing various spamming practices (for a list of the state laws, see *http://www.spamlaws.com/state/*). But in 2003, Congress passed The CAN SPAM Act of 2003, which pre-empted most of those statutes. ("CAN SPAM" stands for Controlling the Assault of Non-Solicited Pornography and Marketing, proving once again that Congress is better at coining acronyms than writing laws.) The Act essentially says that companies can send you unsolicited email until you tell them to stop, as long as they follow a few simple rules—such as including a real return address on each message, as well as a way to unsubscribe from future mailings. If the bulk mailer doesn't follow the rules, it can be sued by ISPs or the Feds (but not by you). Downsides: you'll have to unsubscribe from every company that sends you mail, which could mean doing it thousands of times a year. And it won't do squat to stop scofflaw spammers—many of them located offshore—from flouting the law and continuing to hawk fake prescriptions, work-at-home scams, and other flimflams. In fact, the volume of spam has increased dramatically since CAN SPAM was passed—from around 40 percent of all email to about 70 percent, by most estimates. So yes, spamming is illegal, but the law ain't helping much.

Fight Fire with Water

The Annoyance: I am so sick of spam I could just scream. Blocking the junk isn't enough . How can I fight back?

The Fix: Unfortunately, the CAN SPAM Act does not allow individuals to sue spammers (don't blame me, blame Congress). But it does allow Federal agencies and ISPs to sue the bastards. In March 2004, AOL, EarthLink, MSN, and Yahoo filed their first suit against spammers under the new law. You can add fuel to their fires by forwarding spam to your ISP's abuse department (usually something like *abuse@yourisp. com*) and to the Federal Trade Commission's spam "refrigerator" at *uce@ftc.gov*. If the spam is also a scam, you can also register a complaint with the Internet Fraud Complaint Center, which is run by the FBI and the National White Collar Crime Center. You'll find a link to the complaint form at *http://www.ifccfbi.gov/cf1.asp*. But remember, they don't accept anonymous complaints, so you'll have to surrender a fair amount of personal info, like your name, phone, email, and date of birth.

SPAM DOESN'T PAY

Howard Carmack, the "Buffalo Spammer," got a double dose of spam justice. In May 2003 he lost a $16.4 million dollar civil suit brought by EarthLink, which sued him for using their servers to send more than 800 million pieces of junk email. A year later he was sentenced to serve a term of 3 ½ to 7 years by a New York State judge for violating New York's Identity Theft law. Carmack was found guilty of stealing the credit cards of two Buffalo residents and using their identities to sign up for ISP accounts, which he used to spew out spam.

In November 2004, a brother-and-sister spam team were convicted under Virginia's anti-spam statute. Jeremy Jaynes received a 9-year sentence for sending a high volume of email using fake routing information, while Jessica deGroot got off with a $7,500 fine for helping her brother purchase domain names for use in spamming.

A month earlier, Nicholas Tombros became the first person to be convicted under the CAN SPAM act. The Southern California man pleaded guilty to "war-spamming"—hacking into wireless networks and using them to send pornographic junk email.

Don't Bank on It

The Annoyance: I got an email that looks like it came from my bank asking me to verify my account information. Should I be suspicious?

The Fix: Very. No bank worthy of your business will ask for your account information via email. You've got what's known as a *phisher* spam—email that pretends to be from a financial services firm (or ISP, or online payment site), but is really designed to coax personal information from you. Phisher email can be quite sophisticated; many feature genuine logos and working links to the corporation's actual site. Some even take you to the real site, then pop up a window that asks for your name and account info; that data gets shuttled to scammers who sell your identity to crooks, who then use it to buy stuff and open new accounts in your name—essentially stealing your identity. According to the Anti-Phishing Working Group (*http://www.anti-phishing.org*), phishing attacks are increasing at a rate of more than 100 percent per month. So expect to see a lot more bogus bank emails.

Some spam blocking packages, such as MailFrontier Desktop and Qurb, have filters to identify possible phisher scams. EarthLink offers a free ScamBlocker toolbar (*http://www. earthlink.net/earthlinktoolbar/download/*) for Internet Explorer that warns you when you attempt to visit a site operated by a known phisher gang (see Figure 3-6). Support for other browsers is due later in 2005, but with dozens of new phishers scams emerging each day, EarthLink can't possible track all of them. Be alert!

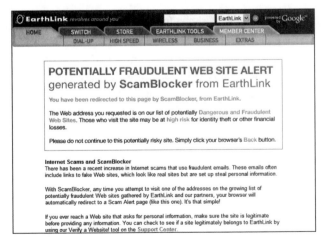

Figure 3-6. So despite all my warnings you clicked the link in that phisher email after all, eh? If you had EarthLink's ScamBlocker toolbar installed, this is what you'd see.

Another option is to download Corestreet's free SpoofStick toolbar (*http://www.corestreet.com/spoofstick/*), which installs into Internet Explorer or Firefox and displays the name of the web site you're really on—a fast way to separate phisher sites from the real McCoy.

To install SpoofStick in IE, click the download link on the Corestreet site, and in the File Download window click Open. Follow the prompts in the install wizard. IE will shut down automatically. When you re-launch IE, the SpoofStick toolbar should be prominently displayed below the address bar.

In Firefox the steps are a little different. If Firefox prevents sites from installing new software (as it should by default), click the Edit Options button in the banner that displays across the top of the page. In the Allowed Sites dialog, click the Allow button, then OK. When Firefox asks you to confirm your choice, click the Install Now button. Restart Firefox, then select View→Toolbars→Customize, find the SpoofStick icon, drag it onto the toolbar of your choice, then click Done.

If you use a different browser, your best recourse is to never click any links inside an email message that claims to be from your bank or other financial institution.

> **tip**
>
> For the skinny on who is behind most of the fake private dick software hawked on the Net, visit the State of Florida's excellent corporations search page at *http://www.sunbiz.org/corpweb/ inquiry/cormenu.html*, click the Name List link, type "Cyberspace to Paradise" and click the Submit button. In the Corporate Name list, click the "Cyberspace to Paradise, Inc." entry. Though literally thousands of affiliate sites sell this software, this is where most of the money eventually ends up. And you don't need detective software to find them.

Always type the name of your bank's web site into your browser, and make sure you arrive at a secure site—the address should begin with https and you should see a tiny padlock icon in the lower right corner of your browser. When in doubt, contact your bank. If there's a phisher scam circulating in their name, they'll likely know about it.

So, is it the real deal or a fiendishly clever spoof? Check the following five tell-tale signs to see if you've got a phisher mail, as illustrated in Figure 3-7.

1. The message was written by someone who flunked sixth-grade grammar or appears to be a non-native English speaker.

2. It threatens that if you don't take immediate action your account will be terminated.

3. It asks you for sensitive information, such as account numbers, Social Security numbers, or date of birth, or directs you to a web site where you're required to provide this information.

4. The web address link doesn't match your bank's normal web address, or the URL shown on the email doesn't match the address of the site when you roll your mouse pointer over the link.

5. The message lacks other ways of contacting the sender, such as a toll-free number. Some phisher emails do include an 800 number, so call it. If your bank answers, ask to speak to someone who can verify the email is legit.

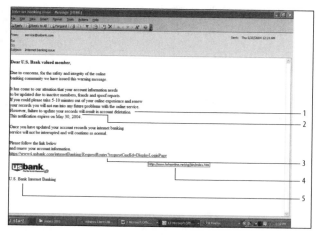

Figure 3-7. Anatomy of a phisher scam.

DON'T BUY THE PHARM

As if phishing wasn't bad enough, there's a variant on the scam that's even more insidious and harder to detect, called pharming. When you've been pharmed, you can carefully type in the address of your bank's web site yet still wind up at a bogus page, handing over your account information to a band of identity thieves.

Pharming attacks the *hosts.txt* file on your hard drive, which your browser uses to translate domain names (e.g., *www.oreilly.com*) into the numbers (208.201.239.36) used by Internet routers. When you enter a URL, your browser looks first at the hosts file and then at your ISP's domain name server (DNS) to turn the words into numbers. Spyware and hack attacks can rewrite your hosts file, so that when you type *www.my-bank.com*, your browser is redirected to a look-alike site run by scammers. (A large-scale version of pharming, called DNS poisoning, does the same thing to your ISP's server—though that type of attack is very rare.)

ZoneAlarm Security Suite lets you protect your Hosts file from being corrupted. (To turn it on, launch ZoneAlarm's Control Center, select Firewall from the list of security apps, select the Main tab and click the Advanced button. Check the "Lock hosts file" box, click OK, then close the Control Center.) Anonymizer.com's Anonymous Surfing app ($30, *http://www.anonymizer. com*) can also thwart pharming attacks by creating a secure connection to the company's servers that bypasses your Hosts file.

If you fear your Hosts file has been corrupted, load it into a word processor. (You'll find it in your *C:\windows\ system32\drivers\etc* folder.) Delete any entries that look suspicious, such as any site that requires a name and password to log in. And, as always, keep a close eye on your credit report, and ask your bank about any transactions that look a little phishy.

Watching the (Digital) Detectives

The Annoyance: I'm bombarded by spam that claims I can find out anything about anybody, simply by buying a $30 software package. Are these things for real?

The Fix: Well they're real in the sense that the people who sell these things really do take your money. But no software product can turn you into a virtual Philip Marlowe, or conversely, expose your secrets to the world. The "detective" software products I've seen consist largely of text files explaining how to find and use public records databases, along with links to paid search sites (such as the ones discussed in "Fend off Cyber Stalkers"). Because the data is public—and largely available for free at sites like Search Systems (*http://www.searchsystems.net*) and Public Record Finder (*http://www.publicrecordfinder.com*)—there's no earthly reason to spend 30 bucks. And since you can't do much to suppress public records (such as property ownership or professional licenses), it makes little sense to worry about it.

Swat Web Bugs

The Annoyance: I've heard that it's possible for spammers to tell if you've read email they've sent you. That just creeps me out. How do they do this, and how can I stop them?

The Fix: You heard right—provided they're sending you HTML mail. In fact, this is becoming standard practice for all bulk emailers, legitimate and otherwise. The trick involves embedding a tiny transparent graphic—often a single pixel—in the message that's tied to a bit of HTML code. When you open the message, that little bit of HTML code tells the page to go fetch a picture from another server out on the Net. But there's no picture to fetch; the server on the other end craftily records that the email was opened, the email address of who opened it, their IP address, browser used, and potentially more. Many web sites use the same technology to determine what pages people open when they visit a site.

To turn off web bugs in email, follow the steps outlined in "Nix Those Nasty Pix" above. To detect the little critters in web pages, download the free Web Bug Detector from Bugnosis (*http://www.bugnosis.org*). Two caveats: it only works inside Internet Explorer 5.x or later, and you may quickly grow tired of the little noise the detector emits as it encounters bug after bug after bug...

Enquiring Minds Don't Really Want to Know

The Annoyance: I received a message from a web site claiming that other people have made inquiries about me. But to get more information, they want $25. Should I pay up to find out what people are saying about me?

The Fix: Not unless you want the word "sucker" tattooed on your forehead. This is an old scam that comes from a variety of domains, such as *http://www.word-of-mouth.org* and *http://www.shareyourexperiences.com*. (See the Snopes Urban Legends page at *http://www.snopes.com/computer/internet/wordofmouth.asp* for more details.) Even if someone was investigating you (doubtful), all these sites do is let you contact them anonymously via email. That's hardly worth 25 bucks.

Free Web Mail, Free Spam

The Annoyance: I signed up for one of those free webmail accounts so I could use it as a spam repository. Now I'm getting spam sent *from* the web mail provider to my primary email account!

The Fix: You didn't think those accounts were really free, did you? The price for using a "free" email account is to be pelted with ads and the occasional spam (see Figure 3-8). Netscape Mail is particularly egregious—it automatically signs you up to receive all types of marketing sludge, including junk mail and telemarketing calls, and not only from Netscape but from its cousins in the Time Warner mediopoly, such as like America Online, MapQuest, and *Fortune* magazine.

Fortunately you can tell them to bug off. With Netscape, sign into your webmail account, click the My Account button below your sign-in name, then select Tools & Services from the menu on the left of the screen, and click the Preferences link under the Communication heading. Change all the Yes answers on that page to No, then click Save, then OK.

Yahoo isn't quite as bad; a free Yahoo Mail account opts you into Yahoo marketing slop, but only the electronic kind. To remove your name, sign in to your mail account, click the My Account link just to the right of the Yahoo Mail logo (you'll have to sign in again), then click the "Edit your marketing preferences" link in the Member Information area, and uncheck all the boxes. Click the Save Changes button, and then sign out.

With Hotmail, the only dreck you're automatically signed up for is email from MSN about new services. Unfortunately, the only way to stop it is to cancel your Hotmail account. The good news? At least half the time, Hotmail's own spam filters shunt such messages to its Junk folder, where they disappear after 7 days.

Or you might just sign up for a free Gmail account, which comes 100 percent free of marketing sludge. However, Gmail's servers will scan the content of your email, then serve up text ads based on keywords inside your messages (see Figure 3-8). This can lead to some interesting juxtapositions—such as ads for baby products showing up inside porn spam. For some folks, having anyone read their email, even if it's only a machine, constitutes a privacy violation.

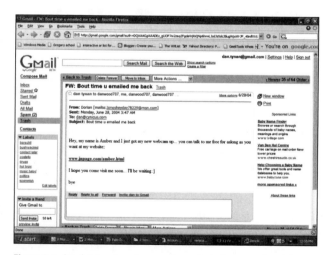

Figure 3-8. Google's Gmail service scans the content of your email, and then delivers ads based on keywords inside the message.

HACKERS, VIRUSES, AND WORMS—OH MY!

Attack of the Data-Eating Zombies

The Annoyance: My computer seems to have a mind of its own. The drive light is flashing and it seems to be busy doing things when I'm nowhere near it. Have I been hacked? Do I have a computer virus? What can I do to keep from being hacked or infected?

The Fix: Your machine may well have a virus. (Then again, maybe Windows is having one its regular nervous break-downs.) Some viruses and worms announce themselves by displaying a silly message on screen; some make themselves known by destroying data or disabling your system. But in the past year we've seen an epidemic of attacks that turn PCs into so-called zombies—machines that are remotely controlled over the Internet and used to launch attacks against other sites, forward spam, or do virtually anything else the hacker desires. Another big threat is keystroke loggers—software that captures what you type and sends it to a remote location. These are extremely handy for stealing passwords, credit card numbers, and other confidential information.

The only way to prevent zombification is to follow safe email practices (such as not opening file attachments; see "Don't Get Too Attached"), keep your operating system up to date, and get software that protects you from digital delinquents (see the sidebar "Ten Essential Privacy Tools").

Think your PC is safe just the way it is? A visit to Steve Gibson's ShieldsUP! (*http://www.grc.com/default.htm*) may change your mind. (Scroll down to the "Hot Spots" area of the page to reveal the ShieldsUP! link.) The site will perform a benign probe of your PC's ports—the communications gateways it uses to send email, get web pages, and so on—and tell you whether you're vulnerable to attack. If you aren't running some kind of firewall or connected to a router, your system is wide open.

A BRIEF FIELD GUIDE TO MALWARE

So you think a virus is a bug that makes you sick and a worm is a bug that lives in your garden? In the digital world, these words have entirely different meanings—and they ain't pretty.

Simply put, a virus is malicious code that attacks other programs. A virus may simply display a silly message on your screen, destroy all the data on your computer, or steal your personal information and shoot it off to a ring of identity thieves. Viruses typically attach themselves to executable files (EXE) and are spread by human actions—like double-clicking that unknown email attachment. A current popular species of virus turns your computer into a zombie that a hacker can control remotely via the Internet, using it to send spam or overwhelm web sites with traffic, effectively shutting them down.

A worm is a kind of malware that's designed to spread itself far and wide, typically via email. Most worms are blended threats, combining a destructive payload with spreadability; i.e., they infect your system, and then transmit themselves using your email account. (And the havoc they wreak can be considerable. In January 2003, the Slammer worm spread across 90 percent of the Internet in less than 30 minutes, according to the Cooperative Association for Internet Data Analysis (CAIDA). It hit a wide variety of computer systems, knocking out everything from airline computers to bank ATMs.) One popular conduit is, you guessed it, Microsoft Outlook. If your system isn't properly protected, a worm could easily exploit a flaw in Outlook and send itself to everyone in your address book—giving you yet another reason to love Microsoft.

A third form of malware is the so-called Trojan Horse, a seemingly innocuous program with a hidden payload (you know, like the soldiers hiding in the big wooden doorstop in that Brad Pitt movie). Trojans can steal personal information or let the machine be controlled by a remote user (see "Attack of the Data-Eating Zombies").

There's no such thing as *good* malware (hence the name), which is why every computer needs a solid security system—including personal firewalls, spam filters, anti-virus programs, and regular software updates—as well as a little bit of luck.

At a bare minimum, you want a firewall to keep hackers from installing software that takes over your system or steals your data. Windows XP comes with a very basic firewall, but the firewall is not enabled by default unless Service Pack 2 (SP2) is installed. To turn on XP's firewall, open the Network Connections control panel and right-click the connection you want to protect. Select Properties, click the Advanced tab, and check the Internet Connection Firewall box. (If you've upgraded to SP2, or bought your computer with SP2 already on it, the steps are slightly different. On the Advanced tab, you click the Settings button in the Windows Firewall section, and in the subsequent dialog box, click the General tab, then "On (recommended).") Click OK to confirm your choices and close Network Connections.

The Windows Firewall should keep Internet hackers from probing your system for openings, but that's about it. It won't, for example, keep applications on your PC from accessing the Internet behind your back, as many Trojan Horses and keystroke loggers do. A better choice is ZoneAlarm Pro ($30, *http://www.zonelabs.com*), which controls which apps can and can't access the Net, blocks pop ups, and lets you manage cookies. (ZoneAlarm also comes in a more limited free version, and as part of a $40 suite that includes a virus scanner, anti-spam tools, and other useful goodies.)

Mac OS X's firewall settings are found in System Preferences→Internet & Network→Sharing. Select Firewall, click the Start button, and close the Sharing window to turn on the Mac's digital bodyguard.

Don't Get Too Attached

The Annoyance: I just received an "email undeliverable" message. But there's a file attached. What should I do with it?

The Fix: Follow Tynan's Golden Rule of Computing #2: when in doubt, delete. (Golden Rule #1: when things go wrong, blame Microsoft.) If you get an attachment you're not expecting, 9 times out of 10 it's a worm or some other digital nasty. Do not (I repeat, DO NOT) save or open this sucker. Opening the file will infect your computer; saving the file can be dangerous if you forget it's there and open it later. Delete it with prejudice. And get yourself an anti-virus program that will automatically detect and neutralize such attachments before they land in your inbox.

If you don't already have antivirus software installed, Panda Software's Active Scan (*http://www.pandasoftware.com/activescan/com/activescan_principal.htm*) will perform a free one-time scan of your system. You'll have to download an applet, surrender your email address and agree to receive e-newsletters as part of the deal, but that's a small cost for some peace of mind.

Friends Don't Let Friends Open Attachments

The Annoyance: My best friend in the whole world just sent me a message with a file attachment. I know the person, so it's okay to open it, right?

The Fix: Not necessarily. (See Tynan Rule #2.) One reason viruses spread like, well, viruses is that once they infect your system, they often mail themselves to everyone in your address book. If you get an attachment from somebody that you trust, call and ask them if they sent you something and if so, what it is. Only if you're convinced the file is benign should you take the plunge—and even then, scan the attachment with your antivirus software the second it lands on your hard drive.

MAKING THE MOVE TO SERVICE PACK 2

If you haven't already upgraded XP to Service Pack 2, now would be a good time. Released in August 2004, SP2 patches some gaping security holes in XP and Internet Explorer. It also adds a pop-up blocker to IE and automatically turns on XP's Internet Connection Firewall. (XP's default setting was off—does the word *duh* mean anything to Microsoft?) ICF can make your computer invisible to hackers and remote attackers, though unlike Zone Alarm or other third-party firewalls, it won't alert you if your PC is already a zombie or stop malware from phoning home.

You may be able to download and install SP2 using XP's Automatic Updates feature (see "Make Updates Automatic"). Or you might not—Windows is just finicky that way. And at 266MB, you'd spend quite a while waiting for the file to download. An easier method is to order the CD from Microsoft. Visit the XP page at *http://www.microsoft.com/windowsxp/sp2/default.mspx*, click the "Order a CD" link under "Get Windows XP Service Pack 2," and fill out some web forms. It's free, and you can use it to upgrade more than one computer (but only if it runs XP). The page claims that shipping will take 4 to 6 weeks, but I got my disc in less than a week. The downside? SP2 doesn't always play nicely with other programs, including some versions of AutoCAD and Symantec AntiVirus. (For a list of known problems and ways to address them, see *http://support.microsoft.com/kb/842242*). You might also experience system slowdowns, especially if you're upgrading an older computer. And because SP2 has flaws of its own—notably, a hole that could allow your files to be shared with the entire Internet—you may need to download patches for it as well. For most users, though, SP2's additional protection is worth the trade-offs.

Antivirus Software Is Not Enough

The Annoyance: My antivirus package scans incoming and outgoing mail, so I can open attachments with no worries, right?

The Fix: Don't let that lull you into a false sense of security. Digital nasties can fool AV programs in a number of ways. For one thing, there's always a lag between the time a virus is set loose in the wild and when your antivirus vendor comes up with a fix—an average of around 10 to 12 hours, according to German virus researcher Andreas Marx (*http://www.av-test.org*). And then you've got to remember to download the fix and install it, which can add several days to the tally—plenty of time for you to get infected. Major AV packages like Norton AntiVirus and McAfee VirusScan let you schedule automatic updates, though after a certain period (which ranges from 90 days to a year) you'll have to pay an annual fee for future virus definitions. My advice: update your software at least once a week and whenever you hear of a big virus outbreak (which seems to happen at least once a week).

Better yet, set your AV software to automatically update itself whenever new virus definitions are available. In Zone-Alarm Security Suite, you do this by opening the suite's Control Center. Select Antivirus from the list on the left and click the Antivirus Options button. Under Advanced Settings select Updates, and check the Enable Automatic Updates (Recommended) box. Then click OK.

Stop Spreading the News

The Annoyance: Ooops, I think I've just infected every member of my family and all of my close friends by sending them a virus. What do I do now? Do I have to enter the witness protection program?

The Fix: No, but you might consider the witless protection program. First, send an email to the family and (former) close friends you may have infected, alerting them (sending flowers and candy couldn't hurt either). If you haven't already installed an AV program, now would be the time—it should be able to isolate and kill the virus, assuming your system hasn't been damaged too badly. You should also update your operating system, as security holes are constantly being discovered and patches issued.

Windows XP makes this easy: make sure you're connected to the Internet, then click Start→All Programs→Windows Update. On the Windows Update web page, click Custom Install. Microsoft will present you with a list of patches to install; pick the ones you want (certainly, all the critical "High Priority Updates"). Click the "Go to install updates" link, then click the Install button. When the install is done you may need to reboot your system.

Make Updates Automatic

The Annoyance: Virus scanners really slow down my system. I figure as long as I don't open attachments I'll be fine, right?

The Fix: Wrong. In March 2004, clever virus fiends released variants on the Bagle worm that could infect systems when a piece of email was opened—no strings (or files) attached. Opening the noxious message caused the victim's PC to secretly download and install malicious code. In this case, the worm only infected Windows machines whose users failed to install a critical security patch for Internet Explorer that Microsoft had released five months earlier. (To find out if your copy of IE is still vulnerable to such attacks, you can run a test at *http://secunia.com/MS03-032*.)

Of course, keeping up with Microsoft's critical security patches can be a fulltime job (and the pay sucks). Rather than fetching each update manually, simplify your life by telling Windows XP to automatically download and install updates as they become available (see Figure 3-9).

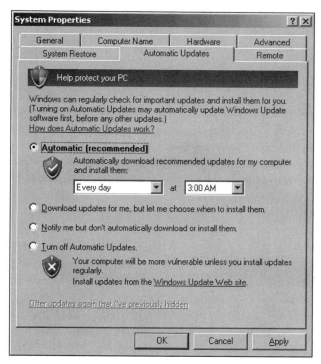

Figure 3-9. Tired of keeping track of Window's critical updates? Let XP download and install the patches for you automatically.

Open the System control panel, click the Automatic Updates tab, and check the "Keep my computer up to date" box; if you're using XP with Service Pack 2, click "Automatic (recommended)." You can tell Windows to automatically download and install the updates; download the update and ask if you want them installed, or simply have it notify you when updates are available.

ONLINE SHOPPING

Give Credit Where Credit is Due...

The Annoyance: The idea of typing my credit card number onto a web page gives me the willies. I feel like I'm inviting people to rip me off.

The Fix: It shouldn't. Though e-commerce sites do occasionally get hacked (and shady sites might steal your data, see Table 3-2), using a credit card actually offers you some protection if you get ripped off. Thanks to the Fair Credit Reporting Act, if someone steals your credit card information to make purchases, you're only liable for $50 of the total—even then, many banks and merchants will credit the entire amount when online fraud is involved, provided you catch the mistake in time.

But you'll want to make sure the site is legitimate (see Table 3-2) and that it uses Secure Socket Layer encryption to protect your credit info as it zips through cyberspace. Even then, you'll need to monitor your account carefully to make sure nobody's "cramming" your card—adding bogus extra charges to the account. Most banks put a limit (like a couple of months) on how long after the initial purchase you can dispute a charge, so examine your monthly statements or check your account more often online. An alternative is to get a separate credit card with a low limit and use it exclusively for online purchases. If crammers do max out the account, you'll be less exposed.

Whatever you do, don't ever send a check or cash to a web site, unless you don't care about losing money. (And if that's how you feel, could you send me some, too?)

Table 3-2. Is that online store a legitimate business or a snare for the unwary? Look for these warning signs.

Shop with confidence	Buyer beware
Store accepts credit card or PayPal payments.	They ask you to mail cash or a check.
Site uses SSL encryption to protect customer data en route to the site.	Doesn't encrypt data, or encryption certificates produce error messages when you double-click them.
Site sports logos from trusted authorities such as VeriSign and the Better Business Bureau Online	Logos are missing or faked (i.e., they don't take you to the logo owner's site when you click them).
Store lists its real world location, including phone numbers and a street address.	Street address is missing, or leads to a P.O. box or private mail drop; you can never reach a human by phone.
Site offers a detailed privacy policy describing the information it collects and what it does with the data.	Privacy policy? We don't need no stinkin' privacy policy.

...But Don't Take Undue Credit

The Annoyance: Sorry, I'm not convinced. I'm still afraid somebody's going to hack into that e-commerce site and rip off my Visa number.

The Fix: Technically, your card number can be stolen even when shopping at secure sites. For example, someone could install a keystroke logger on your computer. Worse, the e-commerce site could be hacked. Over the last few years, attackers have stolen customer data from such high-profile sites as CD Universe, Egghead Software, and Playboy's online store.

The solution: get a disposable credit card number. Citibank (*http://www.citibank.com/us/cards/tour/cb/shp_van.htm*) and Discover (*http://www2.discovercard.com/deskshop*) offer credit card numbers that are good for a single transaction, so even if the number is stolen it won't do thieves much good. Another alternative: online merchants such as Amazon let you place your order online, then provide your credit card number over the phone. If you're still allergic to using plastic online, sign up for a PayPal account (*http://www.paypal.com*)—assuming the e-commerce site you're shopping at accepts such payments. PayPal acts as the middle man: you put money in your PayPal account, the seller contacts PayPal to get paid, and your credit card information never changes hands (provided, of course, you haven't fallen for a PayPal phisher attack—see "Don't Bank on It").

HOW TO READ A PRIVACY POLICY

Any commercial web site worth a damn offers a privacy policy that governs the kind of information it collects from you and what it does with your data. But does that privacy policy really protect you?

A June 2003 study by Annenberg Public Policy Center (*http://www.appcpenn.org*) reports that more than 60 percent of netizens either don't understand or completely misinterpret web site privacy policies. In fact, most of those surveyed believed that if a site had a policy, it meant it was protecting user privacy—a far cry from reality. The same users said if they better understood what companies were actually doing with their personal information, they'd be more careful about sharing it.

You don't have to read the policy of every site you visit, but you should definitely read one for any site where you're asked to provide personal information—especially commerce sites where you must cough up an address, credit card, or other sensitive data. Here's what to look for.

Where's the policy? Reputable sites put a link to their policies on the home page, usually at the bottom near any copyright notices. If the policy is buried—or nonexistent—there's probably a good reason for it. Be wary.

What data is it collecting? Are you just another anonymous user, or is your entire surfing history being recorded? Does the site deposit cookies on your hard drive? If so, do these cookies track you as you wander the Web? To avoid plowing through pages of legalese, search the policy for the phrase "personally identifiable information" (often shortened to "PII") to get the skinny on what data you're giving up.

Who's it sharing with? Some web sites collect information and do nothing with it, but others are in the data-mining business and will sell you out to anyone who meets their price. Look for phrases like "we do not share information with third parties without your consent," and make sure they require your explicit consent (i.e., you must tell them you want your data shared).

How can you opt out? It should be easy for you to tell the site to stop contacting you or sharing your information with its partners, either via email or a web form where you can specify your privacy preferences. If a site makes you write them a letter to opt out, it's most likely because they really don't want you to do it. Do it anyway.

How does it notify you of changes? Privacy polices can change in the blink of an eye, and sites vary widely on when (and if) they notify you. Some sites, such as eBay, send email to registered users when their policies change. Others (such as Amazon) say nothing—although with big companies like Amazon, significant policy changes are usually headline news. With smaller sites, it pays to check back periodically to see if their key policies have changed (most will note when the policy was last updated).

They Know When You've Been Shopping

The Annoyance: When I visit Amazon.com, it says "Hello Bob!" (Which happens to be my name.) This creeps me out. How does it know me? Do all web sites know who I am?

The Fix: Not exactly. Amazon knows you because at some time in the past you registered with the site—most likely when you bought something. The site then deposited a small text file called a cookie on your computer's hard disk. Cookies work like a kind of ID tag. Every time you visit the site, it looks for the cookie, reads the text string inside, and then uses it to call up your record in Amazon's database. The site then loads pages containing your preferences, billing address (if you've provided that), new products that you might be interested in buying (based on past purchases), and that friendly greeting at the top of the screen. This is Amazon's attempt to act like the neighborhood merchant who has known you for the last 15 years.

But most web sites are limited in the amount of information they can glean from a simple visit. They can tell what browser you're using and your IP address, but little else. If you've never registered for the site and/or don't let your browser accept cookies, it won't know who you are.

You Are What You Buy

The Annoyance: Now that Amazon knows me, it automatically signs me in whenever I visit it. Now I'm worried somebody else can go in and see stuff I've bought—or worse, buy stuff under my name. Can they?

The Fix: First the good news. Anybody trying to use your Amazon account needs to know your password before they can click the "Place your order" or "1-Click Shopping" buttons. But if they do guess it, and you've told Amazon to store your billing information, they can shop 'til the cows come home. (For more on choosing good passwords, see the Chapter 2 sidebar "Pick a Peck of Passwords.")

The bad news is that people can learn a ton about you just by looking at the home page Amazon creates every time you visit (see Figure 3-10). For example, Amazon provides personal recommendations based on what you've bought in the past—a pretty fair indication of you and your interests. Worse, Amazon has added a feature that can tell you *why* it's recommending these items, even if you merely looked at an item

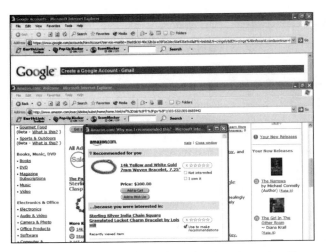

Figure 3-10. Amazon makes recommendations based on what you bought-or even thought about buying-which anyone can look at on your PC when logged onto Amazon's home page (so be careful what you buy there).

but never completed the purchase. All perfectly harmless, until your spouse visits Amazon on your home PC and discovers you purchased intimate gifts for someone else, or your boss notices Amazon's home page open on your computer and sees you've been shopping for books on how to change careers. Suddenly those groovy personalization features don't seem so helpful.

Your options? You can tell your browser to reject all cookies so Amazon remembers nothing about you, but that means retyping your shipping and billing information with every order—a bit drastic, in my opinion. To temporarily suppress Amazon's personalized greetings, you'll need to formally sign out after every session (that's especially important if you use a public or shared Internet terminal to shop).

Unfortunately, Amazon buries the sign-out button under a maze of pages. You'll have to click Help in the upper right corner, scroll down to the Privacy & Security area and click More, then click "Signing out." Then, redundantly, click the yellow "Sign out" button. The next time you (or anyone else using your computer) visits Amazon, it will greet you with a generic home page. To see the friendly, personalized site of old, click the "personalized recommendations" link at the top of the page to log in under your own name and password. If you leave the site (instead of formally signing out) and return the next day, Amazon will "recognize" you, with all that personal information there for snoops to relish. So don't forget to sign out at the end of every session.

IS THAT SITE SECURE?

Before you hand over your plastic, make sure the site uses Secure Socket Layer (SSL) encryption to scramble the data en route. You'll know the page is protected when you see the letters "https" in the web address and a tiny padlock icon in the bottom right corner of the browser. Some web con artists have been known to fake the padlock icon; you can verify it's the real deal by double-clicking it. If a valid certificate from an authority like VeriSign or Thawte isn't present, don't shop there.

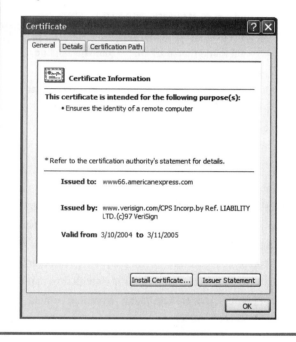

Would You Like Spam with That?

The Annoyance: I just bought something from an online store, and now they're spamming me on a regular basis.

The Fix: What you're describing may look, smell, and taste like spam, but technically it's not. Because you purchased an item from the site, you now have a pre-existing business relationship—a big fat exemption under most anti-spam laws. The solution is simple: If the biz is legit, there should be a valid unsubscribe link in any marketing message they send you. (And if the business isn't legit, you've got bigger problems than spam.) You may also be able to change your marketing preferences by visiting your account page on the site.

For example, on Amazon.com you'd click the Your Account button, log in, scroll down to the Account Settings area and click the "Update your communication preferences" link and pick the kinds of messages you want to receive. At the very least, check the "Send me only those messages relate to my orders, listings, and bids" box, then click the Set options button.

Most stores provide the skinny on how to opt out of obnoxious marketing in their privacy policies. But the next time you buy something, the store may feel free to send you more mail—until you tell them to take another hike.

HOOKED ON MARKETING

Companies that believe they can ignore their own privacy polices should take a lesson from Gateway Learning (no relation to Gateway Computers). The Santa Ana, California company, best known for its Hooked on Phonics series of learning products, got its wrist slapped by the FTC for selling consumer data to marketers—including the gender and ages of customers' children—despite a privacy policy stating the company would not sell information without first obtaining its customers' consent, nor share any data about children. (For the full skinny on the FTC action, see *http://www.ftc.gov/opa/2004/07/gateway.htm*.) Worse, Gateway Learning allegedly tried to change its policy after the fact—another violation of FTC rules. The company agreed to return the $4,608 it made selling the customer data and has pledged to obtain permission before selling an individual's data in the future.

99.44% Hacker Safe

The Annoyance: I visited an online store that had a logo claiming it was "hacker safe." Is it really safer to shop there than at online stores that don't have this logo?

The Fix: All that logo really means is that they pay another company a few hundred dollars a month to look for common site vulnerabilities. That's probably safer than a store that doesn't test anything, but it's no guarantee the site can't be hacked. Such logos tend to boost the site's sales (which is why they pay the money) but may also attract more attention from hackers who want to prove them wrong—one reason why the companies that put the most effort into securing their systems rarely advertise that fact. If the CIA can't create a site that's hack-proof, what chance does bobs-discount-electronics.com have?

The big danger from hackers (or crackers, who are hackers with criminal intent) is they could steal your personal information stored on the site's servers and sell it to the highest bidder, max out your credit limit, or use the data to open accounts in your name, essentially stealing your identity. Not pretty. But if someone's going to steal your ID, they're far more likely to do it by stealing your purse or riffling your postal mail than filching it online, so the odds are in your favor. Your best defense against bogus charges and identity theft is to keep a close eye on your accounts and to order credit reports at least annually, so you can see if anyone out there is pretending to be you (see Chapter 2, "Check Your Reports" for more details on how to contact credit reporting agencies.)

Hate having to give a login name and password to access certain sites (like *http://www.nytimes.com*)? BugMeNot (*http://www.bugmenot.com*) lists working logins and passwords for more than 13,000 web sites, all contributed by other people who hate compulsory web registration as much as you do.

ONLINE FILE SWAPPING

I Share the Songs That Make the Whole World Sing...

The Annoyance: I just downloaded the entire Barry Manilow MP3 Collection using my favorite file-sharing network. These networks are anonymous, right? The record companies can't possibly find out who I am, right?

The Fix: Wrong and wrong. Some of your fellow file swappers aren't really file swappers—they're firms like Ranger Online that are employed by the Recording Industry Association of America (RIAA) and the Motion Picture Association of America (MPAA) to catch file-sharing scofflaws. Exactly how these companies operate is a trade secret, but essentially they log onto peer-to-peer networks like Kazaa or Gnutella, initiate downloads, and record the IP addresses of computers containing large numbers of illegally copied songs. The RIAA's crack legal team then sends a letter to the Internet Service Providers who control these IP addresses, demanding the ISPs identify the swappers using them. Under the safe harbor provision of the Digital Millennium Copyright Act (DMCA), ISPs that cooperate with this request can't be prosecuted for violating copyright laws. Among the recipients of an RIAA subpoena were a 12-year-old honors student in New York City and an 83-year-old grandmother in West Virginia who'd been dead for a month.

Privacy in Peril: Aloha, Kazaa

According to a report in the *Honolulu Advertiser*, agents with the FBI's Cybercrime unit asked computer repair shops on the island of Oahu to report on any machines containing child porn, threats to national security, or file-swapping software. Next time you vacation in the islands, you may want to leave your laptop at home.

Still, some large ISPs like SBC and Verizon refused to comply with the RIAA's demands. In December 2003, a DC district court ruled the RIAA didn't have the authority to force ISPs to identify their customers under the DMCA. So the RIAA's legal eagles changed tactics and began filing "John Doe" suits under other provisions of Federal evidentiary law, making it harder for ISPs to avoid cooperating. (For a good summary of the legal issues, see the Privacy Resolutions PC page at *http://www.privacyresolutions.com/laws/RIAA/RIAA.htm*.) Bottom line? Don't expect your ISP to protect you.

Once the RIAA has your name and number, you're grist for their legal mill. For an overview of the issues sympathetic to file sharers, check out the Tech Law Advisor blog at *http://techlawadvisor.com/riaa/*. For the record industry's point of view, see *http://www.riaa.com/issues/piracy*.

PRIVACY IN PERIL: MAKING A FEDERAL CASE OUT OF FILE SHARING

Fans of file swapping may soon have bigger things to worry about than being sued by the RIAA. At press time, Congress was considering a bill that would make it a Federal offense to share copyrighted files.

The Protecting Intellectual Rights Against Theft and Expropriation (PIRATE) Act of 2004 (S.2237) would allow Federal prosecutors to sue individual file swappers for civil and statutory damages. The bill was passed by the Senate, and referred to a House committee, where it sits to this day. (A 1997 law, the No Electronic Theft Act, made it a crime to engage in file swapping, but no one's ever been prosecuted under it because the burden of proof has been considered too high—not to mention the bad press a prosecutor would get for hunting down file-swapping teenagers). The PIRATE Act could lower the burden of proof and jump-start prosecutions. It may also allow Federal wiretaps to be used to obtain evidence of infringement.

The Sue Me, Sue You Blues

The Annoyance: I don't want to get sued, but I'm also tired of paying $17.99 for crappy CDs with only one decent song on them. How do I keep the RIAA off my back?

The Fix: Well, there are an estimated 40 to 60 million people swapping files online, and the RIAA had sued around 11,500 of them at press time, so the odds are definitely in your favor. Just the same, you can reduce your risk even further by following a few simple precautions.

First, check out the Electronic Frontier Foundation's page on how to avoid being sued by the RIAA (*http://www.eff.org/IP/P2P/howto-notgetsued.php*). The tips include such things as not sharing copyrighted files (duh), turning off file sharing entirely, and not allowing your computer to serve up massive numbers of files. You could also change the names of your files so they're harder to identify (though that also makes them harder for your online buddies to find), or swap only independent music published by companies that aren't members of the RIAA (to find such songs, check out the RIAA Radar site at *http://www.magnetbox.com/riaa/search.asp*). Or you could simply sign up for one of the legal sites (e.g., Apple iTunes, Napster, Sony Connect, etc.) and fork over 75 to 99 cents a pop for your Pop.

> Are you willing to pay to thumb your nose at the RIAA? For $10 a month ($100 a year) you can sign up for AnonX (*http://www.anonx.com*), a service that provides anonymous access to popular file-sharing networks like Kazaa and Gnutella. AnonX manages this feat by employing an encrypted, virtual private network operating from the Pacific island nation of Vanuatu. At press time, the island had not yet been invaded by an armada of record company attorneys—possibly because they've been unable to locate Vanuatu on a map.

Want to find out if there's a record industry subpeona out there with your name on it? Dial up the EFF's subpeona search page *http://www.eff.org/IP/P2P/riaasubpoenas/* and run a search by your name or IP address. If you are unlucky enough to be sued, be sure to check out Subpoena Defense (*http://www.subpoenadefense.org/*) for help with legal issues. And look on the bright side—you might end up in an Apple iPod commercial.

Avoid P2P Vermin

The Annoyance: I like to swap audio and video files on the Net (so sue me). But sometimes these files aren't what they seem. Am I getting viruses or other electronic vermin when I download media files?

The Fix: You could be. Last year British technology site The Register (*http://www.theregister.co.uk*) reported a P2P virus on the Kazaa network masquerading as nude photos of actress Catherine Zeta-Jones (at least they've got good taste). When opened, the file installed a Trojan Horse on the user's system that allowed hackers to gain access to the machine and steal or destroy its data. The Virus Information Library (*http://www.viruslibrary.com*) lists 15 different virus strains that spread via P2P networks.

And even if you don't get a virus, you may download a file that's simply not what it appears to be. Among various other nasty tricks, record companies have been known to seed P2P networks with decoy files featuring 20 seconds of music followed by loud screeching. So, naturally, a pair of enterprising file swappers compiled these songs and put them on an RIAA Remix CD ($7.99, *http://riaamix.com/*).

The moral? If you do download files, be sure to scan them first with your antivirus utility before trying to open them. Think about turning your speakers down, too, the first time you try to play one.

KIDS AND THE NET

Let Internet Explorer Play Web Cop

The Annoyance: I don't want my kids growing up to be fry cooks at McDonald's, so I got them a computer with a fast Internet connection. Now I'm afraid they'll become a little too worldly, too soon. How do I shield them from the Net's nasty, dark underbelly?

The Fix: The first thing you can do is set up separate logons for each child, with settings appropriate to each age group. You'll also want to set yourself up as the adminstrator for that computer, so you can control what they can and can't do with it. (For the skinny on how to set up accounts, see Chapter 2, "One Computer, Many Eyeballs") If you share a computer, this will help keep them from eyeing your browser history or snooping around in your private files.

Once you've done that, you can log on as your child and adjust his or her browser settings to limit what sites they can visit, based on their content. (Though my advice is to use such content filters sparingly; see "Hire a Nanny.") Internet Explorer 6.x comes with an older ratings system devised by the Recreational Software Advisory Council (RASCi), which is now part of the Internet Content Ratings Association.

To turn the Ratings system on, select Tools→Internet Options and click the Content tab, followed by the Enable button. In the Content Advisor dialog box select the Ratings tab and click OK. If you've never enabled the Content Advisor you'll be prompted to create a password. Once you've got a password, click the Settings button in the Content Advisor section, enter your password and on the Ratings tab, use the sliders to choose the levels of sex, violence, nudity, and language you're willing to have your kids exposed to online (the strictest setting is Level 0, all the way to the left). Click Apply, then OK. The default setting is to have all filters turned to Level 0, which is probably what you want with smaller children, but probably not with Net-savvy teens.

Of course, site labeling is entirely voluntary and the vast majority of web sites are unrated. To keep your kids from wandering onto the wrong site, select the General tab and make sure the "Users can see sites that have no rating" box is unchecked. If you want to give kids the option of visiting an unrated site (with your approval, of course), check the box next to "Supervisor can type a password to allow users to view restricted content." You will quickly grow tired of doing this for unrated sites they like to visit over and over. The easiest way to avoid this problem is to select the Approved Sites tab, type the names of sites the kids can visit whether they're rated or not, and click the Always button. (To ban sites you never want them to see, you can simply type the URL and click the Never button.) When you're done customizing the settings, click OK twice to confirm your choices.

SafeSurf offers a free plug-in for IE that's easier to use and customize than IE's default ratings system. You can select an overall filter by age range or specify up to nine settings for each content area, including such topics as gambling, drug use, and intolerance. But first you must download a small safesurf.rat file and install it into your browser, then customize the settings to your liking. (For more information on incorporating SafeSurf into IE, see *http://www.safesurf.com/iesetup/.*)

Hire a Nanny

The Annoyance: My kids already know more about my computer than I do—including how to get around the browser settings. I need a better strategy.

The Fix: You've got a couple of options. One is to use an ISP that offers more control over what your progeny can and can't do online. AOL and MSN both fit that description nicely (see Figure 3-11). You can set up profiles based on their age, which send your kids to special child-friendly home pages, with prebuilt filters for browsing, chat, instant messaging, and email. MSN has a neat feature where if your child is surfing and encounters a web site that's blocked by the parental controls, he or she can email you a note asking for instant approval to visit the site.

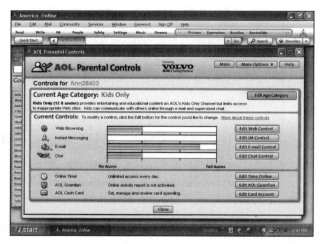

Figure 3-11. Worried about your kids' online wanderings? Let AOL play digital babysitter.

ZoneAlarm's Security Suite comes with a built-in web filter, though it's turned off by default. To turn it on, launch the Control Center and select Web Filtering from the list of integrated applets. On the Main tab, check the "On" box under Parental Control. If you want Zone to assess sites that don't provide a rating (most of the nasty ones don't) and block the bad ones on the fly, check the "On" box under Smart Filtering DRTR Technology. Then click the Categories tab to pick the types of site you want to block. When you're done, close the Control Center. Be warned, however, that Zone's web filter is an extremely blunt instrument. You can't create exceptions within a blocked category. For example, if you choose to block "Adult: Pornography" sites, you won't be able to watch any

videos on iFilm.com, regardless of how innocent they might be, because iFilm contains some adult material. And Zone's filter blocks anyone using the computer, regardless of what name they used to log on.

If you want more control over your kids' web surfing, invest $30 to $50 in a program such as Content Protect (*http://www.contentwatch.com*), CyberSitter (*http://www.cybersitter.com*), or Net Nanny (*http://www.netnanny.com*). This type of software lets you create custom profiles for each user, and lets you police instant messages, email, file downloads, and virtually any other type of Net activity. (For more details, check out the chart at *http://www.internet-filter-review.toptenreviews.com/*.) Many security suites (like those from Norton, McAfee, and Zone Labs) also come with limited web content filters.

However, relying on any third-party monitoring solution can be problematic. For one thing, no software can possibly keep up with the constant flow of nastiness that is on the Net, so you'll need to constantly update the program's filters—and even then there will always be ways to find sites they've missed. The other problem is that you're relying on someone else's idea of what's acceptable. Since these programs first appeared in the mid-90s, critics have documented instances of them mistaking medical sites for porn content or blocking controversial (usually left/liberal) political sites. (For more on the anti-monitoring point of view—and ways to defeat major filtering programs—visit the Peacefire site *http://www.peacefire.org*.)

My advice: if you're configuring Net access for a young child, create a list of sites you'd allow them to visit and block everything else, then gradually add to the list over time. If you've got a tween or a teen who needs the Net for research, I'd suggest a product like Net Nanny (or AOL Guardian) that lets you monitor web use without necessarily blocking access—and a serious discussion about appropriate online behavior. AOL Guardian can limit access to sites and other content based on your child's age, shut down the connection after a specified period of time, and give you a detailed report on their online activity. If your weekly report shows they've been visiting sites they shouldn't have, then it's time for a talk. Another good idea is to put the computer in the living room or some other common area where you can keep an eye on it—they're less likely to do anything risky or risqué if you're in the room.

Thanks for Not Sharing

The Annoyance: I don't mind my kids roaming the Net, but I'm afraid they'll tell some stranger where we live or start sharing my credit card information in a chat room.

The Fix: Use your firewall's privacy protection feature, if it has one, to prevent your kids from spilling specific information over the net—like your home address, phone number, and so on (see Figure 3-12). For example, to do this with Zone-Alarm 5 Security Suite, launch the ZoneAlarm control panel (Start→All Programs→Zone Labs→Zone Labs Security), and select ID Lock in the left-hand area of the panel. On the Main tab move the slider bar to High to prevent any sensitive information from leaking out. Then select the myVault tab, click Add, fill in the description field, then type the information you want to keep secure. Put a checkmark in the boxes next to IM, Web, and Email to secure all outbound communications, then click OK. If you want some sites to have access to this information (like Amazon.com), click the Trusted Sites tab, then Add, and type the URL of the sites you trust with your personal information.

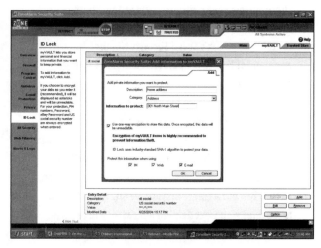

Figure 3-12. Don't let the half-pints spill the beans. A good security suite (like ZoneAlarm 5.0, pictured here) will let you specify what information your kids can and can't share over the Net.

Every so often ZoneAlarm freaks out and warns me that some web site is trying to steal my Social Security Number. In every case it has turned out to be a web site requesting a cookie that happens to contain a random series of numbers that match some (but not all) of my SSN. (ZoneAlarm only watches for the last four numbers of your SSN.) The solution: simply tell the firewall to not allow this data to be sent. One less cookie won't harm anybody.

Watching where your kids wander on the Web is only half the job of protecting them. To keep spam, worms, and other nastygrams from polluting their inbox, turn to a service like Kidmail ($30 a year, *http://www.kidmail.net*). A handy web interface lets you see each message before they do, so you can winnow out the bad stuff. Kidmail also uses a challenge/response system to thwart spambots and worms. (See "Spamology 101"). As you approve mail, the senders get added to the approved list, and any of their subsequent messages go directly to your child's inbox (although you can read a 'blind carbon' of messages from particular senders). There are also enough animations, sound effects, and silly jokes to keep the sub-9-year-old crowd amused for quite a while. If your kids are tweens, Kidmail's big brother Incredimail (*http://www.incredimail.com*) can fill in with even more animations and effects. An ad-supported version is free, or you can forgo the advertisements for $30 a year.

I H8 IM

The Annoyance: When she's not sleeping or talking on the phone, my teenage daughter is Instant Messaging her friends. She's even started talking in IM lingo. How do I keep the online creeps away from her without ruining her fun?

The Fix: Both AOL and MSN let you specify who your kids can and can't communicate with via IM. If kids want to add someone to their list, they'll have to go through you first (see "Your Own Private AOL"). But a truly determined teen will figure out a way to get around any restrictions you put in her way—for example, by downloading a separate copy of AOL Instant Messenger and creating a new screen name. Your best strategy is to discuss appropriate online behavior with your kids and stress the importance of caution and good judgment, especially when dealing with strangers. The Wired Teens site offers good advice on dealing with IM (*http://www.wiredteens.org/teensim.html*), while Larry Magid's Safe Teens site (*http://www.safeteens.com*) offers general guidelines for both teens and their beleaguered parents.

PRIVACY IN PERIL: STEALING CHILDREN'S IDENTITIES

Children are an increasingly attractive target for ID thieves, in part because they're easy prey for smooth-talking predators in chat rooms, and because the crime can go undetected for years. According to Linda Foley, executive director of the Identity Theft Resource Center (*http://www.idtheftcenter.org*), a lot of child identity theft is committed by estranged parents who have ruined their own credit ratings and decide to "borrow" their children's. If data collection notices and pre-approved credit offers for your kids start showing up in the mail, order a credit report for your child. Unless you gave them a gold card for their last birthday, most kids shouldn't have any records at the Big Three credit reporting agencies.

Children aren't the only people at risk. The recently deceased are also easy pickings for skilled ID thieves. These vermin read obituaries and obtain death certificates (often available for free online), which usually contain the victim's Social Security Number. Before any creditor knows the person is dead, the scammer has applied for credit using the deceased person's information and run up big charges. Fortunately you can halt this crime by signing up with the Global Will Registry (*http://www.emergency-and-will.com*). For $15 a year ($10 annually thereafter), the service will alert the major credit reporting agencies when you pass on, so they can put a freeze on your credit. That way your loved ones won't get dunned long after you're done.

YOUR OWN PRIVATE AOL

Using America Online used to be like visiting the county fair—you'd see barkers to the left, carnies to the right, and nothing but balloons and cotton candy everywhere else. AOL 9.0 has toned down the blatant marketing and other in-your-face features, but there are still things you can do to ratchet up your privacy, just by tweaking a few simple settings.

- *Lower your profile.* AOL lets you build quite a detailed dossier about yourself for your online buddies to peruse. (To get there, click Settings→About Me→Create/Edit My Profile.) But if your friends can see it, so can 30 million other AOL subscribers. If you feel you must maintain a profile, be as vague as possible. Don't put your full name or phone number; for location, list North America; and be careful about listing your gender, marital status, or photos (especially you gals out there). The same goes for AOL's home page and blogging tools (Settings→About Me→Create/Edit My Home Page). Imagine that creepy guy from high school looking at your page, and edit it with him in mind—not your trusted friends.

- *Tighten your IM Security.* AOL lets you control who can and can't send you an Instant Message, but the default setting is open to anyone who knows (or can guess) your AOL screen name. To change that, select Settings→IM Privacy and Security, and click the Privacy and Security tab. Select any option, from allowing all Instant Messages to blocking them all; if your universe of IM pals doesn't change much, choose "Allow only People on my Buddy List," then click Save.

- *Drop the Pop Ups.* To minimize annoying pop ups (especially those coming from AOL itself), select Settings→Pop-Up Control Settings, and make sure all the boxes on that screen are checked. You may want to specify some exceptions for those few sites (such as Amazon.com) where you actually welcome pop-up windows.

- *Dam the Spam.* To keep junk from filling your inbox, go to Settings→Spam Controls, and click the sliding bar to indicate spam-catching strength (If you really want to be strict, you can choose to allow mail only from people you know or from a custom sender list. Click the "Sender Filter" link) Make sure you comb through your inbox for any spam that's slipped through, and click the Report Spam button to delete the junk and to help fine-tune AOL's filters.

- *Cover your tracks.* You can tell AOL to stop keeping track of where you've been browsing by selecting Settings→Toolbar and Settings, and checking the "Clear History trail and Auto-complete after each time I Sign Off or Switch Screen Names" box, then clicking Save. This is especially useful if you're sharing one AOL account with other family members, and you don't want them following your footsteps.

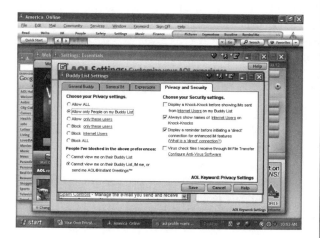

PRIVACY @ LARGE

Whois Stalking Me?

The Annoyance: I'm starting up a web site for battered women, but I don't want abusers to find out how to reach me by searching the Whois database. Is there a way I can register anonymously or tell my registrar to suppress my contact information?

The Fix: There is, though it's not exactly obvious. The Grand Poobah of Internet policymaking, the Internet Corporation for Assigned Names and Numbers (ICANN) (*http://www.icann.org/*), requires anyone who registers a web site to make their contact information available to the public via the Whois database. There are plenty of good reasons for this—for example, if you need to track down somebody making libelous comments about you on their site, you can search Whois and locate the blighter. But you can get around the public record requirement in a couple of ways.

For example, domain registrar Network Solutions, Inc. (NSI) will provide alternate contact information for the Whois database (such as a private mailbox maintained at NSI and a temporary email address). They'll then forward any email, letters, or calls to your real address while keeping that info safe from spammers, direct marketers, and others who troll the Whois rolls. The cost for this service? A mere $9 a year on top of whatever domain registration fees you're paying (for more information, see *http://www.internetprivacyadvocate.org*).

You could also use a service like Domains by Proxy (*http://www.domainsbyproxy.com*), which also charges $9 a year to register the web site for you (thus providing the company's contact info, not yours) while giving you control over domain transfers. But this type of protection can be fairly limited. According to the site's terms of service, if you engage in "morally objectionable activities" (like sending spam), or your site is simply the subject of a legal dispute, Domains by Proxy will remove its name from your record and expose your real contact information to the world.

Even if you forgo a proxy or forwarding service, be careful about the information you put in the Domain Name Service database. Don't enter your home address or phone number (a P.O. box is a much better choice), and avoid using your primary email address.

PRIVACY IN PERIL: ANTI-SOCIAL NETWORKING

The premise of social networking sites is incredibly attractive: Create a profile on a site like Friendster or Tribe.net listing your deepest thoughts and fascinating hobbies, and before long you'll have 400,000 new friends. The problem is that some of those folks might not really be so friendly—or even who they say they are.

Social networks are rife with tales of identities being hijacked, profiles being sabotaged, and users who've had highly personal entries re-posted in highly public places. That's in large part because security and privacy are often secondary concerns to the folks who created these sites.

For example, privacy consultant Alan Chapell claims he logged onto Classmates.com and set himself up as reunion organizer for 16 separate classes in 8 schools, just to show how lax the site's authentication was. Johnathan Moore, a 27-year-old software engineer, hacked his way around Friendster and other networks to demonstrate their security flaws. According a report in *Wired*, he was able to mine the network for users' ZIP codes and last names, which he could then use to track down their home addresses.

Chapell and Moore's intentions were benign; others won't be. Does that mean you should shun social networking sites? Not necessarily. If you're looking to connect with others—whether for business or pleasure—giving up some degree of privacy is a given. But choose your networks carefully; those that make it easy to contact just anyone are also the most prone to abuse. And remember, you don't have to tell the world everything in your online profile. A little mystery can be a good thing.

Antidotes for Domain Poisoning

The Annoyance: I registered a domain name, and suddenly I'm getting all this junk mail from other domain registrars and web hosting services.

The Fix: One reason may be because ICANN requires registrars to sell Whois records in bulk to other interested parties (charming, no?). If you don't want your domain registration information to be sold, you must tell your registrar. For example, to opt out at Network Solutions, you must log into your account page, click Edit User Info in the left menu and check No next to the statement "I choose to have my name included in the Bulk WHOIS data licensed to third parties for domains for which I am the Account Holder or Primary Contact." Click Save and you're done. For other registrars, you'll need to check the privacy policies and/or email customer support for instructions on how to opt out. And if they don't let you opt out, maybe it's time to switch registrars, eh?

Bloggers are from Mars, Lawyers are from Venus

The Annoyance: Someone I know posted a web log entry about me that contained information I'd rather keep out of the public domain. Now I'm afraid it will start to show up in Google searches.

The Fix: Bloggers usually surrender a lot of their personal privacy. That's their choice, and that's fine. Unfortunately, a lot of bloggers also compromise the privacy of others—and that's not so fine. An informal survey conducted by researchers at MIT's Media Lab found 66 percent of bloggers reveal personal information about others—and use those peoples' real names—with nary a thought about securing permission first. Many bloggers also seem to think they can publish anything they want about anyone with impunity, which is a good way to get themselves sued.

For example: Irish blogger Gavin Sheridan (*http://www.gavinsblog.com*) was threatened with legal action by San Francisco attorneys representing John Gray, author of *Men Are From Mars, Women Are From Venus*. (Apparently Dr. Gray doesn't cotton to being called a "fraud," even on a relatively obscure web site.) Sheridan shot back a reply (posted on his blog, of course) reminding Gray's attorneys that: a) he's an Irish citizen and thus not bound by the California courts, and b) Gray is a public figure and enjoys fewer libel law protections. At press time, nearly a year later, Gray's attorneys had yet to respond.

But as a private citizen, you are protected by libel laws—and can sue bloggers who slander or defame you, if you have the stomach and the budget for it. A better solution is to contact the blogger and politely but firmly ask him/her to correct, retract, or remove the offending statements (although this material may still show up in Google searches if those pages have already been cached). According to that same MIT survey, about a third of bloggers have gone back and edited or removed entries because they were too revealing or too negative, so the odds of a positive response are pretty good.

If you maintain your own blog, respect other peoples' privacy. Ask permission before writing about someone who's not a public figure. If you can't ask, then don't use their real names. And remember: you *are* liable for what you say online, no matter what your blogger buddies tell you.

Usenet or Lose It

The Annoyance: Ok, I admit it, I'm a bit of a hothead. I've posted more than my share of flames and outrageous statements on various newsgroups across the Net. Now I regret many of the things I typed in haste. Is there any way I can expunge them or otherwise "take it back"?

The Fix: Sorry. All the stupid things you've posted on Usenet over the years are preserved for posterity on Google Groups, assuming someone else is bored (or malicious) enough to look for them. But you can save yourself future embarrassment by using an anonymous remailer to post comments from now on. These are especially helpful to people who need to discuss highly personal issues (like sexual or substance abuse) without the stigma of having their identities attached to their comments. You'll find a list of anonymous newsgroup posters at *http://www.nemasys.com/ghostwolf/Resources/asarian. shtml*. For more information about anonymous speech on the Net, check out the Global Liberty Internet Campaign (*http://www.gilc.org/speech/anonymous/*).

PRIVACY BY THE NUMBERS

1 in 2
Male Internet users who admit to having visited an adult site

428,579,418
Spam emails blocked by AOL in a randomly selected 12-hour period in July 2004

70%
Online users who say they are concerned about online privacy

40%
Netizens who say they read online privacy policies

1.8 million
Users who were tricked into giving up personal information by phisher email scams

75%
Netizens who reveal personally identifiable information on their web blogs

36%
Bloggers who've posted things that have gotten them in trouble with family, friends, or employers

12 minutes
Average time required for unprotected PC to suffer a hack attack on the Net

30,000
Number of new zombie PCs discovered each day, from January to June 2004

Sources: EarthLink/Harris Interactive, AOL, Messagelabs, Electronic Frontier Foundation, Gartner Research, MIT Media Lab, SANS.org, Symantec

4

Privacy at Work

In the 21st century, the phrase "workplace privacy" has become something of an oxymoron. If you work in the public sector, you may be able to lean on the U.S. Constitution and other state and federal laws for a modicum of protection. If you're slaving away for a private firm, your privacy rights can essentially be summarized as "their property, their rules."

In the past, workplace monitoring was spurred by a desire to increase productivity. These days, corporations are more worried about attackers than slackers. Worms, viruses, spyware, and other malicious code can reach into the network of computers at any corporation, and cost billions of dollars in lost income and time spent cleaning up the mess. Hackers and electronic eavesdroppers can compromise a company's internal networks and steal confidential data—if employees don't accidentally leak the information first via email or instant messaging. Concerns about security lead human resource executives to employ in-depth background checks and pre-employment screening. And that's barely scratching the surface.

But different companies have different cultures. Some may strictly forbid extracurricular web surfing; others may allow it as a perk for break times, or encourage you to explore the Web because it makes for more informed employees. Some firms record every call you make or scan every email message; others only monitor randomly or in situations where they suspect wrongdoing. And, of course, a few benighted firms don't monitor at all but rely on their employees to act appropriately.

Clearly, it pays to figure out what kind of company you're working for. What activities does your employer monitor and how? You'll want your company to put its policies in writing, so everyone knows where the lines are drawn. You should ask your boss what he's doing to *protect* your privacy, not just invade it. And while you're at it, you should find out what's legal, what isn't, and what's unknown. This chapter will give you those goods, and more.

THE INTERNET AT WORK

Surfing on Company Time

The Annoyance: I think my boss is watching where I go on the Web. Aren't employers required to notify you if they monitor your web activity?

The Fix: In general, no. With very few exceptions, private employers can monitor everything you do in the workplace and aren't required to tell you a thing about it. (Government employees actually enjoy a few more rights; see the sidebar "Better Fed than Dead?")

Some employers include vague language like "we reserve the right to monitor your activities," either on a splash screen when you turn on your computer or buried deep within the employee handbook. Of course, that doesn't tell you whether they *are* monitoring or how they might be going about it. Only Connecticut and Delaware require employers to notify employees before monitoring their online communications. In other states it's entirely up to each company.

Lewis Maltby, president of the National Workrights Institute (*http://www.workrights.org*), says that while there's little you can do to prevent your boss from monitoring your online behavior, you can make monitoring less intrusive and more transparent:

- Ask your boss whether your company monitors employee communications, and if so, what types of communication and how. If your boss doesn't know, ask her to inquire further about this and get back to you.

- Once you find out what's monitored, decide how you want to communicate personal information. For example, if your company routinely scans email traffic but not phone calls, you may want to call your spouse or your doctor the next time you need to discuss a personal issue (although a better idea would be to use your cell phone or another line not owned by your company).

- If you don't like being monitored, make your objections known. If enough employees complain, the company may alter its policies (don't hold your breath). At the very least, insist your employer add a written policy to the employee handbook detailing which online activities are allowed and what the company does to ensure compliance.

Find out why your company is monitoring employees, and see if there's a less intrusive method of achieving its security goals. For example, instead of using web monitoring software to log every site an employee visits, your employer could use the same program to block employees from visiting objectionable sites—such as porn and hate speech sites—that could cause the company legal headaches. Companies concerned about productivity loss could adjust the software to allow access to certain types of sites at specified hours—say, news or travel sites during lunch or after work—or for a certain number of minutes each day. Maltby says many firms would happily embrace policies that protect their needs without alienating their employees. "Most employers are not interested in spying on you," says Maltby. "They're just trying to avoid sexual harassment suits, prevent the loss of their trade secrets, and keep people from spending all day on the Net when they should be working. [But]...companies don't have to violate your personal privacy to protect their legitimate business interests."

TEN WAYS YOUR BOSS CAN SPY ON YOU

Feel like someone's watching your every move at work? Someone probably is. Surveys by leading research organizations consistently show employee monitoring is on the rise. Here are some of the ways Corporate America watches its workers. (Unless otherwise noted, the stats that follow derive from surveys conducted by the American Management Association.)

Web monitoring: Nearly two-thirds of U.S. firms actively monitor their workers' web activity, according to the AMA. Most use software made by companies such as Websense or SurfControl, which sits on the company's network servers and logs every URL visited by every employee. The software could also be used to simply block attempts to reach forbidden sites without recording all of your web activity.

Email scanning: Almost half of American firms scan the content of employee email. Many use software, such as ClearSwift's MIMESweeper, that scans message text for keywords and blocks internal or external email containing sensitive information (e.g., company secrets or potentially harassing messages); other firms hire people to do the job.

Phone recording: Around one in ten businesses record employee conversations, although legally, companies aren't allowed to eavesdrop on private conversations. About 8 percent tap into your work voice mailbox.

Hard drive snooping: More than a third of surveyed firms admit to digging through their employee's hard drives. Most companies can do this over the company network without you ever knowing.

Capture and logging software: One in five companies records what users are doing at their machines in real time. Some install software that logs every keystroke or periodically captures what's on your screen. Software such as Chronicle Solutions' netReplay or TrueActive Monitor can record every single thing you do, all day long.

Surveillance cams: Think those security cameras are there for your protection? Some 15 percent of companies routinely videotape employees to measure job performance.

Personal searches: If you work in the public sector or in an industry that requires security clearances, you probably pass through a metal detector when you enter and leave the office every day. You might also be searched on your way in or out. At companies—especially retailers—where employee theft is rampant, going through your purse or backpack is standard operating procedure.

Background checks: Some employers merely check references and make sure you really did get that degree from Harvard. But if you're going for a high-level executive position, don't be surprised if the firm hires a private investigator to pry into your life.

Drug tests: At nearly all Fortune 500 companies and many smaller ones, applying for a job means peeing into a cup. Many companies also conduct random blood tests of current employees, although this practice appears to be declining.

Other employees: The guy in the next cubicle may be ratting you out. The 2003 National Business Ethics Survey found that 65 percent of employees reported misconduct to management.

Want to surf from work but still cover your tracks? Using Anonymizer's free proxy server (*http://www.anonymizer. com*), you can surf to any site while hiding its address from your employer's web monitoring software (see Figure 4-1). Your boss will know you visited Anonymizer.com, but won't know where you went beyond that. Anonymizer is available as a free toolbar for Internet Explorer; support for Firefox and other browsers is due later this year.

But the free toolbar is just really a demo—many sites either don't display or are deliberately blocked. That's because Anonymizer really wants you to fork over $30 for its Anonymous Surfing app, which installs on your hard drive. (Of course, if your employer already blocks access to Anonymizer.com or prevents you from installing browser plug-ins or software, you're out of luck.) Your company might also be able to suss out your surfing habits in other ways, using keyloggers or screen capture utilities.

For an explanation of how anonymous proxy servers work, as well as directories to free proxies around the world, visit the Public Proxy Servers site (*http://www.publicproxyservers.*

com) or Anonymity Checker (*http://www.anonymitychecker. com*). The Electronic Privacy Information Center provides a long list of tools you can use to privately surf the Web, send email, or engage in online chat at work; see *http://www.epic. org/privacy/tools.html*.

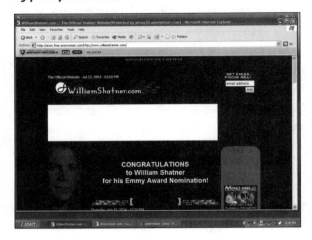

Figure 4-1. Anonymizer lets you surf at work without revealing where you've gone on the Web-say, to your favorite Shatner fetish site.

Visit NasteePix.com, Get Fired?

The Annoyance: I work hard, but I like to do a little recreational web surfing during break times. Can I get fired for this?

The Fix: You might. It all depends on your employer's policies and what you mean by "recreation." If your definition includes gambling, viewing photos of scantily-clad models, downloading MP3s, or trolling hate-speech blogs, you stand a pretty good chance of getting canned. According to a 2001 survey by the American Management Association (AMA), 62 percent of companies monitor Internet content, and more than a third of those firms disciplined employees for breaking their Net policies. (The AMA doesn't say how many of those folks got fired, but you can be sure some did—see "Privacy in Peril: Prurient Interest.")

The trouble is that many corporations lack any kind of written guidelines on what's acceptable behavior. Porn is an obvious no-no, but what about news, political, or travel sites? A study by The Center for Business Ethics at Bentley College found that over 90 percent of companies allow "reasonable personal usage" of the Web, but only 42 percent define what "reasonable" means. So find out what your employer does and doesn't allow (see Table 4-1.) Some questions to ask:

- Are employees allowed to use their work Internet connection for personal use?

- If so, is personal use restricted to certain times of day (like lunch breaks or after 5 p.m.)?

- Are there limits on the amount of time employees can surf each day?

- What types of sites are prohibited?

- What penalties will be assessed if employees break the rules?

- Are there procedures in place for employees to dispute claims made against them? (For example, your computer was infected with spyware that drove it to illicit sites.)

Mark Rowe, one of the authors of the Bentley study, says a degree of recreational use is permissible in many organizations, but "companies are not being sufficiently explicit in terms of their policies. There need to be very clear guidelines for employees."

Table 4-1. Let's be reasonable...

Activities allowed	% of companies that allow them
Job searches	25
Online Trading	28
Online shopping	51
Online banking	54
News sites	84

Source: Reproduced with permission by the Center for Business Ethics at Bentley College.

Out of the Office, But Not Out of Sight

The Annoyance: I telecommute from home two days a week. I keep my Quicken checkbook, digital photos, and other personal stuff on the computer at home I use for work. Does my boss have a right to snoop around my home PC?

The Fix: It depends on whose gear you're using. If your employer furnished the computer you use for telecommuting, then it has the right to look at anything on it.

If you're using your own computer, you have more privacy rights, but you're far from in the clear. If you're logging into the corporate network and using that to connect to the Internet, your employer can monitor where you go and what you do online, though it probably can't legally look at what's on your hard drive. Even if you're on your own dime when paying for Net access, if you're checking a corporate email account, your employer can certainly monitor your inbox and outbox.

Privacy attorney Parry Aftab (*http://www.aftab.com*) advises her corporate clients to set up web kiosks in employee break areas that are exempt from company monitoring. That way, employees would have the freedom to access the Web without penalty, and employers would avoid liability for what the employees do online.

"If the company supplied it, they have the right to do anything they want," says privacy rights attorney Parry Aftab (*http://www.aftab.com*). "Those same rules apply to other employer-supplied gear like laptops, cell phones, pagers, handheld PCs, Blackberries, and so on. It's much broader than computers, which is something most people tend to forget."

You may have also waived your privacy rights as part of a work-at-home agreement, says Aftab, which could give your boss unfettered access to your home computer (though probably not other machines on your home network). If you signed a telecommute agreement, now's the time to examine the fine print.

PRIVACY IN PERIL: PRURIENT INTEREST

Even the boss can be caught with his, umm, pants down—and end up paying a stiff penalty. Michael Soden, chief executive of the Bank of Ireland, was forced to resign in June 2004 after porn was found on his office PC during routine maintenance. Although the adult content broke no laws, Soden's behavior violated internal bank policies.

Soden might consider applying for work at LL Media. According to a report in *The Register*, a UK-based technology site (*http://www.theregister.co.uk*), the Danish IT firm has given employees free subscriptions to porn sites as a form of fringe benefit. However, certain types of porn sites aren't allowed, and company employees can only use the subscriptions on their home PCs.

Whose Email Is It, Anyway?

The Annoyance: I sometimes use my work email for personal use. I don't want my boss reading it.

The Fix: Join the club. Nearly 9 out of 10 people use work email to send or receive personal messages, according to a 2004 survey by the AMA. That same survey found that 60 percent of companies monitor email communications with the outside world, and one in four companies has fired someone for violating their email policies.

If you must send personal mail at work, you could use a webmail account such as Yahoo Mail or Hotmail instead of your corporate account. But remember, when you're using your work PC and/or your employer's network, your boss still has the legal right to read your outbound or inbound messages. And she could do it in a variety of ways.

For example, your IT department could have a "sniffer" device on the network that captures unencrypted data as it passes over network wires. It might employ software such as netReplay that lets them view what's on users' screens—kind of like a closed circuit TV camera trained on your PC. The office geek squad might install a keylogging program on your machine that captures everything you type. At the very least, companies concerned about employee communications can use web monitoring software to log the time you spend on these webmail sites and/or limit your access to them.

One way to defeat a sniffer is by encrypting your mail so that only you and the intended recipient can read it. (See the tip below.) Encryption is especially useful when you need to share confidential business information across the wires. But if your employer has installed a monitoring device on your computer, there's little you can do short of disabling the device—which is likely to get you in far hotter water.

As with web monitoring, find out what kinds of messages your employer looks at and how, suggests NWI's Lewis Maltby, and see if you can carve out some personal use that won't infringe on company policies. For example, you could ask your bosses to fine-tune the scanning software to make exceptions for messages that are almost certain to be personal—like email you send to your spouse.

HUSH HUSH, SWEET EMAIL

Need to send personal email from work but don't want the boss to sneak a peek? Encrypt (scramble) your messages so that only you and your intended recipient can read them. There are a zillion email encryption products out there, but one of the easiest is Hushmail (*http://www.hushmail.com*), a webmail service based on the Pretty Good Privacy (PGP) encryption technology. (To send encrypted mail, your recipient must also use Hushmail or a compatible product, such as PGP Mail.) To create a free Hushmail account, simply pick a username, provide a passphrase (such as "To err is human, but it feels divine"), and jiggle your mouse pointer around on screen to create a random number sequence that Hushmail will use to encrypt your messages. That's it.

The free version of Hushmail includes a meager 2MB of storage. For $30 to $90 a year you get customer support, from 32MB to 128MB of storage, and the ability to access your Hushmail account using Outlook and other POP3 email programs. You can also stick with your existing email package and just use PGP encryption software, such as PGP Personal Desktop ($59, *http://www.pgp.com*) or the free (but harder to use) PGP 8.1 (available at *http://www.pgp.com/products/freeware.html*). For more email encryption tools, see the Electronic Privacy Information Center's list at *http://www.epic.org/privacy/tools.html*.

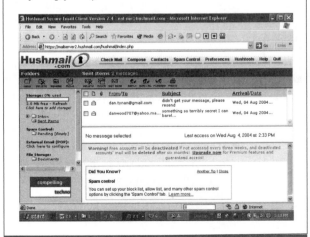

Beware of IT Spies

The Annoyance: I know my company is scanning my email. But I also suspect the little twerps in my company's IT department are reading my messages just for kicks, and then blabbing about it to the world.

The Fix: They very well might. A recent survey by Forrester Consulting and Proofpoint found that 44 percent of large companies hire people to scan outgoing email looking for trade secrets, copyrighted material, or anything else that could get the company in legal trouble. The problem with this, says NWI's Lewis Maltby, is that few companies have anyone assigned to watch the watchers. Slightly more than half of the companies surveyed by Bentley College had written guidelines on how Internet monitoring is supposed to be conducted. Only a third required company monitors to sign a confidentiality agreement, and one in four performed no oversight at all. The survey only included companies that employed ethics officers—so if these folks aren't thinking about keeping email monitors in line, imagine what the rest of Corporate America is like (see Table 4-2).

Again, your best solution is to ask management. Do they have written guidelines that govern monitoring procedures? Are monitors bound by a confidentiality agreement? What's done to ensure they are following proper procedures?

The bottom line, says Frederick S. Lane III, author of *The Naked Employee: How Technology is Compromising Workplace Privacy*, is to be very careful about what company resources you use. "If you don't want your employer reading email you send to your buddy at Alcoholics Anonymous, or your doctor, or your child, don't use your employer's computer to send that mail."

Table 4-2. Who's watching you online?

Title	% with access to monitoring data
Security guards department	58
Human resources	56
Internal auditors	38
Chief Information Officer	36
CEO	12
Individuals being monitored	8

Source: Reproduced with permission by the Center for Business Ethics at Bentley College.

Chewing the Fat on Chat

The Annoyance: I use instant messaging to check in with my friends and family while I'm at work. Can my boss see who I'm talking to and when I'm logged on?

The Fix: He sure can. For the moment, instant messaging is slightly more private chat than email. The Forrester survey found only 21 percent of companies are keeping an eye on IM communications, but that number is likely to grow as more companies adopt IM as a business tool and realize the potential havoc that IM could wreak. For example, the SEC now requires securities dealers to archive business IM records for three years; healthcare companies may also be required by federal statutes to preserve any electronic communications regarding patient health records, including IM.

With software such as FaceTime Communications' IM Auditor or Akonix L7 Enforcer, your company's IT department can log the amount of time you spend on IM, record all your conversations, and/or block certain activities on IM such as file sharing. They can monitor all the major chat clients (so don't think using AOL's or MSN's IM software makes you safe). They can also log when you're online; so if you set your messenger software to indicate that you're not at your desk when you really are, your boss may think you're goldbricking.

You may be able to keep your IM private by using products such as Hushmail's Hush Messenger (*http://www.hushmail.com*), which uses PGP encryption to scramble private conversations with other Hush Messenger users, or IMpasse (*http://www.im-passe.com*), which likewise automatically encrypts and decrypts messages sent via AIM, Yahoo Messenger, and MSN Messenger. Otherwise, when you use IM, assume someone's listening—because even if they aren't now, they probably will be soon.

PRIVACY IN PERIL: DONE IN BY IM

If you think your boss eavesdropping on your instant messaging chats is bad, consider this. At a technology conference in June 2004, IMLogic managing director Derek O'Carroll told a story about an executive whose IM client was infected by a virus. The virus proceeded to record all his IM conversations and email them to everyone in his buddy list. The conversations included negative comments about coworkers—who were included on his IM buddy list (apparently they weren't *close* buddies). Next thing the exec knew, he was looking for a new job. Thus inspiring a twist on the old adage: if you can't say anything nice, don't say it on IM.

You want to notify the SEC that your company is breaking the law, but you don't want your boss to find out who squealed. Or maybe a coworker has a personal hygiene problem, but you just don't have the heart to tell him to his face. Anonymizer.com offers a free email service (*https://www.anonymizer.com*) that lets you send messages that are completely untraceable. Of course, anonymous services like this can also be used to harass or stalk people—so please use your anonymity for good, not evil.

Do Your Hunting From Home

The Annoyance: I hate my job, so during breaks at work, I've been posting digital résumés on job boards like Monster.com. There's no way my boss can find out, is there?

The Fix: There is. If your company has installed web filtering software like Websense or SurfControl—or even just looked at the network server logs—your boss could easily find out exactly how much time you've been spending at Monster.com or any other online job board. If the company uses an email security program such as ClearSwift's MIMESweeper, it could scan outgoing email looking for telltale signs (like file attachments with "résumé" in the title). If they use a keylogger, they can detect what you've been typing on your PC at any time. And so on.

One solution may be to use an anonymous proxy server and email encryption, assuming you can get them to work through the office firewall. But a better idea is simply to avoid using your work PC for anything involving a job search—unless you want your boss to help you in your quest by firing you. (For more tips on Net job hunting privacy, see "Who's Reading Your Résumé?")

APPLYING FOR WORK

This is Your Job on Drugs

The Annoyance: I just applied for a job at a prestigious company, but before they'll even consider me they insist on a urine sample. Can I legally refuse?

The Fix: You can always refuse, but you probably won't get the job. Since the "Just Say No" campaign of the early 80s, drug testing has become an unfortunate part of life at many companies. It's also been used for more than just keeping addicts off the payrolls. According to a 2001 survey by the American Management Association (AMA), employers also use such tests to deny employment based on an applicant's medical history, HIV status, presence of sexually-transmitted diseases, and whether they're pregnant. Companies have also successfully used drug test results to deny workers' compensation claims. And even if you're perfectly clean (and healthy, and not with child), you could still get nixed due to false test results (see Table 4-3).

Table 4-3. You could be a druggie...or you may just have a head cold.

Legal Substance	May show up as...
Ibuprofen	Marijuana
Cold remedies or diet pills	Amphetamines
Novocain	Cocaine
DHEA	Anabolic Steroids
Poppy seeds	Opiates

Sources: Erowid, Community Health Gate

TEA, BUT NO SYMPATHY

What's the cost of a false positive drug test? How about nearly three years of unemployment? That's the price paid by Charmaine Garrido, a former investigator with the Cook County Sheriff's Department.

In 2001, Garrido tested positive for cocaine at work and was forced to leave her job. In June 2004, the Illinois Court of Appeals ruled that the positive test results were more likely caused by Garrido drinking large amounts of a coca-tinged tea she had purchased while visiting Peru. The mate de coca tea (cost: 120 bags for $45) contains trace amounts of cocaine and is used for treating altitude sickness. The lesson here: if you feel you've been failed by a false drug test result, you may have to sue to get your job back.

If you'd rather collect unemployment checks than undergo a drug test, you still have a few options. To wit:

- Check local laws. Some municipalities (such as San Francisco) prohibit drug screening for people in non-safety-related professions. For a guide to drug laws by state, visit the Drug Policy Alliance site (*http://www.drugpolicy.org/statebystate/*) or the National Conference of State Legislatures (NCSL) site (*http://www.ncsl.org/programs/employ/drugtest.htm*).

- Find an employer that doesn't test. According to AMA surveys, 67 percent of companies test for drugs, down from a peak of 81 percent in 1996. (The AMA study also notes that the level of pre-employment screening remains high; most of the decline is due to companies conducting fewer tests on current employees.)

- If you already work for a company that tests, try to convince your employer to substitute "impairment testing" in place of drug screens. Impairment tests measure reaction times and other factors that determine how well individuals actually perform their jobs, instead of simply scrutinizing the contents of their bloodstream. For more on impairment testing, see The National Workrights Institute's page at *http://www.workrights.org/issue_drugtest/dt_impairment_testing.html*.)

An extensively researched (but unofficial) FAQ about drug tests and the ways people have tried to defeat them can be found at the Erowid site *http://www.erowid.org/psychoactives/testing/testing_faq.shtml#3.* Be aware, however, that several states make it a crime to falsify the results of a drug test.

The Background on Background Checks

The Annoyance: I am inches away from getting a big job, but my future employer insists they need to do a background check on me first. I don't like the idea of my prospective employer digging into my past. Can I do anything about it?

The Fix: Well, you can say no. Under the recently revised Fair Credit Reporting Act, a prospective employer has to obtain your permission before it can run a background check on you. (The bad news is that if you refuse, you're less likely to get the job.) If the company decides not to hire you because of something that turned up in the report, it must give you a copy of the report, as well as the opportunity to dispute anything you feel is inaccurate. But if the employer says it made the decision based on factors other than your background check, then all bets are off.

If you live in California, you can get a copy of the report regardless of whether it was a factor in their decision. Other state laws may provide further rights (see the National Conference of State Legislatures' page on laws concerning job applicants and credit checks at *http://www.ncsl.org/programs/employ/jobapplicantcreditchecklaws.htm*). The Privacy Rights Clearinghouse (PRC) offers an extensive fact sheet on background checks at *http://www.privacyrights.org/fs/fs16-bck.htm.*

But the law only applies to information gathered by third parties. So, for example, if a company does its own background checks—and never uses information from a credit reporting agency—it's not subject to the limitations of the FCRA. Any company that wants to be exempt from these restrictions could hire its own gumshoes as employees. According to Frederick S. Lane, author of *The Naked Employee,* one-third of the nation's 40,000 investigators are employed by corporations.

Here's a tip from the PRC: if you agree to a background check, ask your potential employer what background screening company they use. By law, that firm must give you access to the dossier they compile—which can include information not provided in the report given to the employer.

For many jobs, such as those dealing with child care and virtually all governmental positions, background checks are mandated by state or Federal law. For tips on how to keep a background check from coming back to bite you, see the sidebar "Be Your Own Gumshoe." Table 4-4 lists what a background check can reveal.

Table 4-4. What can a background check reveal? A lot.

What may be part of a background check	What's left out [a]
Driving records	Bankruptcies more than 10 years old
Employment history	Civil suits more than 7 years old
Property ownership	Tax liens more than seven years old
Court and Criminal records	Accounts on collect after 7 years
Medical records [b]	Arrests (but not convictions) after 7 years
Credit history & bankruptcies	
Personal and character references	
State licensing records	
Military records [b]	
Workers compensation history	

[a] Applies only to background checks using a third-party consumer reporting service, as per the FCRA.
[b] In most instances, your permission is required before employers can access this information.
Source: Privacy Rights Clearinghouse

BE YOUR OWN GUMSHOE

If a potential employer plans to sort through your sordid past, it's a good idea to run your own background check first, says Tena Friery, research director for the Privacy Rights Clearinghouse. That way you can ferret out errors and correct them before your future boss sees them. Here's how:

- *Order your credit report.* Credit reports contain a lot more information than just how good you are at paying your VISA bill. They can include information about the property you own, your marital status, legal proceedings, and more. According to the Public Research Interest Group (*http://www.pirg.org/consumer/credit/*), more than 25 percent of reports contain errors that have caused people to be denied credit or employment. For the scoop on how to order yours, see Chapter 2, "Check Your Reports."

- *Check your court records.* Some state databases report every time you've been arrested; others only include your name if you've been convicted. If you've had a felony changed to a misdemeanor, or had records expunged, double-check to make sure the court has a record of it. Unfortunately not all court records are online, so you may be forced to visit the courthouse and comb through its files.

- *Drive by the DMV.* Many employers will check your driving record, especially if your job involves operating a vehicle. If you've got a DUI/DWI conviction, you might still get the job. But if you lie about that on your application—and your employer uncovers the falsehood—you probably won't. You can usually request your driving records by contacting your state DMV (see *http://www.dmv.org*) or you can order a copy directly from DrivingRecord.com for $30 a pop.

- *Peruse your old personnel files.* Some states (like California) allow you to request your HR files from former employers, provided you make your request within a certain time period. Even if they don't, your old boss might let you see them anyway.

- *Hire a pro.* If you're applying for a big money gig, you might want to hire a private investigator to see what misinformation is floating around with your name attached. A cheap alternative is to spend $60 to $100 on an online search using a site like US Search (*http://www.ussearch.com*) or Intelius (*http://www.intelius.com*). It won't be as thorough, but gross errors will leap out.

- *Notify your friends and neighbors.* In-depth background checks involve phone and on-site interviews with neighbors and other associates—and not just the ones you put down as references. Alert them before they're called, so they're less suspicious and more helpful when the phone rings.

- *Be honest.* Check that résumé one more time for any overstatements or inaccuracies. A 2001 survey by executive recruiters Christian & Timbers revealed that one out of four executive résumés contained falsehoods—and being caught in a lie can kill your chances right from the start.

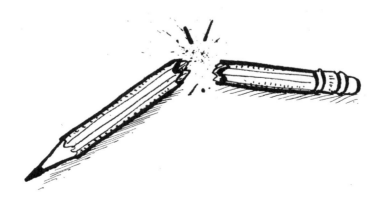

> **t i p**
>
> The Americans with Disabilities Act was designed to prevent employers from discriminating against physically challenged but otherwise qualified candidates, yet its privacy protections can extend to anyone seeking gainful employment. For example, the ADA prohibits employers with 25 employees or more from asking health-related questions that could indicate evidence of a disability prior to the job offer. Banned questions include:
>
> - Do you have a heart condition?
> - How many days were you sick last year?
> - Have you ever filed for worker's compensation?
> - Have you ever been treated for mental health problems?
> - What prescription drugs are you currently taking?
>
> For more on what employers can and can't ask under the ADA, see *http://www.eeoc.gov/facts/jobapplicant.html*.

Bury the Dirt

The Annoyance: So once they dig up all this dirt on me, what happens to it?

The Fix: That depends on how big a job you're applying for, as well as where you live. The Fair Credit Reporting Act requires companies that use a third-party consumer reporting agency (e.g., Experian or ChoicePoint) to properly dispose of the records after the check is completed. That includes electronic copies as well as paper. Sounds good, right? But in this law there are some gaping holes that still allow some employers (and potential employers) to hang on to your personal information.

For one thing, the law never defines what it means by "proper disposal." So, for example, a firm could merely throw out the paper report and delete electronic copies, which, as we know, doesn't really erase anything (see Chapter 2, "Complete Delete"). A dumpster diver or a moderately knowledgeable computer snoop could easily gain access to your report.

Worse, the law doesn't apply to anyone who's up for a job that pays more than $75,000 a year, which is where the most extensive background checks are performed. It may not apply to some smaller businesses (those details were still being worked out as this book was being written). And if your employer ran a check on you a year ago, tough luck—the law only applies to background checks that took place after December 1, 2004.

The solution: ask to see what's in your file. Though most private employers aren't obliged to show you, they might do it anyway out of goodwill. And be sure to quiz your company's HR department about how it secures personnel records (see "Beware Employee ID Theft,").

Avoid Questionable Questions

The Annoyance: Before I took a job at my company, I was asked to take a 200-question personality profile that probed me for all kinds of invasive information. What can happen to my answers?

The Fix: Just about anything, so be careful what you say. Tena Fiery of the Privacy Rights Clearinghouse advises job applicants to beware of open-ended questions, such as "Have you ever been arrested?" The Federal Credit Reporting Act limits employer queries about arrest records to the last seven years (though there is no time limit for convictions). Equal Employment Opportunity laws also limit questions relating to gender, race, sexual orientation, and certain medical conditions (such as pregnancy).

WHO'S READING YOUR RÉSUMÉ?

Posting your résumé online is faster, easier, and a lot more efficient than printing cover letters and licking stamps. But according to a November 2003 report by the World Privacy Forum, it's also far less private. Many omnibus job sites ask for sensitive information they're not entitled to and share it with third parties. Some have been found guilty of selling résumé data without permission. And some offer minimal protection from hackers or identity thieves.

- When you can, post your résumé directly to a prospective employer's web site, not via a third-party job board. The fewer stops your résumé makes along the way, the less likely your information will be lost or misused.

- If you're applying for jobs at large companies that handle thousands of applicants, it may use a third party (e.g., Monster.com or CareerBuilder.com) to process résumés. Find out who handles applicant data, and read that site's privacy policy carefully.

- Don't post your résumé to any site that lacks a privacy policy or whose policy is deficient. For example, if the policy states the site now owns your résumé information and/or shares your data with third parties, don't use it.

- Check the policy to see how long your résumé will be stored on the site, and only use sites that let you edit or delete you résumé at any time.

- Avoid using your real name or email address. Some job sites let you mask your identity until a potential employer indicates interest. If the job board doesn't let you mask yourself, use a disposable email address for your primary contact info. Yahoo Mail Plus, Zoe Mail, and Hushmail all let you create temporary mail IDs.

- Never put your Social Security Number or date of birth on your résumé. You can always provide these to the employer later when they offer you a job. If a site requires you to submit your SSN—as many government job boards do—you may want to mail in your résumé or find an alternate way to apply.

- Check out professional résumé writing services very carefully before hiring one. They may also be in the business of selling your information to marketers.

- Don't put names or contact information for your references on your résumé. If you do, don't expect a glowing reference from someone whose privacy you've just compromised.

- For more information on how to protect your privacy at online job boards, see Pam Dixon's Job Search Privacy site (*http://www.jobsearchprivacy.org*).

If the questions are inappropriate to the job you're applying for, you could sue the employer under several privacy torts, says Don Harris, principal of HR Privacy Solutions (*http://www.hrprivacy.com*), which advises multinational corporations on personnel privacy issues. (Fear of lawsuits may be one reason why the number of companies requiring psych tests for job applicants dropped from one-half in 1998 to one-third in 2001, according to those relentless survey-takers, the American Management Association.)

In July 2000, Rent-A-Center paid a $2.2 million settlement to some 1200 applicants who were asked to fill out a 502-question form that asked, among other things, whether they had ever engaged in "unusual sex practices" (making one wonder exactly what kind of appliances Rent-A-Center carries). In December 2001, Wal-Mart agreed to pay a $6.8 million settlement after the Equal Employment Opportunity Commission sued the mass-market retailer for using a questionnaire to discriminate against handicapped applicants—a violation of the Americans with Disabilities Act.

Of course, some companies will still ask illegal questions, intentionally or otherwise. A reasonable response is to side-step questions that make you feel uncomfortable without making a Federal case out of it. If a potential employer asks if you've ever been arrested, you can say something like "They keep trying, but they've never been able to catch me" or "my record is clean," without going into the details of some youthful mistake from 20 years ago. (The Technical Job Search site offers more tips on how to handle unlawful questions at *http://technicaljobsearch.com/interviews/illegal-questions. htm*.) Then again, if a company insists on asking nosy questions about your past (or your unusual sex practices), maybe you don't want to work there.

If your boss asks you to take a lie detector test, you can tell him (or her) to go stuff it. The Employee Polygraph Protection Act prohibits private employers from requiring applicants or employees to submit to lie detector tests, or disciplining those who refuse to take such tests. The exceptions? If you're applying for certain jobs (armed guard, pharmaceutical rep) or if you're accused of theft or embezzlement, you can be asked to strap on the electrodes. (For more on the law, see *http://www. dol.gov/dol/compliance/comp-eppa.htm*.)

HR/PERSONNEL RECORDS

When Personnel Gets Personal

The Annoyance: My personnel file is a Pandora's Box of personal information about me—background checks, drug tests, and psychological profiles—that I'd rather not share with the world. How do I know my employer isn't sharing this information with the world—or that it will stay private after I leave the company?

The Fix: You don't. In fact, there are no legal limits on what a private firm can do with the information in your file, says HR Privacy Solutions' Don Harris. In most cases you don't have a legal right to see your file, let alone dispute inaccuracies inside it.

"For the most part, employers can pretty much do what they want with employees' information, says Harris. "For example, it's perfectly legal for an employer to sell its entire database of employees to a commercial party that wants to market products and services to them. I don't know of any employer who would do such a thing, but there's no law against it."

Harris adds that common sense and a desire to not alienate employees keeps most companies in check. If your employer doesn't already have a written privacy policy, ask it to create one that spells out what the company does with your personnel records while you're employed and after you leave the company. The policy should also detail how your employer protects the security of its files—not only from unethical bosses, but also against hackers, internal spies, or simple carelessness. (See "Beware Employee ID Theft.") If your company doesn't have a security plan, your questions may spur it to create one.

You should also check your personnel file every six months or so, to make sure there's nothing inaccurate in there, advises Tena Fiery of the PRC. Public sector employees are allowed access to their files by law; approximately 20 states have rules allowing private employees to see all or part of their HR files. In California, for example, employees have the right to see any documents in their files they've signed, but some states aren't even that generous. As far as I can determine there is no central clearinghouse for state laws on the topic, so you'll need to check with the appropriate hide-bound bureaucracy in your area.

PRIVACY IN PERIL: SORRY, WRONG NUMBER

Verifying employment and salary histories is both painstaking and mind numbing, which is why many companies hire automated services like The Work Number (*http://www.theworknumber.com*) to do the job for them. The Work Number claims to house some 80 million records that can be accessed by potential employers, mortgage brokers, property managers, and others to verify employment or eligibility for public assistance programs. But according to a July 2004 report by The Privacy Rights Clearinghouse, some of those records are wrong—they misreport job titles or indicate employees have been fired when in fact they left under their own steam.

Tom Werner, general counsel for TALX, The Work Number's parent corporation, says the site gets all of its information directly from employers, and that mistakes are rare. Employees who want to check the accuracy of their records can search the site's directory for their employer's name, then log in using their Social Security Number and PIN, or call 800-367-5690. To dispute information in your record, you can call 800-996-7566 and The Work Number will try to resolve the differences with your former employer. However, Werner adds, "The final decision on the accuracy of the data contained on a verification of employment or income resides with the employers, since they maintain the primary source of employment information."

If you've got a beef with the information contained on The Work Number, the PRC would also like to hear about it; contact them at *http://www.privacyrights.org/inquiryform.html*.

Avoid Bad PR from HR

The Annoyance: I just left a job under trying circumstances. Can negative reports in my HR file follow me around to my next job?

The Fix: Yes, they could. However, employers tend to be fairly gun-shy about sharing too much information because they can be sued if a negative report causes someone to lose out on a job, says HR Privacy Solutions' Don Harris.

"A lot of employers have gotten burned in court, so they tend to give just name, rank and serial number—essentially dates of employment—and not give away sensitive information," says Harris. "If the employer shares negative information about you, you can sue them under a privacy tort such as libel or defamation. But the burden of proof is on you, as well as the expense and the bad publicity."

Harris says this is what leads many executives to resign instead of being fired. The advice here: If you fear a negative recommendation, strike a deal with your (soon-to-be-ex) boss. Agree to go quietly, as long as your employer agrees to not say bad things about you after you're gone.

PRIVACY DOWN UNDER

Australia is famous for doing everything on a large scale (e.g., beer, waves, crocodiles), so it shouldn't come as a surprise that they're also big on workplace privacy. In early 2004, the government of New South Wales passed a law that would ban most forms of employer snooping. According to a report in The Register (*http://www.theregister.co.uk/2004/03/31/nsw_bans_workplace_cybersnooping*), the Exposure Bill would forbid employers to spy on employees without having a reasonable suspicion of wrongdoing. The rules cover video surveillance, email snooping, and other forms of tracking. Companies that demonstrate a need to conduct surveillance will also have to inform employees ahead of time. Good onya, mate!

Beware Employee ID Theft

The Annoyance: The admin who works in HR hates my guts. How do I know she's not sabotaging my employment records?

The Fix: You don't. She very well may be doing nasty things to your records, including stealing your identity.

Professor Judith Collins of Michigan State's Identity Theft Crime Lab investigated more than 1000 cases of ID theft, and found that up to 70 percent could be traced to employees or people posing as employees. A 2002 study by credit reporting giant TransUnion cited stolen employee records as the number one source of identity crimes.

Whether you'll find out if your personal information has been compromised depends on where you live. As of 2002, California law requires companies doing business in California to notify employees when the security of their personal information has been breached. So if you live or work in the Golden State, your boss must tell you when its HR records have been exposed or pilfered—assuming it knows about the deed and that telling you won't impede a criminal investigation. (For more information on California's privacy protections, see *http://www.privacy.ca.gov/*).

This is another situation where you may have to nag your employer to follow smart security precautions to protect your personal data. HR Privacy's Don Harris suggests every business take a few simple steps:

- Only allow authorized personnel to access HR records.

- Password-protect and encrypt sensitive computer files.

- Require hefty background checks for those with access to such records.

- Discourage the use of temporary employees in HR.

- Avoid using Social Security numbers on ID badges, timesheets, payment stubs, or any other document that circulates in public.

- Shred sensitive materials once they're no longer needed.

On a personal level, your best defense is to keep a close eye on your credit reports, so you can suss out if your ID has been swiped. (For more on how to do this, see Chapter 2, "Check Your Reports.")

PRIVACY IN PERIL: GOT PAYROLL?

According to a June 2004 report in *Computerworld* magazine, officials working in Northern California's Contra Costa County inadvertently sent hundreds of highly sensitive emails to an Internet company in Sweden over a period of two years. The messages, which contained employee payroll and benefits information, were apparently sent to the Swedish firm by accident because of errors in county officials' email address books. The firm's owner attempted to contact the county for two years before giving up and turning to *Computerworld*, which successfully intervened and turned off the spigot of unwanted email. Legal experts speculate this case may become the first test of California's 2003 identity theft law (SB1386), which requires companies to notify individuals when their personal information has been compromised. So far, no county employees have reported purchases of Volvos or fermented Baltic herring on their credit card statements.

MISCELLANEOUS WORK ISSUES

Dish the Dirt, Lose Your Job?

The Annoyance: My employer "monitors calls for quality assurance" between me and the company's customers. If I happen to say something nasty and vile about my vile, nasty boss, can he fire me?

The Fix: It depends on whom you're talking to. Businesses that monitor phone calls aren't legally allowed to eavesdrop on private conversations. So if you call your boss names while you're on the phone with your spouse, technically they're not allowed to listen. Of course, your supervisor could overhear you saying it at work, or the tattletale in the next cubicle could repeat this information to your boss. That's all perfectly legal.

According to the NWI's Lewis Maltby, as long as employers aren't violating your civil rights, they are free to fire you at any time for whatever reason. "Your boss could fire you for writing a letter to the editor," Maltby says. "He could fire you because he doesn't like the way you part your hair or because his wife burnt the toast that morning."

The exception: a company can't fire you if doing so would violate a federal or state law. For example, your employer is forbidden to fire you simply because you filed a worker's compensation claim against it. Your boss also can't fire you for refusing to do something that's against the law (like cooking the books or lying to the SEC). And if you have an agreement with your employer that lays out grounds for dismissal, your boss has to follow it, though you might have to go to court to enforce that contract. Your options? Negotiate a work agreement that describes exactly how and when your employer can terminate you, or keep your lips zipped until the boss is truly out of earshot.

PRIVACY IN PERIL: BLOGGING YOUR WAY TO UNEMPLOYMENT

Your boss may eavesdrop on your conversations at work, but what you say on your own time is your business, right? Well, not if you do it on the Web. Michael Hanscom, a temporary employee doing a stint at Microsoft, discovered that simply publishing a photo is enough to get you fired. In October 2003, Hanscom snapped a shot of some Apple PowerMacs being unloaded from a truck at the company's Redmond, Washington headquarters and published it on his personal blog. A few days later he was contacted by his supervisor and asked to not return. He had apparently violated internal Microsoft policies prohibiting photographs taken on company property. (Microsoft has never revealed how it happened to find out about the photo.)

Still, that's small potatoes compared to Jessica Cutler, a former staffer for U.S. Senator Mike DeWine (R-Ohio). The 24-year-old Cutler got canned after publishing a scandalous blog under the name "Washingtonienne," detailing her many affairs with office coworkers, including a paid sexual arrangement with an agency head in the Bush administration. The official reason for Cutler's termination was misuse of Senate computers. They should probably be happy she didn't publish photos.

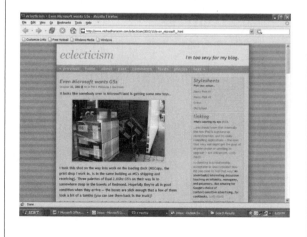

DO EMPLOYEES NEED A BILL OF RIGHTS?

In his book *The Naked Employee*, author Fred Lane describes a how a benevolent corporation should treat employee privacy. Short of Congress enacting an Employee Bill of Rights (don't bet on that one), there's nothing to force any private employer to follow such rules. But you might want to photocopy this page and put a copy in the company suggestion box—or on the CEO's desk.

- *Get permission first.* Companies should obtain employees' consent before acquiring personal information about them. As part of the process, employers should disclose what types of information they're seeking and how it relates to job performance.

- *Provide full disclosure.* If you're going to spy on your employees, tell them first. Be specific about what you're monitoring and why you're doing it—before applicants agree to take a job there.

- *Limit the spread of information.* Train employees in sensitive positions to avoid disclosing personal information unnecessarily to third parties. A landlord might need to verify that Hercule in accounting is gainfully employed; he doesn't need to know that Hercule is a total slob who's been late to work every day of his career.

- *Don't misuse medical data.* If you're going to seek information about an employee's medical history or lifestyle choices, make sure that data is directly related to the work he or she is being hired to perform—not to its potential impact on the company's health insurance premiums.

- *Avoid needless drug tests.* If you must test, do so only in cases where suspected drug abuse may be hurting an employee's ability to perform. A better alternative is impairment testing, which measures actual abilities, not trace elements in the bloodstream (see "This is Your Job on Drugs").

- *Preserve boundaries between work and home.* Telecommuters shouldn't have to give up more of their privacy just because they're no longer within their supervisor's field of vision.

"In most companies there is a potential for dialog about how workplace privacy should be handled," says Lane. "Most companies want to create a good environment for employees, and they recognize that too much surveillance damages that."

(Adapted by permission of the publisher from *The Naked Employee* by Frederick S. Lane III, copyright 2003, Frederick S. Lane, published by AMACOM Books, New York, New York. *www.amacombooks.org*.)

Medical Records May Be Hazardous to Your Job

The Annoyance: My child has a chronic health condition. I've used my employer's health insurance plan to cover part of the costs of his treatment. Now I'm looking to switch jobs. Can my new boss find out about my child's health history and use that to as an excuse to hire someone else or deny my family insurance coverage?

The Fix: Legally, your new boss shouldn't find out, but that doesn't mean he won't. The Health Insurance Portability and Accountability Act (HIPPA) prohibits health care providers from sharing identifiable information with your employer without your written consent. So in theory, your new boss need never know about your child's health history. But naturally there are exceptions. If your employer is paying for your health care costs out of its own pocket, it would have access to your medical records, though it can't legally share them with other parties or other employees not involved with administering the health plan.

On the other hand, if your employer isn't providing health care (i.e., a third-party insurer is paying the claims) and it obtains your medical information via other means, HIPPA doesn't apply. While your boss can't go to your doctor and demand your medical records without your consent, he can find out in other ways—for example, if you sign up for an employee assistance program to deal with a substance abuse problem. Information you provide on job applications or via work-related physicals, anything that turns up in a background check, health secrets you disclose in ordinary conversation—all are fair game.

"One of the biggest workplace privacy risks is employer access to medical records," says author Fred Lane. "That one is harder to quantify because it's not supposed to happen. But with the growth of self insurance by employers and rising medical costs, there's a tremendous incentive for employers to gain access to that information."

If your boss violates your rights under HIPPA, you can file a complaint with the U.S. Department of Health and Human Services Office for Civil Rights (*http://www.hhs.gov/ocr/hipaa*). For more information on your rights under HIPPA and how to file complaints, visit the Health Privacy Project web site (*http://www.healthprivacy.org*). There you'll also find summaries and links to various state laws, which may offer more medical privacy on the job, depending on where you live.

BETTER FED THAN DEAD?

If you work for Uncle Sam, you probably have more workplace privacy rights than the rest of us. Federal, state, and local government employees are protected by the Constitution's limits on unreasonable search and seizure, which can keep bosses from snooping around you or your computer without sufficient cause. Government workers also enjoy greater access privileges to information, such as their own personnel records. Strange as it seems, these Constitutional protections end when you walk through the doors of Corporate America, though a handful of states (such as California, Florida, and Massachusetts) have statutes that apply Constitutional limitations to all employers. Otherwise, private sector employees have few legal privacy rights. For more information, see the Workplace Fairness site (*http://www.workplacefairness.org*).

PRIVACY IN PERIL: NEXT TIME, TAKE A TAXI

If you're taking a company car on a personal outing, be careful where you park it. According to a March 2001 story in the *New York Times*, an employee at a car alarm company in Dallas lost his job thanks to a Global Positioning Satellite tracking device the owner had placed in the car. Using GPS data, the owner discovered one of his Dakota pickup trucks was spending a fair amount of time in the parking lot at the Million Dollar Saloon, a local strip club. The employee was forced to secure alternate means of transport—as well as income.

Cameras, Cameras, Everywhere

The Annoyance: I can't go to the bathroom without passing under the ever watchful eye of a surveillance camera. Company management says the cameras are there for our protection, but I can't help feeling like I'm being spied on. Is there anything I can do to stop it?

The Fix: With few exceptions, employers are free to videotape you if you're in a public or open area, or if you've given your consent to be taped. (You may have given consent without knowing it; for example, by accepting an employee handbook that had information about the company's monitoring policies buried inside it.) If they're filming you while you're in your skivvies, though, the law may be on your side.

According to privacy attorney Parry Aftab, "when the video surveillance is hidden, or records areas generally considered 'private,' such as rest rooms or dressing rooms, the courts have been divided on whether an invasion of privacy has occurred." The key is where the court is located and whether it determines you have a "reasonable expectation of privacy."

For example, in January 2002 the U.S. Supreme Court let stand a decision barring Consolidated Freightways from placing hidden cameras in employee restrooms, despite a collective bargaining agreement with a local Teamsters union that allowed such surveillance. The cameras were found to violate a California state law barring such "toiletcams." The state of Connecticut also bars video cameras from areas such as employee lounges or locker rooms. If your state has statutes prohibiting invasions of privacy (as California, Connecticut, and Massachusetts do), your odds of prevailing in court are much better. Of course, bringing suit is a last resort. You may have better luck by banding together with similarly aggrieved coworkers and asking your employer to remove cameras placed in sensitive areas. (For more on monitoring, see Aftab's site at *http://www.aftab.com/videotapinglaw.htm*.)

The Searchers

The Annoyance: My employer insists on searching my office, my desk, even my backpack. What gives her the right?

The Fix: The real question is, what can prevent her from doing this? And the sad answer is, not much. A 1999 survey by the Society for Human Resource Management and *The Wall Street Journal*'s CareerJournal.com site found that nearly half of HR managers thought it perfectly acceptable for an employer to search an employee's office or desk. (Not surprisingly, only one in five job seekers considered this a reasonable search.)

In this area, public sector employees may be able to lean on Fourth Amendment protections against unlawful search and seizure. With private companies, the law leans the other way. Your employer generally needs a valid reason for the search—such as suspicion of theft. And, as with video and electronic monitoring, the search shouldn't impinge on reasonable expectations of privacy. If you work in an office where personal searches are rare, and your employer has no reason to suspect you of wrongdoing, your expectation of privacy may be fairly high. If you work in a jewelry store where employee bags are periodically checked, your expectations should be much lower.

PRIVACY BY THE NUMBERS

$776,000,000
Projected sales of web monitoring software by 2007

1 in 5
Companies had business email subpoenaed in 2003

1 in 4
Firms that have fired employees for violating written email policies

86
Percentage of management employees who send or receive personal email at work

1 in 3
Employees send sexual content to coworkers over email

68
Percentage of U.S. corporations that require employees to take drug tests

$77,000
Estimated cost of identifying one employee with a substance abuse problem

8
Percentage of companies that have analyzed the effectiveness of their drug testing programs

---

Sources: Frost & Sullivan, American Management Institute, SurfControl plc, ACLU

Privacy in Public

Not long ago, being out in public meant being just another face in the crowd. Unlike at home or in the office, you could wander for hours and never meet anyone who knew your name or anything about you. You could walk into a store, browse library shelves, attend classes, and drive anywhere with near-perfect anonymity. You could pay cash for a one-way airplane ticket and simply disappear.

Those days are gone. Now when you walk into a store, a retailer can create a richly detailed profile of who you are, based on what you buy. The very items in your shopping cart can tattle on you, thanks to radio transceivers embedded in their packaging. Under the specter of the Patriot Act, the books you read and the classes you attend can become part of a secret dossier the government compiles about you. You can no longer fly anonymously, and soon you may be unable to drive without a tracking device recording your movements. Fear of terrorism has turned airports into armed checkpoints where you can be stopped and frisked at any moment for virtually any reason. Your most private medical records can be shared with literally thousands of others—legally, without your consent or even your awareness.

Your credit records are routinely swapped like baseball trading cards between a morass of interconnected banks, brokerages, and insurance companies. Get stopped by a cop? Better be ready to hand over your ID, even if you're nothing but an innocent bystander. Even walking down the street is no longer a private activity, thanks to a forest of public and private surveillance cameras.

You can't defeat all these intrusions. But you can fight back. And the solution can be as simple as knowing your rights and being willing to stand up for them. In this chapter, you'll learn how to battle identity theft and reclaim your good name, keep stores and marketers from profiling you, keep your medical records from snoops, and much more.

AT THE STORE

Don't Get Cashiered

The Annoyance: At my local electronics boutique the cashier always asks me for my home zip code or phone number. Should I give it? What happens to this information?

The Fix: These may seem like innocent questions, but this data—and, really, any personal information that isn't related to payment—is none of the store's business. In California it's illegal for cashiers to ask for personal information when you pay by check or credit card, but most states aren't that strict. About half the states have some laws regarding retail privacy, but most regulate whether a merchant can demand to see your credit card when you write a check, or if they can record your phone number or address when paying with plastic. The answer in most cases is usually no. (For a state-by-state guide to retail privacy laws, see the Privacy Rights Clearinghouse fact sheet at *http://www.privacyrights.org/fs/fs15plus.htm*).

Some businesses ask for your Zip code to help them determine where to build new stores—if a large percentage of customers drive 20 miles to shop there, that area could be a good candidate for expansion. The phone number question is more insidious. A phone number is a unique identifier that can be used to create a profile of you and everything you buy from a particular store, even if you always pay in cash. This profile in turn can be used for a whole host of purposes, most of them not for your benefit (see "Your Shopping Cart, Yourself"). Fortunately this is one of those privacy traps that are easy to avoid, says Larry Ponemon, CEO of the Ponemon Institute (*http://www.ponemon.org*), which advises corporations on ethical ways to manage personal information.

"When the guy at the register at Radio Shack asks you for personal information like your phone number, stop and ask why they're asking for it," says Ponemon. "Do they really need to create a record of me just because I'm buying a battery? If it's not really essential for the transaction, don't give it."

Meanwhile, if you frequent an establishment that still prints your entire card number, ask them if they're aware of FACTA, and when they're planning to buy a machine that will substitute X's for all but the last four or five digits. And be sure to take any receipts you're planning to throw away and run them through a paper shredder—before some lucky dumpster diver emerges with your number in hand.

TEN ESSENTIAL PRIVACY WEB SITES

These 10 sites give you a crash course in 21st century privacy issues. Most are also nonprofit volunteer organizations that could use your financial support (assuming you have any money left over after buying copies of this book for all your loved ones, of course). All are worthy of a bookmark in your browser.

Center for Democracy & Technology (http://www.cdt.org). An advocacy group for hot-button digital issues, the CDT serves up the latest news about privacy issues, as well as a quick guide to Federal legislation, including all bills that are pending, passed, or passed over.

Consumer Privacy Guide (http://www.consumerprivacyguide. org). Sponsored by Common Cause, the Center for Democracy and Technology, the Privacy Rights Clearinghouse, and others, the Guide is an eminently practical (if brief) how-to manual on protecting your privacy online and off.

Electronic Privacy Information Center (http://www.epic.org). These Washington, DC-based wonks fight for your privacy rights on Capitol Hill. EPIC's site is a great source of information; it also links to software you can use to surf the Web, send email, and chat anonymously.

Electronic Frontier Foundation (http://www.eff.org). A kind of ACLU for geeks, the Electronic Frontier Foundation has been defending consumers' cyber rights since 1990. The EFF site provides in-depth information on cases involving topics such as censorship, Federal surveillance, file swapping, and RFID tags, among others.

FirstGov for Consumers (http://www.consumer.gov). The friendly face of your Federal government on the Web, FirstGov tells you how to sign up for the FTC's Do Not Call registry, report cyberfraud to the FBI's Consumer Sentinel, or handle issues from children's privacy to Identity Theft. You can also easily look up the Web sites of hundreds of government agencies.

Health Privacy Project (http://www.healthprivacy.org). The HPP gives you the scoop on state and Federal laws that protect your medical privacy (or don't, as is more often the case). The site provides an easy-to-understand guide to the intricacies of the Health Insurance Portability and Accountability Act (HIPAA).

Junkbusters (http://www.junkbusters.com). Are you sick to death of spammers, telemarketers, junk mail, junk faxes, and the like? So was Dr. Jason Catlett, who created Junkbusters to help consumers combat these vermin. You'll find scads of practical tips, "buzz-off" letters you can send to marketers, and much more.

Privacy International (http://www.privacyinternational.org). This London-based group provides a global perspective on privacy issues. It's especially handy for travelers, offering data organized by country and updates on the use of national ID cards and biometric passports.

Privacy Journal (http://www.privacyjournal.net). Meet Robert Ellis Smith, who's been writing about the history, philosophy, and future of privacy for 30 years. His site contains excerpts from his monthly newsletter ($125 per year) as well as tips on how individuals and organizations can protect themselves.

Privacy Rights Clearinghouse (http://www.privacyrights. org). The San Diego nonprofit provides a series of detailed yet clearly written fact sheets on topics like credit bureaus, background checks, medical privacy, and much more. It's especially good at explaining privacy protection laws in the Golden State. The PRC urges consumers with privacy questions to contact them at *http://www.privacyrights.org/inquiryform. html*.

Your Loyalty Is Not Rewarded

The Annoyance: I've been shopping at the same supermarket for years, using the same discount card. (So far I've saved nearly $87). Do they now have a record of everything I've purchased over that time?

The Fix: They sure do. Supermarket "loyalty" cards are the black holes of retail privacy, sucking in everything in their path. Yet according to a November 2003 survey by ACNielsen Homescan, 81 percent of shoppers now carry one, up from 35 percent in 1997. But the cost of loyalty programs can far outstrip the 29 cents you save on a box of Ho Ho's. Every time you use that card, the store—and the data mining companies that manage loyalty programs for many different stores—is adding to a minutely detailed profile of you and your shopping history that can be sold to marketers, subpoenaed by attorneys, and shared with law enforcement agencies. (For real-world examples of how this data has been used and abused, see "Your Shopping Cart, Yourself.")

"Since 1990, when the first shopping cards appeared, the cash register has morphed from a quaint adding machine with a cash drawer into a powerful computer hooked to the Internet and able to transmit massive amounts of data," says Katherine Albrecht, director of Consumers Against Supermarket Privacy Invasion and Numbering (CASPIAN) at *http://www. nocards.org*. However, she says, there are a few practical things you can do to avoid the wholesale harvesting of your shopping history:

- Shop at stores that don't use loyalty card programs, such as Publix Super Markets, Stater Brothers, and Trader Joe's. Mom and pop grocers, and Hispanic or Asian food stores are also a good bet, says Albrecht. Not only will the store not be profiling you, but you may end up actually saving money. Those well-advertised 'loyalty reward' discounts are usually offset by higher prices elsewhere.

- If you can't find a store nearby without a loyalty card program, get a card and fill it out with bogus personal information (I use the name Krusty T. Clown, myself). Then always pay in cash. If you use a bogus card but pay with credit or a check, your genuine identity will replace the fake one and be tied to all previous purchases made with that card. And if they ask for your phone number, don't slip up and tell them, or they can use it to identify you.

- When paying with cash is inconvenient or simply impossible, Albrecht suggests you carry a second loyalty card you can use when purchasing by check or credit card. This will limit the recorded history of your purchases. Mark the card "check/credit" so you know when to use it. Every six months or so toss that card and apply for a new one, to limit the amount of data in your profile.

- If a store requires you to provide some form of ID such as your driver's license or Social Security Number when applying for a card, don't do it. (In California, it's illegal for stores to ask for this information.) Take your business somewhere else.

Inconvenient? You bet. That's why most people just go ahead and use their cards, despite runaway data harvesting. But if this data comes back to bite you, don't say we didn't warn you.

Checked your receipts lately? If you pay by credit or ATM card, many retail outlets and restaurants still print your entire card number and expiration date on the slip. That's not only a written invitation for identity thieves, it may also be in violation of the Fair and Accurate Credit Transactions Act. Under FACTA, businesses must truncate the expiration date and all but the last five numbers, or face fines of $5,000 to $50,000 per violation. But there's a catch: depending on when the payment machine was placed in service, businesses may have up until July 2008 to comply. Your state may also have laws limiting the use of account numbers on receipts (for a guide to state truncation laws, see *http://www.merchantequip.com/ truncation.php*).

YOUR SHOPPING CART, YOURSELF

So you go to the local super mart, use your frequent shopper card, and get a few discounts in return—no big deal, right? Well, maybe not. There's a lot more going on with that card than you've probably imagined.

The Ponemon Institute's Privacy Trust Surveys gauges public attitudes towards airlines, banks, grocery stores, and pharmaceutical companies. The industry that gets the lowest marks from consumers? Grocery stores, says CEO Larry Ponemon. Small surprise. Consider how your shopping data can be used and abused:

- *Criminal investigations.* In August 2004, Washington state firefighter Philip Scott Lyons was charged with attempted arson after police examined his Safeway Club Card records, which indicated he'd purchased the same type of firestarter that was used to ignite the blaze. Five months later, someone else confessed to starting the fire.

- *Civil suits.* In 1995, 62-year-old tow-truck driver Robert Rivera slipped and fell in a Vons supermarket, shattered his kneecap, and sued the chain. Rivera claims Vons' attorneys threatened to use his shopping history—specifically his purchases of alcohol—against him in court. Vons denies this, but the case has become a poster child for the potential use of shopping records in civil suits. (The case was later dismissed for other reasons.)

- *Racial profiling.* Florida-based Catalina Marketing Corp. (*http://www.catalinamarketing.com*) handles loyalty card programs for some 21,000 grocery stores and boasts a database of more than 100 million households. In 2003 Catalina announced that, through careful analysis of shopping data, it had identified 6.4 million Hispanic households in the U.S. (Catalina spokesperson Rachel Keener says the firm used a third party company to merge the shopping histories with shoppers' identities, and that the company has recently gotten out of the direct marketing business.) Catalina's client used the data to send mailers to 150,000 Hispanic shoppers in Southern California. Conceivably, the Feds could use the same techniques to identify every Arabic household, or every gay one, and so on. The possibilities are virtually endless—and ominous.

- *Pharmaceutical profiling.* Under HIPPA, your prescription drug purchases are supposed to be confidential. But if you get your prescriptions filled at your supermarket's in-store pharmacy and pay for them at the checkout stand (not at the pharmacy counter) that information could find its way into your loyalty card profile. (Pharmacies—even in a grocery store—are covered by HIPPA, but grocery stores per se, aren't.) Ponemon says a leading baked goods company analyzed shopping data and found a strong correlation between customers who favored a particular type of chocolate cookie and those who were taking antidepressants. (You can imagine the marketing slogan: "If you like Zoloft, you'll love our new Double Fudge Oreos.")

- *Federal surveillance.* In the weeks following the 9/11 attacks, Ponemon says at least one major supermarket chain voluntarily gave up its entire database of customers to the FBI. (Ponemon knows this because an attorney for the supermarket chain consulted with him before doing it—though the store ultimately ignored his advice that they notify customers.) The supermarket handed over the data because it believed some of the 9/11 hijackers had loyalty cards at one of its stores, and thought the Feds could use this data to create a "shopping profile" of a terrorist. Under the Patriot Act, law enforcement agencies can also demand business records (such as shopping histories) regarding anyone it deems relevant to an investigation. (For more on the Patriot Act, see "...Except When the Feds Step In.")

The next time you pick up a product that costs 20 cents less for loyalty card holders, think about what that discount might cost you in the long run.

My Soft Drink Is Spying on Me!

The Annoyance: I've read that some stores (such as Wal-Mart) are implanting tiny little radios in every product so they can track who's buying what and where it goes. Is this true? How can I stop my Twinkies from tattling on me?

The Fix: It may be too late. In the next few years, we're likely to see more and more products with embedded Radio Frequency Identification (RFID) chips. When read by a scanner the chips emit a unique ID number, which can be matched to records in a database—to, say, identify the name and price of the item at a cash register. Starting in 2005, Wal-Mart will require all of its suppliers to embed radio chips in shipping pallets, so it can track products from the manufacturer to each store's warehouse. Wal-Mart believes RFID will save the company millions of dollars by preventing theft, lost inventory, and other supply chain snafus.

But the real controversy comes when RFID chips become so cheap that they are used to identify each individual product. That RFID scanner at the cash register could not only record that you just bought a can of Coke, but that you bought can #27654 from Wal-Mart store #437. RFID scanners are expected to replace cash registers; you'll be able to walk out with that can of Coke in your purse and the store will deduct the cost from your bank account (see Figure 5-1). That also means the store would have a detailed record of all your purchases, even if you never signed up for a loyalty card. And if can #27654 turns up at a crime scene or the *pied-a-terre* of someone who's not your spouse, that information could prove quite interesting to law enforcement or a divorce attorney.

Mark Roberti, editor of *RFID Journal* (*http://www.rfidjournal. com*), says the potential benefits of RFID tagging far outweigh the dangers. For example, Roberti notes that millions of people already have RFID chips embedded in the plastic housing on their car keys; this helps prevent auto theft by allowing a scanner inside the car's steering column to identify and reject counterfeit keys. RFID chips encased inside tires may be used to notify car owners in case of a product recall—before the tires blow out and cause you to flip your SUV. Chips placed in meat packaging can be used to find out what animal your filet mignon came from, which could prove comforting when there's another outbreak of Mad Cow disease. They can also prevent the use of counterfeit products in things like pharmaceuticals or commercial aircraft, as well as

a host of other benign applications. And RFID tags can be disabled as you leave the store, if the retailer chooses to do so, which could prevent them from tracking what you do with stuff after you bring it home.

But privacy advocates like CASPIAN's Katherine Albrecht see a world in which our very possessions spy on us (what the wags at the MIT Media Lab have dubbed "things that fink"). So the same chips that identify unsafe tires can be used to monitor the movements of your car, clock your speed, and issue you a ticket. The chips that ensure your prescription medicine is the real deal may also help create a pharmaceutical profile of you—useful for marketers, law enforcement, or civil attorneys. (For more scary uses of the technology, see "All RFID, All the Time.") That's why organizations such as the ACLU, the Privacy Rights Clearinghouse, and the Electronic Frontier Foundation have called for a moratorium on tagging individual products until the privacy issues can be hammered out (see *http://www.privacyrights.org/ar/RFIDposition.htm*).

Given the long history of companies and government agencies gathering data for one purpose (e.g., consumer safety) and using it for another (e.g., product marketing, personal profiling) consumers have reasons to worry. The best thing you can do is get informed and get active, before the chips become an inescapable part of modern life. Contact companies involved in RFID research and ask them how they plan to use the chips. (You'll find a list of more than 100 firms testing the technology at *http://www.spychips.com/rfid_sponsors. html*). For more information on the movement to halt RFID deployment, visit Albrecht's site at *http://www.spychips.com*. And if you want to hear what some of the pro-RFID crowd has to say, visit the Information Technology Association of America's RFID page at *http://www.itaa.org* and search for "RFID."

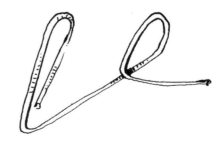

ALL RFID, ALL THE TIME

Radio Frequency Identification (RFID) chips may not have had much of an impact on your life yet, but just wait. This technology can be used in a seemingly infinite number of ways, many of which will cost you some privacy. For example, RFID tags can follow a product from production to destruction, as shown in Figure 5-1. Here are some of the most common—and creepiest—ways RFID is and will be used.

- *Packaging.* Originally developed for tracking inventory, RFID chips in product packaging could eventually replace cash registers. Walk out of the store with your goods and the system automatically deducts their cost from your bank account. (And, like a loyalty card, keeps a detailed record of everything you buy.) Don't even think about shoplifting.

- *IDs.* The U.S. State Department had planned to include RFID chips in new U.S. passports, until privacy advocates raised a storm of protest over the chips' lack of security. But that's just the beginning. Radio chips are already being used in security badges, student IDs, driver's licenses, transit passes—virtually any type of item used to identify you. Scanners can be set to read the chips at a distance, so you won't even need to take the card out of your pocket. The phrase "Can I see some ID, please" (as well as "no, you may not") could become a thing of the past.

- *Money.* The European Central Bank is working to embed radio chips in banknotes by 2005, according to Katherine Albrecht. If other banks follow suit, you can kiss "anonymous" cash transactions goodbye.

- *Cars.* Automated toll payment systems use the chips to allow cars to pass through booths without stopping. Michelin is testing radio chips in tires, while a UK firm is building RFID into license plates that can be read at a distance of 300 feet. Such chips could broadcast the vehicle identification number to a roadside scanner as you zoom by at 60 mph. By strategically placing scanners at key locations, it's possible to create an instant record of everywhere you've driven, how long you stayed in each place, and even how fast you were going.

- *Appliances.* Run out of Ben & Jerry's Chunky Monkey again? So-called "smart" refrigerators could scan for the container's radio chip and, when it can't find one, place an order for a pint at your local grocery. (Of course, it may also send a note to your HMO telling it you've gone off that low-fat diet your doctor prescribed). Your TV set could scan the products in your house so it knows what kind of commercials to send you. Your medicine cabinet could know what meds you're taking and how often. These and other goofy ideas are now being studied by such mainstream companies as Proctor & Gamble and Pfizer.

- *Weapons.* VeriChip, a subsidiary of Applied Digital Solutions in Palm Beach, Florida, is exploring the use of RFID in so-called "smart guns," which would prevent weapons from being fired by anyone but their registered owners. Of course, that would also require the gun owner to have a radio chip implanted in his or her body (see "I've Got You Under My Skin").

- *Books.* Chips are being embedded in books by libraries and book publishers. Of course, O'Reilly would never do that. (By the way, we noticed you skipped Chapter 1. You should go back and read it, it's really quite interesting.)

- *Your Body.* Subcutaneous chips have already been implanted in hospital patients (to match them to their medical records), government employees (to allow access to restricted areas), and night clubbers in Barcelona (to serve as a payment system for the quasi-clothed). The possibilities are endless and terrifying. But all of these uses have been voluntary...so far.

1 Radio tag placed on carton.

2 Dairy ships carton to grocery store.

3 Consumer purchases tagged carton.

4 Consumer recycles milk carton.

5 Carton arrives at recycling center. Manufacturer produces replacement.

A Manufacturer tracks product through wireless radio communication.

Figure 5-1. Want to see how RFID works? Visit HowStuffWorks.com and get the skinny.

My Identity Has Been Swiped!

The Annoyance: Every time I go to my favorite bar, they run my driver's license through a barcode scanner to verify my age. I'm not only old enough to drink, I'm old enough to know that they must have other reasons for swiping my license.

The Fix: Officially, bars do this to verify that you're not using a fake ID, but they may end up learning a lot more about you than your legal age. Over 40 states issue driver's licenses containing either a 2D barcode or a magnetic strip on the back, according to SWIPE (*http://www.we-swipe.us*), a group of performance artists (yes, performance artists) that seek to publicize how swipe cards are used for data harvest-

Want to disable RFID chips inside consumer packaging? The Stop RFID site (*http://www.stoprfid.org*) has a few suggestions. First, look for the chip's antenna; in most consumer goods it's typically a thin black or gray wire at least a quarter inch long, and often hidden under a paper label or sticker. You can kill the chip by removing the antenna using a knife or scissors. You can also destroy an RFID chip by popping it in a microwave oven, though Stop RFID doesn't recommend this method—the tag could spontaneously burst into flames.

ing. Barcodes can contain up to 2K worth of compressed data and, depending on where you live, may include your digital mugshot, fingerprint scans, your Social Security Number, and organ donor information. (For more on what kinds of data the DMV has crammed onto your license, see Chapter 6, "Taking License with Your License.")

And it's not just bars—retailers, airports, convenience stores, hospitals, and government agencies are also installing driver's license scanners to verify identities. While it's illegal under Federal law for businesses to sell this information, only a handful of states limit what kind of information they're allowed to store or what *else* they can do with it. Theoretically, a bar could hold onto this information indefinitely and use it to create a profile of you and your drinking habits (which could come back to haunt you if, say, your boss or soon-to-be-ex-spouse got their hands on it). On the plus side, they could use it to mail you two-for-one margarita coupons.

In some cases having your license scanned may be unavoidable. For example, to buy booze from a state-run store in Philadelphia you must get swiped; your data is sent to the Pennsylvania Liquor Control Board database in Harrisburg. But if you go into a bar down the street, you can prove you're old enough by declining the scan and simply showing your ID.

"Most bars would rather have your business than your data," says Brooke Singer, a co-founder of SWIPE. Besides just saying no, she advises consumers to ask the establishment why they're swiping cards, what kind of data they're collecting, and what they're doing with it. Because your favorite bar doesn't really need to know what's happening to your kidneys after you die.

Be Anti-Social

The Annoyance: I just signed up for cable service, and the application form asked for my Social Security Number. Why do they need this number? What happens if I refuse?

The Fix: Legally, you're not required to hand over your Social Security Number to get cable access, rent an apartment, obtain insurance, or do most things you need to do in your life. (Conversely, you can be legally denied a service or product if you don't fork over your SSN, as long as they're not discriminating against you based on race, disability, and so on.) Many businesses collect your SSN without even knowing why. But this can be a huge privacy risk, because your SSN is the key that can unlock all kinds of personal information about you.

There are, however, some big exceptions: transactions involving the Federal or state government—such as the IRS, the Department of Motor Vehicles, or benefits programs such as Medicare—almost always require you to give up your SSN. Anyone who has to report interest or income to the IRS, such as your employer or the bank that holds your mortgage, is required to collect your number.

And many private businesses will simply turn you down unless you provide it. For example, a bank can't legally demand you turn over your SSN in order to obtain a credit card, but it won't likely issue you one without it. That's because your credit report is tied directly to your SSN—and the bank needs it to determine whether you're a good credit risk.

When in doubt, don't give out your number. Leave the form blank, feign memory loss, or say "I decline to state" if asked. If the business demands your number, ask them why they need it and what they plan to do with it, advises Rod Griffin, spokesperson for Experian. "If they can't give you a good reason," he says, "I'd be cautious about giving it out."

Want to find out what's hidden on that bar code on the back of your drivers license? SWIPE offers a service and downloadable program (*http://turbulence.org/works/swipe/barcode.html*) that can read barcodes on the licenses from 36 states. You'll need to scan the barcode using a flatbed scanner or a digital camera, then upload the image to SWIPE's site or download a small (90K) applet to decode it on your computer. The site also shows you how to request your consumer profile from the major data mining corporations like ChoicePoint and Acxiom, calculate how much your data is worth to them, and send them a bill. (Reading the mag stripe on driver's licenses is a bit more involved. For those with a strong DIY jones, check out the premiere issue of MAKE magazine (*http://www.makezine.com*) for advice on making your own mag stripe reader.)

If the business merely wants your SSN so it will have a unique way to identify you, ask if it will substitute another number in its place. If the business says it wants your SSN so it can run a credit check on you, see if it will run the check without the number. Griffin says Experian doesn't necessarily require an SSN, but if the agency can't clearly identify that the credit information belongs to a single person—for example, if a father and son share the same name and address—Experian won't return any report. In that instance, you will have to give up your SSN or go elsewhere.

For more information on which private organizations can and can't legally force you to hand over your SSN, see Chris Hibbert's excellent FAQ at the Computer Professionals for Social Responsibility site *http://archive.cpsr.net/cpsr/privacy/ssn/ssn.faq.html*. You'll also find information about how to protect your SSN at the Privacy Rights Clearinghouse (*http://www.privacyrights.org/fs/fs10-ssn.htm*) and the Social Security Administration's site (*http://www.socialsecurity.gov*).

I'VE GOT YOU UNDER MY SKIN

They call it "getting chipped," and so far about a thousand people have done it. Applied Digital Solutions' VeriChip is an RFID transmitter no bigger than a grain of rice that can be injected into the fatty tissue under your right arm. As it leaves the syringe, the chip is coated with a synthetic scar tissue that keeps it from floating around inside your body. The cost? A mere $150 to $200 per chip, says company CEO Scott Silverman.

Like all RFID devices, the VeriChip transmits a unique ID number that, when scanned, can be matched to records in a database. The chips can be removed, but once they're in your body, they can't be turned off.

Subcutaneous chips are being used as replacements for credit cards, to control employee access to restricted areas, and to help hospitals identify patients. Silverman says ADS is talking to Federal agencies about using VeriChips at border checkpoints, to replace military dog tags, and other applications he's not allowed to talk about.

For a low monthly fee, ADS can also maintain your medical, financial, or other data. Silverman says users will be able to control who can get access to their records, but admits there's nothing to prevent ADS from complying with a government subpoena or sharing the data with third parties. In November 2004, ADS announced a set of privacy principles that stated, among other things, the use of RFID implants should be strictly voluntary, and that people who have been "chipped" should have the right to disable the chips at any time. They also appointed a chief privacy officer to work with consumers and privacy advocates.

Silverman argues that injectable chips enhance individual privacy by thwarting identity theft and credit card fraud. "I suppose in theory the government could come and take over our business," says Silverman. "But we've done everything we can to protect the privacy of our subscribers. Every technology has privacy issues. We don't believe RFID poses any greater risk than using the Internet, databases, or cell phones."

Source: Verichip. Used with permission.

Improving Your Rental Health

The Annoyance: I just rented "Texas Cheerleader Massacre" and "Delilah Does Detroit" at my local video store. Now I'm afraid my employer will uncover this when he does a background check on me. Can people find out what movies I've rented?

The Fix: Not legally. In fact, movie rentals are one of the few things in our lives that enjoy strong privacy protection. For that, you can thank Judge Robert Bork. Back in the late '80s, a reporter for the *Washington City Paper* published a list of 146 movies rented by the ultra-conservative Supreme Court nominee, apparently in an attempt to embarrass him. (Though not a very successful attempt. According to published accounts, the list contained only one R-rated movie—The Who's *Tommy.*) This prompted Congress to pass the Video Privacy Protection Act of 1988, which bans video stores from disclosing what movies you've rented without your consent.

Naturally, there are a few exceptions. The records are still subject to subpoena from law enforcement—and, one presumes, under the Patriot Act. The video store must delete your rental records, but only those more than one year old. For marketing purposes, the store may link your name and address with the movie genres (but not specific titles) you like and share that information with other parties unless you specifically tell them not to. It's also unclear whether the law applies to rentals of DVD and video games (it should, but no case has tested this yet). However, some state laws go further in protecting your rights. (For a good summary of the law, see EPIC's page at *http://www.epic.org/privacy/vppa*.)

If some halfwit video store employee shares your records anyway, you can sue the store for $2500 per offense. The ACLU did just that in 1997, when it sued the city of Oklahoma City for obtaining the names of people who rented *The Tin Drum* after a local judge decided the film was child pornography. The ACLU won that case, by the way.

t i p

If your identity has been stolen, or you're a victim of domestic violence who needs to hide from an abuser, you can request a new SSN from the Social Security Administration. You'll need to provide a fair amount of documentation, and you can't do it if you've filed for bankruptcy, you're trying to evade the law, or you can't prove someone else is using your number or that your life is in danger. For more information, contact the agency at (800) 772-1213 or visit *http://www.ssa.gov/ssnumber*.

LIBRARIES AND SCHOOLS

Beware Public Net Terminals

The Annoyance: I use the computers at my local library to access my email and do a little word processing. Can the people who use the machine after me see what I've done?

The Fix: They might be able to do that—and a lot more. The security of such public Internet terminals varies wildly from library to library. Some lock down everything on the system, leaving you nothing but access to a browser and a few basic commands. Other libraries think they've protected their systems from snoops when they really haven't.

As an experiment, I visited the public library down the street from my office. In less than 15 minutes, on a system the library thought was secure, I found Word documents containing résumés with complete street address information (including phone numbers and addresses of their references), letters someone had written to their insurance company (complete with their Social Security Number), and an account of someone's first pregnancy. I was able to view the browser history, which produced not only a record of recent site visits (including some truly nasty ones) but also AOL chat handles and Yahoo email addresses. I could also look at the cookies folder to see what sites the people before me had visited, and so on. Had I been a stalker, an identity thief, or just your average psychopath, this data would have been a goldmine. Meanwhile, the librarian in charge of the terminals had no clue you could save files to the hard drive; he believed the system was completely wiped of data every time someone new logged on.

The lesson: be particularly careful when using a public Internet terminal, especially if the terminal prevents you from deleting files, clearing the browser's cache and history, and so on. Be careful where you surf, and never save anything to the hard drive on a public terminal. If you use one to edit your résumé or write letters, you can usually save your files to a floppy. Delete temp files, cookies, and your browser history, if you can. (For instructions on how, see Chapter 2.) Don't take the librarian's word that your privacy is protected—it may not be.

t i p

An easy way for a snoop to steal your passwords or other personal information at a public Net terminal is to sneak a peek at what's on your screen—a practice known as "shoulder surfing." Some libraries put terminals in carrels or recessed cabinets that are hard to spy on. If you're planning to view sensitive information on a public terminal, pick one that's in a corner or another less open area. If possible, push the monitor back into the wall or at an angle that makes it hard for anyone else to get a good look. And always be aware of those who might be loitering nearby with nothing better to do than stick their nose in your business.

Your Reading Habits Are Private ...

The Annoyance: I like to check out books on radical topics, but I'm worried this could affect my reputation if word got out. Can anyone just walk in and demand to see my library records?

The Fix: In most cases, no. At last count 48 states have laws on the books protecting library confidentiality, but the particulars vary. To find out the rules in your neck of the woods, visit the American Library Association's home page (*http://www.ala.org*) and type "state privacy laws" into the site's search engine. A page listing relevant codes in each state should be the first page on the list.

...Except When the Feds Step In

The Annoyance: Wait—can't the FBI find out what books I've checked out?

The Fix: It certainly can try. All library records are subject to court order, which must be approved by a judge and can be challenged by the subject of the investigation (i.e., you). The 2001 USA Patriot Act makes this much more invasive by allowing the FBI to request "business records" from libraries and bookstores for anyone they deem "relevant" to an investigation. The requirements for judicial approval are much lower, and libraries are also prohibited from notifying the subject of the investigation, so you'd have no chance to challenge such an order. Records could include the titles of books and other media you checked out or purchased, as well as any data relating to your use of public computers and even the questions you ask reference librarians, assuming the library maintains that information.

The American Library Association and the American Booksellers Association strongly objected to these provisions of the Act, and many libraries made it a policy not to retain this information so that such requests can't be fulfilled. Your first step toward protecting your privacy is to find out what kind of records your library keeps and how long it keeps them. Some key questions to ask:

- Does the library have a written policy about patron confidentiality? If so, ask for a copy.

- Does the library keep a record of all the material you've ever checked out, all activity for a certain period, or just the items you have out right now?

- Does the library keep patron information in offsite backups or data archives? Even if they delete your information when you return a book, this data could be backed up somewhere—and available to the Feds.

- Are individual books linked to records of everyone who's ever taken them home, squirreled away in some computer database? That's important for rare books, in case librarians discover that parts are missing and need to hunt them down, but otherwise there's no practical use for this information.

- What kind of identification does your library require for access to Internet terminals? How long does it save sign-up sheets? The ALA advises libraries to delete and/or shred this information when it's no longer needed.

- How much information does the library keep about your Internet activity? Is computer use or browsing history linked to personally identifiable information? Who manages this information? Many libraries use outside companies to provide Internet access; such firms could be approached directly for information without the library (or its patrons) ever knowing.

The ALA offers guidelines for implementing library privacy policies and procedures at *http://www.ala.org/ala/oif/iftool-kits/toolkitsprivacy/Default4517.htm*. If your library is clueless when it comes to privacy, print out a copy and give it to them.

Hate the thought of the FBI peeking over your shoulder as you read? You could curse and gnash your teeth, or you could ask Congress to do something about it using the petition from the Campaign for Reader Privacy (*http://www.readerprivacy.org*), shown in Figure 5-2.

Figure 5-2. The Campaign for Reader Privacy petition.

PAY THAT FINE!

If you're planning to check out *The Anarchist's Cookbook* or some other volume you don't want the world to know about, don't return it late. Even though the confidentiality of library records is protected in nearly every state, the fines that you pay on late books (and, in some cases, the books you paid them on) could become part of the public record.

Your reading habits may also be shared if the library hires a private agency to track you down. For example, Unique Management Services of Jeffersonville, Indiana, is a collection agency that specializes in tracking down library scofflaws. In a FAQ on its web site (*http://www.unique-mgmt.com/*), the company urges libraries to collect patrons' Social Security numbers, birthdates, and other sensitive personal information when they sign up for a library card, making them easier to find. Think about that before you decide to keep that borrowed copy of *Sex for Dummies*.

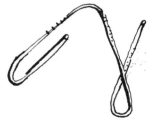

READING GETS RAILROADED

In October 2002 the ACLU, the Electronic Privacy Information Center, the American Library Association, and the American Booksellers Association filed a Freedom of Information Act suit against the U.S. Department of Justice. Their purpose: to compel the DOJ to release information on how the Patriot Act has been used to spy on what books Americans are reading. The following January, the DOJ released a six-page document listing all the National Security Letters—which can demand the release of private business records without judicial oversight—it has sent since October 2001. All the information, including the number of letters, had been blacked out for "reasons of national security."

In July 2004 the Freedom to Read Protection Act, which would have nullified provisions of the Patriot Act pertaining to library records, was narrowly defeated in the House of Representatives thanks to some last-minute maneuvering by conservatives. After the 15-minute time limit for electronic voting had expired, the Act was ahead 219 to 210. But according to published accounts, House Republicans kept the vote open while they worked on members to change their votes. The Act ultimately failed to pass, ending on a 210 to 210 tie.

But the battle isn't over yet. As this book was being written Vermont Congressman Bernie Sanders re-introduced the Freedom to Read Protection Act. Here's how you can help fight for your right to read:

- Bone up on how the USA Patriot Act can invade your privacy. You'll find extensive backgrounders and news about the Act at the web sites of the ACLU (*http://www.aclu.org/patriotact*), the American Library Association (*http://www.ala.org/ala/pio/mediarelations/patriotactmedia.htm*), and EPIC (*http://www.epic.org/privacy/terrorism/usapatriot/default.html*).

- Sign the Campaign for Reader Privacy's online petition at *http://www.readerprivacy.org/?mod[type]=sign_petition* or download a PDF copy and print it out for your unwired friends.

- Write or call Congress and urge its members to let section 215 and other noxious parts of the Patriot Act expire at the end of 2005. The ACLU offers an online form that makes it easy to send your thoughts directly to your Congressional representatives (see *http://www.aclu.org/SafeandFree/*.

- Express support for the "Library, Bookseller, and Personal Records Privacy Act" (S.317), authored by Wisconsin Senator Russell Feingold, and Sanders's Freedom to Read Protection Act. Each seeks to limit the FBI's ability to request business records under the Patriot Act.

So What's Your Major?

The Annoyance: I'm planning to major in Islamic studies when I go to college. Am I going to end up on somebody's watch list? Exactly how private are my college records?

The Fix: It depends on which records and who's asking. The Family Educational Rights and Privacy Act (FERPA) of 1974 prevents any schools that receive Federal funds from releasing "non-directory" information—such as your transcripts or financial aid records—without your consent. (Unless, once again, the school is presented with a court order; more on that in a moment.)

But colleges can publish student directories, which may contain all kinds of information about you, including addresses, phone numbers, photographs, your major, and your date of birth (see Table 5-1). A recent survey by the American Association of Collegiate Registrars and Admissions Officers (*http://www.aacrao.org*) found that about half of all directories contained information such as student names, campus and home contact information, and email addresses. A third of universities shared directory information with other parties, from individuals simply checking on your student status to banks looking to sign you up for a credit card. FERPA allows students to request their information be removed from such directories, though the procedure varies by school. Contact your school's office of public records or registrar for the nitty gritty.

Be aware that opting out could have some unintended negative consequences, says Barmack Nissarian, an associate executive director at AACRAO. For example, employers trying to verify your degree may get an unhelpful response from the university, because you haven't given permission. Or you may not be able to collect your diploma along with your classmates at commencement, because printing your name and major in the graduation booklet could reveal information you've deemed private.

Here's the scary part. According to the same survey, nearly 70 percent of the schools surveyed reported they'd received subpoenas or court orders requesting non-directory information about students, and nearly all complied with these requests. Another 31 percent received improper requests—unaccompanied by a subpoena or court order—and about 20 percent of those schools went ahead and handed over the information anyway.

If that makes you mad enough to feel like suing the Feds, I've got some bad news. Though FERPA forbids such disclosures, it does not allow for private rights of action. In fact, there's little recourse for punishment save withholding Federal funds from the school. That would be a death sentence for most universities, so no government agency is ever likely to pursue it.

Table 5-1. Full disclosure? Many student directories take the term "public education" a bit too literally, revealing a wealth of information about you to anyone who asks.

Personal data	% of student directories that contain this information
Campus address and phone number	73
Email address	66
Permanent address and phone number	51
Field of study	45
Photographs	23
Date of birth	15
Place of birth	6

Source: American Association of Collegiate Registrars and Admissions Officers, March 2004

F IS FOR FOREIGN

Visiting the U.S. on a student visa? Think twice about cutting that physics midterm. Foreign-born students that want to attend American universities must register with the Student and Exchange Visitor Information System (SEVIS), a database of nearly 900,000 students, visitors, and their dependents maintained by U.S. Immigration and Customs Enforcement. (They'll also have to pay a $100 fee to defray costs of maintaining the database.) The database tracks school attendance and disciplinary problems in an effort to identify foreign nationals who register as students but have no intention of attending classes. As of August 2004, SEVIS had produced nearly 1,600 investigations and 155 arrests for such crimes as truancy, being expelled, or failing to maintain a full course load. At press time, no students had been arrested for chewing gum or passing notes in class.

Apply With Care

The Annoyance: I used an online service to send my college application to a bunch of schools. Is my data safe?

The Fix: Not necessarily. Here's a nasty little catch I bet you didn't know about: FERPA only applies to enrolled students. So if you've applied for college but didn't get accepted, the information on your application is completely unprotected. In fact, some states *require* publicly funded institutions to share such information.

For example, the Texas Public Information Act requires state agencies to provide certain information to any member of the public who asks for it. So a bank could request a list of anyone who applied to the University of Texas and get a nice little cache of potential credit card customers. UT is required by law to share only the name and address of each prospective or enrolled student, says Shelby Stanfield, director of student information systems for the Austin campus. But he adds the university doesn't ask who is asking or what they want the data for.

You certainly leave yourself open if you use an online service to apply to multiple schools. Most online services offer no privacy protections at all—indeed, most of their revenue derives from selling your information to marketers. There are a few exceptions, however. One of the largest processing services, CollegeNet, claims to be "one of the rare commercially sponsored college-oriented Websites that DOES NOT collect student data for sale or brokering to third parties," according to a notice posted on its web site. Another popular third-party service, Princeton Review, allows students to opt out of its marketing efforts.

Unfortunately, most applicants will reveal anything if they think it will help them get accepted, says AACRO's Nassirian. "They spill their guts to colleges and universities—they give away tons of financial information, that their grandfather died last year, that they're depressed, all kinds of personal problems," he says. "Even my doctor doesn't have access to the kind of information people routinely fess up to on college applications."

The lesson: before you include that tear-stained confessional essay in your college packet, think twice about who might be reading it. Stanfield advises students to avoid putting their Social Security numbers on applications, since it's not legally required. (Students attempting to qualify for financial aid,

scholarships, or campus jobs, however, will likely have to give up their SSN at some point). If you use an online service to process your application, read the site's privacy policy carefully; don't use any service that shares your personal information with third parties. Most important, says Stanfield, don't share your log-on or password information with friends, roommates, or other significant others—the information they find may prove too juicy to resist.

PRIVACY IN PERIL: SWAP FILES, GO TO JAIL?

Napster was invented by a college student, so it makes sense that many of the nation's estimated 60 million file swappers are matriculating at our nation's bandwidth-rich campuses. But if the Feds have their way, some of these students could be trading their school sweaters for an orange jump suit.

In April 2004 the FBI raided campuses from Arizona to Maryland as part of an international sweep, seizing some 200 computers allegedly used to swap copyrighted material (although no arrests were ever made). To keep anti-swapping storm troopers from swarming over their campuses, universities are starting to police their own networks. One solution, jointly developed by Universal Music Group and Vivendi Universal Entertainment, is the Automated Copyright Notice System. According to reports published on CNET.com, the ACNS can monitor campus network traffic, identify copyrighted material being illegally downloaded, and cut off Net access for the alleged scofflaws. At press time, no university had publicly admitted to using the ACNS.

Meanwhile, in an effort to wean students off file sharing networks, an estimated 75 schools have signed up for discounted access to legal music services such as Apple iTunes, RealNetworks' Rhapsody, and MusicNet. In some cases, schools have folded the cost of such services into mandatory student fees. Protecting our nation's record companies from the file-swapping hordes—isn't that what higher education is all about?

According to an April 2002 survey by AACRAO, half of all universities use a student's Social Security Number as the primary student identification number. As schools become savvier about identity theft, they're becoming more flexible about letting you request a different student ID. Procedures vary by school, so check with the campus registrar about what you have to do. While you're there, ask whether you can have your SSN removed from or partially obscured on copies of your transcript. Four out of five schools still put students' SSNs on their transcripts.

High School Confidential

The Annoyance: I had a checkered past in school—some truancy issues, and more than a few run-ins with my high school detention officer. Does this record really stay with me for life, as my teachers were so fond of saying?

The Fix: Your school disciplinary records are considered part of the information protected by FERPA, which applies to students of any age. So the fact you got caught smoking in the boy's room a few times probably won't come back to haunt you. But there are a few exceptions. Records kept by campus police aren't covered by FERPA (though this is more likely to affect college students). If you've been disciplined for a violent crime or sex-related offense, that information can be made public in some circumstances. And when students transfer to a new school, their disciplinary records must transfer along with them.

Other bits of controversial legislation have punched holes in FERPA. A little-known provision of the No Child Left Behind Act compels schools to turn over student contact information to military recruiters, unless parents or students explicitly tell them not to. (So if you don't want the ROTC to come knocking on your door, be sure to ask your school administrator for the form that lets you opt out.) Under the Patriot Act, schools must share information about immigrant students—such as disciplinary problems or changes in their field of study—with the U.S. Citizenship and Immigration Services (formerly called the Immigration and Naturalization Service). Forget about opting out of that one.

And if you apply for Federal aid, you might as well just open your door and invite the G-men in for tea. Among other things, your name will be run through Department of Justice records to determine if you've been convicted of a drug-related offense (if so, kiss that scholarship goodbye). If you're a male, you'll be checked against Selective Service records to make sure you've registered for the draft. Fallen behind on student loans? Your data could be shared with a private collection agency.

Privacy in Peril: Give Me a P!

Thinking about joining your high school's Chess Club? Get ready to fill that cup! In June 2002, the Supreme Court ruled that an Oklahoma high school had the right to conduct random drug tests of students involved in extracurricular activities, without any suspicion of actual drug use. The ruling even described appropriate places for teachers to stand while students provided their specimen.

A 2003 study of 76,000 students by University of Michigan researchers found that 1 out of 4 high schools conducted drug tests, but that testing programs had a minimal impact on students' habits. Researchers also found that use of harder drugs was actually *higher* at schools that conducted random tests.

Some states, however, provide stronger protection against school administrators pawing through your bloodstream. According to the Drug Policy Alliance, a handful of school districts nationwide (out of some 15,000) have explicitly rejected random drug testing. For more information on how to add your school district to that list, visit the DPA's site at (*http://www. drugpolicy.org*).

If you believe a school has violated your or your child's FERPA rights, you can file a complaint with the Department of Education's Family Policy Compliance Office (*http://www.ed.gov/policy/gen/guid/fpco/ferpa/students.html*). You'll need to send a letter to the following address:

Family Policy Compliance Office
U.S. Department of Education
400 Maryland Ave., SW
Washington, DC 20202-5901

Be sure to include all pertinent details, and don't expect a prompt response. You can also call the DOE at (202) 260-3887. For more information on FERPA and other student privacy issues, see *http://www.epic.org/privacy/student*.

So you've been nominated to appear in a national directory of exceptional high school students, despite the fact that you've been pulling straight C's for three years? Don't get all puffed up—it's really just a ploy to make you fill out a marketing survey. The No Child Left Behind Act lets parents and students opt out of school surveys that are really just marketing tools, but it makes exceptions for fundraisers, magazine and book clubs, and "student recognition" programs—like those bogus national directories. Do yourself a favor: when you see a survey that asks questions about your habits, attitudes, religious or political affiliations, or other non-educational topics, put down your number two pencil, close the survey booklet, and read a book instead.

ON THE ROAD

Grounded By No-Fly Lists

The Annoyance: I'm a frequent flyer, and just about every time I go through a security checkpoint some beefy guard pulls me to the side, waves a wand over my entire body, and interrogates me before I can get on the plane. Am I on some sort of government no-fly list? How do I get off?

The Fix: You may well be, though good luck finding out. Since 1990 the feds have maintained a list of passengers deemed a threat to civil aviation. In fact, there are at least two separate lists: one contains "selectees" who must undergo extra scrutiny before boarding; the other contains the names of those who are prevented from flying at all. The terrorist attacks of 9/11 vastly increased the scope of such lists—from a handful of names to more than 20,000, according to an October 2004 report in the *Washington Post*.

In April 2004, the ACLU filed a class action lawsuit on behalf of six individuals who believe they were unfairly singled out, either because their name is similar to one on the list or because of their political activity. For example, attorney David C. Nelson, one of the plaintiffs in the suit, says he's been stopped more than 40 times. (Former TV star David Nelson of "Ozzie and Harriet" fame also reports being stopped at airports.) In documents released last October 2004, Transportation Security Administration officials admit to massive problems with "false positives" resulting from similar sounding names. More than 2000 passengers have filed complaints with the TSA regarding the no-fly lists. The agency plans to introduce a new program in August 2005 (called "Secure Flight") that it claims will reduce the number of false positives but may provoke other privacy concerns (see "Are You Registered to Travel?").

According to published reports, some travelers have solved the problem by changing how their names are spelled on their airline reservations—adding or subtracting a middle initial, for example. You can also request the TSA remove you from the No-Fly list by filling out and returning a Passenger Identity Verification Form listing your SSN, date of birth, and a detailed physical description. You'll also need to submit notarized copies of three forms of ID—such as a birth certificate, driver's license, military ID, passport, visa, or voter registration card. If approved, the TSA says it will contact the airlines and help streamline your check-in process. To obtain this form, call the TSA's Office of the Ombudsman at (877) 266-2837, email them at *TSA-ombudsman@dhs.gov*, or send a letter to:

> Office of the Ombudsman
> TSA Headquarters
> 601 South 12th St. – West Tower - TSA 22
> Arlington, VA 22202

While you're at it, fill out the ACLU's detailed No Fly/Watchlist Complaint Form (*http://www.aclu.org/Feedback/Feedback.cfm?R=40*). The ACLU provides a similar complaint form for people who believe they were singled out by security because of racial profiling (*http://www.aclu.org/airlineprofiling/*). This won't make traveling any easier in the short term, but it could ultimately help make passing through airport security less of a hassle.

My Bag Has Been Flagged

The Annoyance: I just returned from a trip, opened my suitcase, and found a calling card from the Travel Security Administration announcing that my bag had been opened and inspected by hand (see Figure 5-3). (Fortunately, I left my AK-47 at home). Was I just inches away from being thrown into a cell at Guantanamo Bay?

The Fix: In the post 9/11 era there's nothing you can do to stop the Feds from riffling your bags. But you can avoid trouble by not packing certain problematic items. Before you fly, check the TSA's list of permitted and prohibited items (at *http://www.tsa.gov/interweb/assetlibrary/Permitted_Prohibited_8_23_2004.pdf*); you may be surprised by what you can bring. For example, nearly all forms of weaponry are allowed in checked baggage (so that AK-47 would have been fine, provided you declared it to the TSA officials at check-in, and packed it inside a locked case, separate from your ammo). But

flammable materials and most other hazardous chemicals are verboten. The rules for carry-on luggage are much fussier; essentially anything more lethal than a corkscrew will get removed. You could also be liable for criminal penalties and civil fines of up to $10,000, depending on the item. (For a select list of prohibited items, see Table 5-2.)

Whether an item can go on board is ultimately up to the screener—so even if an item is on the permitted list, the screener may still determine it can't go on the plane. If you have questions about what you can and can't bring with you, contact the TSA at (866) 289-9673, or email them at *TSA-contactcenter@dhs.gov*.

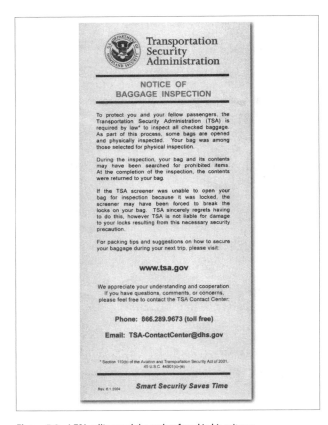

Figure 5-3. A TSA calling card the author found in his suitcase.

Table 5-2. What you can pack—and where.

Item	Carry on?	Checked baggage?
Nail clippers	Yes	Yes
Cigarette lighter	No[a]	No
Pointy metal scissors	No[b]	Yes
Mace or pepper spray	Yes[c]	No
Swords	No	Yes
Hockey sticks	No	Yes
Firearms	No	Yes
Ammunition	No[d]	Yes
Hand grenades	No	No

[a] As of April 2005.
[b] Blunt scissors are OK.
[c] One 4-ounce canister is permitted on board, if fitted with cap to prevent accidental discharge.
* Some airlines may allow small amounts of ammo to be carried on board.
Source: Travel Security Administration

Your Life Is an Open Bag

The Annoyance: Once the TSA screeners have my bag open, what's to keep them from snooping around for—or even stealing—other stuff?

The Fix: Not much. Over the past year there have been several news reports of TSA and private screeners being arrested for stealing valuables from passenger bags. The TSA has processed more than 25,000 claims for damaged or missing goods since February 2002, with an average payout of $110. (If your valuables have disappeared from your bags while traveling, you can file a claim with the TSA by downloading a complaint form at *http://www.tsa.gov/public/display?theme=174*.)

What's more interesting is what happens when the TSA discovers something in your bags that shouldn't be there. For example, if they find flammable materials—including any alcoholic beverage more than 140 proof—it will be handed over to the airlines for disposal.

ARE YOU REGISTERED TO TRAVEL?

The Transportation Security Administration has proposed an interesting way to avoid long security checkpoint lines: join the Registered Traveler program. Last summer select airlines began inviting frequent fliers to participate in pilot programs (no pun intended) in five cities: Boston, Houston, Los Angeles, Minneapolis, and Washington, DC. Volunteers were asked to provide full personal information and submit to a fingerprint or iris scan and a complete background check. Once cleared, they could pass through a special checkpoint where they are scanned to verify their identity, then continue on to their boarding gate. (For more information, see the TSA Registered Traveler fact sheet at *http://www.tsa.gov/interweb/assetlibrary/RT_Factsheet.pdf*).

Meanwhile, the TSA is readying a new passenger profiling system for the rest of us called Secure Flight. Unlike earlier, highly controversial proposals for passenger screening systems, Secure Flight will rely strictly on passenger name records, not consumer data, to identify potential terrorists. TSA officials say Secure Flight will be used only for airport security screening, not to identify other criminal suspects. The agency hopes this program, set to launch in spring 2005, proves more accurate and less problematic than current no-fly watch lists.

If screeners find anything illegal—like, say, a controlled substance—the agency will notify your airline as well as the appropriate law enforcement agency, in which case you might find an unwelcome escort waiting for you after your plane touches down. If you're carrying more than $10,000 in cash, agents (the honest ones, anyway) are likely to contact your good friends at the IRS. What happens if they find a copy of, say, *The Anarchist's Cookbook* or other politically sensitive materials? A spokesperson for the TSA declined to comment.

But the fix is simple: to avoid theft, pack small, expensive items like jewelry or electronics in your carry-on—the TSA won't compensate you if they disappear from your checked baggage. (You can find a list of other valuables not covered at *http://www.tsa.gov/public/interapp/travel_tip/travel_tip_0038.xml.*) If the items are too big or too numerous for your carry on, conceal them inside clothing. Be sure to make a list of all your valuables and check your bags before you leave the airport. Most important: leave wads of cash—and your stash—at home.

> ## t i p
>
> **Making your vacation plans through a traditional travel agent can help keep some of your personal information out of Passenger Name Records, says travel guru Edward Hasbrouck. Standard industry practice is to use the agency's address and phone number when making reservations, making the agents an effective anonymizer for many travelers.**

High-Risk Frisks

The Annoyance: On my last trip through airport security, the guards stopped me and gave me such a thorough pat down that I felt like a criminal. How can I keep this from happening again?

The Fix: Ever since two female Chechen terrorists allegedly brought down two Russian airliners with explosives hidden in their clothing, airline passengers are being subjected to more invasive physical searches. The TSA estimates that 15 percent of airline travelers—or nearly 2 million passengers—get patted down every week.

This has angered some women who feel they've been unfairly singled out for searches—like the 54-year old Michigan woman forced to pull down her pants in Detroit Metro airport in December 2004 so screeners could examine her artificial leg for explosives.

Unfortunately there's no way to refuse a pat-down and expect to get on a plane, but it helps to know the rules airport screeners must follow:

- Women must be searched by a female screener, if one is available.

- Screeners must use the sides or backs of their hands when examining sensitive areas such as between or below the breasts.

- Screeners must allow the search to take place in a private area, if you request it.

You may be able to reduce your chances of getting frisked by avoiding bulky or loose clothing that could be used to conceal a bomb, as well as underwire bras or fashion accessories that could trip airport metal detectors.

According to published reports, the TSA has received around 300 complaints about overly aggressive (or excessively friendly) pat downs. If you feel you've been treated unfairly, you can submit a complaint to the TSA's Office of Civil Rights detailing the nature of the incident, the date and time it happened, the name of the airport, your flight info, and the name of the screener if you have it. Send your letter to:

Transportation Security Administration
Director, Office of Civil Rights
601 South 12th Street - West Tower, TSA-6
Arlington, Virginia 22202
Attn: External Programs Division

For more information, call the TSA's Office of Civil Rights at (877) 336-4872 or send email to *TellTSA@dhs.gov.*

WHAT'S IN A (PASSENGER) NAME?

If you've ever flown in a commercial jet, checked into a hotel, booked a cruise, or rented a car, you've created a passenger name record (PNR). Your PNR contains a wealth of information about where and when you've traveled, and with whom. This information is stored in any of four massive commercial databases and is never purged, so your PNR could theoretically contain your entire travel history.

But that's merely the tip of the iceberg. Edward Hasbrouck, travel privacy guru and author of *The Practical Nomad* (http://www.hasbrouck.org), says your PNR can indicate a lot more than simply who you are and where you've been. For example, your passenger records can reveal:

- *Your religious beliefs.* Did you order a Kosher meal? That information is permanently enshrined in your PNR.

- *Medical Conditions.* Did you order a low-salt meal or request a wheelchair be made ready for you at the gate? If you're especially infirm, your record may indicate your ability to feed yourself or control your bladder.

- *Employment status.* If you travel for work, your job title may be part of the record, as well as the company you work for and the name of the person who made the reservation for you.

- *Income level.* How much did you pay for your ticket? How frequently do you fly? Did you always go first class? All may be indicators of relative affluence.

- *Memberships and affiliations.* Did you receive an AARP discount? Did you book a room as an attendee at an event to get a better rate? Your travel records can show not only your age and interests but whom you associate with.

- *Romantic liaisons.* So you were traveling on business with a colleague, yet your PNR indicates you both checked into a single room with a king-sized bed. What's up with that, lover boy?

Until 9/11, this information was hard to come by because it was scattered among four massive computerized reservation systems and used only by the travel industry. Since then, most of the major U.S. airlines—including American, JetBlue, Northwest, and United—have voluntarily shared more than 300 million PNRs with the FBI and other government agencies, without notifying their passengers. In some cases, PNRs were married to data obtained from Axiom, which collects information about the purchase histories of some 130 million individuals, in an attempt to identify potential terrorist threats.

In fall 2004, the Transportation Security Administration announced it will be collecting and analyzing PNRs for use in its Secure Flight program, which is scheduled to begin testing in late summer of 2005. Privacy advocates warn that such a system could be used to profile individuals based on activities unrelated to terrorism—such as political dissent.

The EZ Way to Track Your Movements

The Annoyance: I bought a pass that lets me drive right through the toll booths on the turnpike without stopping. It saves me a huge amount of time each morning. But does this mean the highway authority can track my movements? Can this come back to bite me in, say, divorce court?

The Fix: You bet. Systems like EZ Pass, which is used on toll roads from Maine to Virginia, I-PASS (Illinois), or FasTrak (Northern California) rely on RFID transponders that attach to your car's windshield and emit a unique ID when read by a scanner (see "All RFID, All the Time"). Every time you drive though a booth, the scanner reads the signal coming off your transponder, identifies your vehicle, and deducts the toll from your prepaid account. Such automated payment systems can provide a reliable record of your movements (or, at least, your car's movements), which is why electronic toll data has become increasingly popular with law enforcement agencies and civil attorneys.

The New York Thruway system reported it received more than 250 subpoenas for EZ Pass records in 2003—roughly double the number of the previous year. It provided the data in roughly half of those cases. Electronic toll information has been used in a murder investigation in Maryland and custody cases in Illinois. It's been used to nab New York City cops who tried to claim overtime pay when they'd already driven home, and to investigate Cook County judges. Anyone who claims to be in one place when they're really in another can get nailed by electronic toll records.

But transit authority officials aren't the only ones who can get at this data. Enterprising students at Texas A&M rigged scanners that collected transponder information to calculate average traffic speeds for Houston drivers. The use was benign (they created a web site that allowed drivers to gauge traffic conditions), but it proved how easily someone can scan your toll pass. A handful of airport parking lots and two McDonald's drive-thru restaurants now accept payments using EZ Pass. This data is also vulnerable to hackers: in October 2000, a security hole in the New Jersey EZ Pass web site exposed the names and account information of thousands of drivers.

The solution is simple but inconvenient: skip the EZ Pass and wait in line to pay cash at the toll booth. Alternately, you can buy a bag such as the mCloak ($30 to $40, *http://www.mobilecloak.com*), which blocks wireless transmissions for such RFID cards and devices, preventing a scanner from reading your card when you don't want your movements to be tracked. Cloaks can also be used for other wireless gizmos, including WiFi Handhelds or cell phones with built-in GPS transponders. Note: some transit authorities, such as FasTrak, provide RF-blocking Mylar bags for free.

We Know Where You Drove Last Summer

The Annoyance: I've just bought a car with one of those new GPS-based directional systems inside. Can someone use this to follow my movements?

The Fix: It depends on what kind of system you have and what you've been up to. Sophisticated telematics systems can keep you from getting lost and help you out of a jam. But they often do so at the expense of your privacy.

There are two major telematics manufacturers: ATX Technologies, which makes systems for Mercedes Benz, BMW, and Rolls Royce, among others; and OnStar, which is available in many GM cars. Both services go well beyond simple navigation. Using a cellular phone connection, you can communicate directly with service operators to dispatch a tow truck or an ambulance if you've been in a wreck. Impact sensors can automatically alert the service when you've been in a collision, and it can use the system's GPS transponder to locate your car virtually anywhere on the globe. They also tap directly into your car's computer controls—so someone thousands of miles away can open or lock your car doors, turn the engine on or off, and even control heating and air conditioning. If you've locked your keys in your car and it is 20 degrees outside, that's a godsend.

According to OnStar's privacy policy, the service only tracks your car's location when you call for assistance, you're involved in a collision and/or your airbags deploy, or when compelled by a valid court order. This is where things can get sticky. The same technology that can locate your car when it's stolen can also be used to track you, if law enforcement agencies deem you worthy of investigation. Worse, the Feds could theoretically use the system's cell connection to bug your car and listen to your conversations.

PRIVACY IN PERIL: RENT A CAR, PAY A FINE?

In 2001, Acme Rent-a-Car of New Haven, Connecticut, fined more than two dozen customers $150 for speeding while driving its cars. How did Acme know? Each car had a GPS transponder and software that alerted the company when customers exceeded 79 miles per hour for two minutes or more. The fines were later overturned by the Connecticut Department of Consumer Protection, which ruled that Acme provided insufficient notice to customers before implementing the penalties, and ordered the company to discontinue the practice.

In 2001, FBI investigators in Las Vegas did just that. For more than a month, agents eavesdropped on suspects in their car using its telematics system, before the unnamed telematics company asked a court to intervene. Ultimately, the 9th Circuit Court of Appeals ruled the eavesdropping was illegal—not because of privacy violations, but because tying up the cellular line interfered with subscribers' ability to access their contractually guaranteed emergency road service. The Federal decision only affects states in the 9th District, which includes California, Hawaii, Nevada, Oregon, and Washington.

OnStar and ATX say the systems they sell today notify passengers when a call is initiated, making it hard to eavesdrop without their knowledge. ATX spokesperson Gary Wallace says the type of notification varies by automaker, and older systems may not have this feature.

Dan Kahn, road test editor for Edmunds.com, a research site for car buyers, recommends drivers concerned about their privacy avoid subscription services like OnStar or ATX and install after-market navigational systems instead. They won't help locate your car if it's stolen, but they can keep you from getting lost—without being tracked.

PRIVACY IN PERIL: CANDID TRAFFIC CAMERAS

You may not realize this, but when a red-light or speed-radar traffic camera detects a car racing through an intersection, it captures images of the driver as well as the car's license plate. In July 2004, a traffic cam in Hawthorne, California, caught a woman in more than the simple act of running a red. When her husband visited the police station and reviewed the video taken by the camera, he saw another man behind the wheel of his car, who turned out to be his wife's lover. Soon afterward, the cuckolded car owner filed for divorce. So if you're thinking about having an affair, do it in a city without traffic cams—or maybe just take the bus instead.

tip

Want to foil traffic cams by covering your license plate? Be careful—many states make it a crime to deliberately obscure your license number. An alternative tactic is a $30 can of spray varnish. Products like PhotoBlocker, Photo Fog, and Photo Stopper claim to foil cams by making your license plate highly reflective—so when the camera's flash goes off, the number is obscured. (We can't vouch for the effectiveness or legality of this practice, however.)

You might also try your luck in court. In September 2001, San Diego Superior Court Judge Ronald L. Styn overturned nearly 300 red-light-camera citations, saying the accuracy of the cams had been compromised because their manufacturer, Lockheed Martin (now Affiliated Computer Services), collected a sizeable percentage of every fine. For more info on camera locations nationwide and tactics used to fight citations, visit *http://www.highwayrobbery.net*.

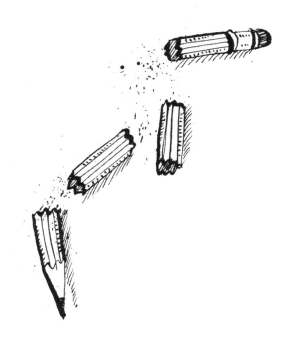

BIG BROTHER UNDER THE HOOD?

Automobile surveillance may soon be available 24/7, if the National Transportation Safety Board has its way. The NTSB has recommended that all cars be required to contain an Event Data Recorder (EDR), similar to the black boxes installed on commercial aircraft. This EDR plugs into your car's diagnostic computer and can record the day and time you drove, how far you went, at what speed, whether you wore a seat belt, and how well the car's safety devices worked.

The idea is that investigators can use this data after a crash to determine its cause, which in theory could lead to safer cars. The practical reality is that such black boxes could become a treasure trove for insurance companies, rental agencies, law enforcement, family law attorneys, employers, and anyone else with a more-than-casual interest in your driving habits.

Many new cars already come with recorders that store only a few seconds' worth of data at a time—so they can record what happened in the moments preceding an accident, but not how fast you were driving a week ago. If you break the law, however, this information can be used against you. In October 2003, a New York driver was convicted of killing a pedestrian based in part on data retrieved from his car's black box. According to accident reconstruction firm Harris Technical Services, EDR data has been used in more than 20 civil and criminal cases since 2000.

Worse, some private firms are promoting boxes that keep a running record of your driving habits. Last August, the Progressive Insurance Group began a pilot program in Minnesota where drivers who agreed to put data recorders in their car could be eligible for discounts on their auto insurance—provided they didn't speed or drive after midnight, and had the recorder plugged in at least 95 percent of the time. Drivers who want the discounts have to periodically upload their driving data to Progressive using a personal computer.

Car manufacturers are installing recorders not merely to improve vehicle safety but to gather information in case they're sued, says Dan Kahn, road test editor for Edmunds.com. If the EDR indicates a driver hit the brakes hard and swerved before his SUV overturned, the carmaker could avoid paying millions in damages in a product liability suit. Kahn says manufacturers can also use the data to void the car's warranty—if the recorder says you've been driving aggressively, you may be out of pocket for repairs.

So far, regulation of such devices has been minimal. California, for example, passed a statute that requires carmakers to disclose the presence of data recorders in the vehicle's owners manual. But that same law allows third parties to access that data in certain circumstances. Meanwhile, California and other states are considering the use of black box data to assess mileage taxes on vehicle owners, check vehicle emissions, or collect information on speeding violations.

Most cars won't work without the recorders plugged in, says Kahn, so disconnecting them isn't an option. The best solution is to do your homework before you buy your next automobile. Find out if the car has an EDR before you buy it, and what kind of information it records. Or shop for an older classic—though GM cars have used very basic event logging since the 1970s, most cars built before 1996 don't have any place to plug in a data recorder.

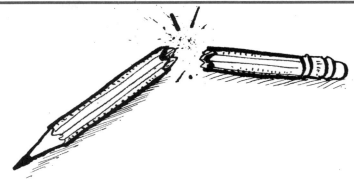

AT THE DOCTOR'S OFFICE

Testing Can Be Hazardous to Your Health Insurance

The Annoyance: I'm thinking about getting tested for HIV. But I'm reluctant to go to my regular doctor, because I'm afraid my insurance coverage could be cancelled if the test is positive. Do I need to worry?

The Fix: You might. The test results will become part of your medical record, which can be shared with a wide range of entities under the Health Insurance Portability and Accountability Act of 1996 (see "Getting Hip to HIPAA"). If you pay for the doctor visit using private health insurance, that information is almost certainly going to end up in medical databases and follow you the rest of your life. The very fact that you had the test, even if it turned out negative, may be a flag to some insurers that you are high risk.

One option is to be tested anonymously at a local free clinic. Such services don't collect personally identifiable information when they collect your blood sample—so you'll be able to get the results without creating a traceable record of them. You'll find a nationwide directory of clinics at the Free Clinic Foundation of America's site *http://www.freeclinic.net* and HIV testing centers at *http://www.hivtest.org.*

Anonymous testing is available in 40 states and the District of Columbia. The remaining ten allow only "confidential" testing, where the results can be shared with other health professionals and state health agencies. States that only allow confidential tests include Alabama, the Carolinas, the Dakotas, Idaho, Iowa, Mississippi, Nevada, and Tennessee. All ten require doctors to report your test results and your name to state health authorities. For more information on the reporting requirements for each state, visit the Henry J. Kaiser Family Foundation's State Health Facts web site (*http://www. statehealthfacts.org*).

Another option is to find a so-called "country doctor." This is a movement of physicians who've declined to become "covered entities" under HIPAA by not transmitting protected health information electronically. (Country doctors can still keep records on computer, they simply can't transmit them.) By definition, such physicians don't accept insurance or Medicare payments, so all medical expenses will come out of your pocket. (However, such doctors are still subject to state reporting rules and disclosures to law enforcement.) Depending on the laws of your state, using a country doctor may mean giving up some of HIPAA's benefits, such as getting copies of your medical records. At press time, the American Association of Physicians and Surgeons was attempting to create a directory of such doctors. Check their web site (*http://www.aapsonline.org*) for updates.

Waiting for lab test results in the mail, but afraid your spouse or your parents will get to them before you do? Under HIPAA you can specify alternate means for your health care professional to contact you—such as a different postal or email address. (Make sure they agree to use encryption before you allow the latter.)

GETTING HIP TO HIPAA

Unlike most areas of American society, your medical records are protected by Federal law. But whether they're *well protected* is a matter of debate. The Health Insurance Portability and Accountability Act (HIPAA) took effect in April 2003 and applies a complex series of guidelines to any organization that handles sensitive health information—like your doctor, your insurance company, and any data clearinghouses they use.

For consumers, HIPAA has three main benefits:

*   *Access*. You have the right to see, copy, and correct your own medical records, with a few limited exceptions. However, you may have to pay for copies and other administrative expenses.

*   *Confidentiality*. Healthcare providers and insurers must keep your information private. Employers can't access your medical history unless they administer an employee health plan, in which case this information is restricted to certain individuals in the organization (see Chapter 4, "Medical Records May Be Hazardous to Your Job"). Law enforcement agencies must obtain a valid court order to see your records.

*   *Security*. Organizations that handle health data must take steps to protect your information and keep it safe from inadvertent disclosure or illegal access.

That's the good news. The bad news is that HIPAA contains many loopholes and exceptions, the law is loosely enforced, and the legislation has been a source of great confusion to patients and medical personnel alike.

One exception allows doctors' offices to share your information with third parties so they can market "alternative treatments" to you. Financial institutions and law enforcement agencies are not covered under HIPAA—so if you pay for a nose job using a credit card or the Feds bust your doctor for illegal drug sales, that information isn't protected.

Worse, many organizations have found it difficult to implement HIPAA rules, or may be breaking them without being aware of it. In a survey published in Summer 2004, healthcare consultants Phoenix Health Systems reports that 4 out of 10 health care organizations say they're not fully compliant with all HIPAA regulations, more than a year after they went into effect. One out of five admit they're not yet following HIPAA privacy guidelines.

Zix Corp., a Dallas-based maker of email security systems for health care providers, reports that more than half of the top health care organizations are violating HIPAA rules every day. A Spring 2003 audit of 4.4 million electronic messages from 7500 health care organizations found that 53 of the top 100 healthcare providers transmitted sensitive medical information using unencrypted email, which could be intercepted en route or read by anyone with access to the recipient's computer. More than a third of top insurers also used unencrypted email. In most cases, says Zix, these companies are probably unaware their employees aren't following good email security practices.

Theoretically, breaking HIPAA rules carries stiff penalties. Violators can be fined $100 per incident up to a maximum of $25,000 per year. If the violation involves fraud or commercial gain, regulators can impose criminal penalties from 1 to 10 years in prison and fines from $50,000 to $250,000. But despite more than 5,000 consumer complaints alleging HIPAA violations, as of April 2004 not a single entity had been penalized, according to Georgetown University's Health Privacy Project. The U.S. Department of Health and Human Services' Office of Civil Rights, which oversees HIPAA compliance, takes a more educational approach to the law, trying to ensure health care professionals are aware of the rules and try to abide by them. (Got a HIPPA beef with your doctor? See "Report Privacy Gaffes.")

Most privacy advocates feel HIPAA offers weak protections at best. Depending on where you live, state laws may offer stronger privacy rules than HIPAA. For a summary of state medical privacy statutes and links to more information, visit the Health Privacy Project web site (*http://www.healthprivacy.org*) and click the State Law button.

Keep Your Hospital Stay Private

The Annoyance: I'm going in for some elective surgery of an extremely personal nature, and I don't want my gossipy coworkers or friends to know about it. How can I protect myself?

The Fix: First, tell the hospital or other care facility to take your name out of their patient directory. Some facilities may ask for your permission before they list you, but they're not required to—so anyone who knows your name can walk up and inquire about what room you're in and your general condition, though not the type of treatment you're receiving. If you've checked into the oncology wing or the maternity ward, however, they can get a pretty good idea of why you're there.

According to HIPAA rules, upon admittance you should be given a form where you can specify the types of medical information you're willing to share and with whom. Even so, your control over this information is ultimately quite limited. Privacy advocate Robert Gellman estimates that if you get treatment at a hospital and pay for at least part of the treatment using an insurance plan, anywhere from 1,000 to 10,000 people—from hospital staff to insurance company administrators to university researchers—could have access to it. Many of them are not covered under HIPAA.

But there's a downside to keeping your hospital stay under wraps, notes April Robertson, corporate compliance officer for ChartOne, a medical records management firm in San Jose.

"You won't get flowers, get well cards, or phone calls, and if your old auntie shows up in the lobby during visiting hours, she won't get to see you," she says. Robertson suggests you ask the hospital if they'll let you choose a password that you can share with your family, so you can choose who gets to visit while you convalesce.

Bottom line? If you don't want anyone to visit or call, don't tell anyone you're going to be in the hospital. If you think someone is looking for you and likely to do you harm, warn the hospital (preferably when you schedule the procedure, not at the time of registration) and they will take appropriate measures. If you really want privacy, don't use insurance and pay the bill out of pocket.

Medical Marketing Migraines

The Annoyance: A few weeks ago I got a prescription filled for medicine to treat a chronic condition. Now I've started to get solicitations in the mail for similar medicines. Who sold my name to these guys, and what can I do to stop them?

The Fix: This is one of those lovely little loopholes in HIPAA. Your doctor or pharmacy can share your information with marketers under the guise of providing information about "alternative treatments." For example, your drug store may contact you at the behest of a pharmaceutical company to see if it can persuade you to switch brands of anti-depressant.

You can opt out of receiving future marketing dreck, but only after you've received the first one. Worse, you'll have to opt out separately for each healthcare provider that sells your information and for each member of your family who is contacted. The law specifies no standard opt-out method, so the procedure for getting your name off a marketer's list will vary.

You might attempt a pre-emptive strike by telling your doctor or pharmacist to not share your contact information with anyone. The Association of American Physicians and Surgeons has developed a model nondisclosure form you can give to your doctor, dentist, or other medical professional that demands they not release your personal health information to third parties. (You can find it at *http://www.aapsonline. org/confiden/patientadvisory.htm*.) If the marketing is allowed under HIPAA guidelines, your physician isn't forced to comply or even acknowledge your request. But if she doesn't honor your requests, you probably don't want her as your doctor.

While you're in a hospital bed zonked out on meds, your medical chart is available to anyone who wanders by. The Health Privacy Project advises patients to discuss concerns about confidentiality with health professionals prior to treatment. Ask your doctor to keep treatment notes and other sensitive material separate from your medical chart, to limit access by strangers.

PRIVACY IN PERIL: DRUG STORE COWBOYS

Have you gotten a letter or a call from your pharmacy offering helpful advice concerning prescription drugs—or even samples of the drugs themselves? Your drug store may be selling you out to Big Pharmaceutical, and breaking the law in the process.

In 2002, at least 300 South Florida residents received unsolicited letters from Walgreens with samples of Prozac inside, part of a promotional campaign instigated by local sales reps of Eli Lilly, makers of the popular anti-depressant.

Meanwhile in California, the Privacy Rights Clearinghouse is suing Albertsons' pharmacy (which includes the Save-On, Acme, and Osco chains) for allegedly contacting its customers on behalf of pharmaceutical companies. The PRC alleges Albertsons was paid up to $4.50 per letter and $15 per call by Big Pharma companies to get customers to switch to more expensive drugs. If true, that may violate a California law requiring companies to obtain customers' consent before using personal health information for marketing purposes. If you've received such a letter, contact the Clearinghouse at *http://www.privacyrights.org/ar/PharmacyAlert.htm*.

MEDS IN BLACK: MEET THE MIB

Do you have high blood pressure? Have you been treated for depression? Do you have a dangerous hobby such as skydiving or smoking? If so, you're probably on file at the Medical Information Bureau. The MIB is a kind of credit bureau for your body, used by more than 600 insurance companies to keep tabs on 15 million individuals and make sure they don't misstate their medical histories in order to qualify for insurance or lower premiums. And like a credit bureau, it has to follow the guidelines set down by the Fair Credit Reporting Act, which means you can obtain a copy of your file and demand they correct any inaccuracies. This is especially important if you've been turned down for insurance because of information in your MIB file. To request a free annual report, call the automated voice line at (866) 692-6901 or write to MIB at this address:

MIB, Inc.
P.O. Box 105
Essex Station
Boston, MA 02112

You'll have to provide your name, Social Security Number, date of birth, birthplace, occupation, home address, and phone number. MIB says it will process your request within 15 days, if they have a record for you on file. For more information, see the MIB web site at *http://www.mib.com/html/request_your_record.html* or send email to infoline@mib.com.

Report Privacy Gaffes

The Annoyance: I've recently changed doctors. My old doctor's office tried to fax my treatment records to my new physician, but they goofed and sent my entire medical history to some stranger's fax machine.

The Fix: Technically, that office has violated HIPAA's guidelines for data security. Fax machines are notoriously insecure devices even when the documents arrive at the correct number—anyone can come by and have a look at what's being printed out. But your doctor's office needs to exercise more caution in how they handle your records.

If you believe your physician's office has violated the HIPAA Privacy Rule, you can report them to the Department of Health and Human Services' Office of Civil Rights by mail, fax, or email. You'll need to fill out a form detailing how the doctor violated your privacy, along with supporting materials and your full contact information. (For forms and detailed instructions, see *http://www.hhs.gov/ocr/privacyhowtofile. htm*.) The offending medical practice can be fined $100 per incident, but the odds of that happening are slim. More likely they'll get a letter warning them to clean up their act.

A better solution would be to request a copy of your medical records from your old doctor—you're legally entitled to it, under HIPPA regulations. Then bring a copy to your new physician and keep one at home for your own records.

Confused by the privacy disclosure forms your doctor asks you to sign? Join the club. An April 2003 study of HIPAA notices, sponsored by the Privacy Rights Clearinghouse, found that most were confusing and way too complicated—clearly not written using the plain language required by the law. Fortunately, you don't have to stay in the dark. Every health care provider is required to have a HIPAA privacy officer on hand who can answer questions and handle complaints. So if you don't understand something, ask to speak to your doc's privacy officer.

Be Careful What You Tell Your Doctor

The Annoyance: Some of my personal habits aren't exactly mainstream or strictly legal. But they do impact my health and I'd like to talk to my doctor about them. Am I protected by rules of doctor/patient confidentiality?

The Fix: Not necessarily. What you tell your doctor isn't as private as you might think. Confidentiality laws vary widely by state, and in many cases physicians are compelled to report certain conditions. For example, doctors may be required by law to report certain communicable diseases such as smallpox or tuberculosis to public health officials. Gunshot or knife wounds and suspected cases of child abuse must be reported to the proper authorities. Six states require doctors to notify their state department of transportation when patients have a condition such as epilepsy that could keep them from driving safely. In August 2004, a Pennsylvania man lost his driver's license after he told his doctor he drank a six pack of beer each night. A court subsequently ruled his license could be reinstated, but only after he installed an auto ignition system that contained a blood alcohol analyzer.

The Bush Administration's Department of Justice has asserted there is no such thing as doctor/patient confidentiality. Last year the DOJ sought the medical records of women who had undergone late-term abortions in California, Illinois, Michigan, New York, and Pennsylvania, claiming that it required these records to defend the late-term abortion ban passed by Congress but overturned by the courts. After being spurned by judges in nearly every state, the DOJ ultimately dropped its demands.

Despite that victory, doctor/patient privacy is hardly assured. Even privacy-conscious doctors may voluntarily disclose information if they believe the health of the patient or of other parties is at stake. And HIPAA puts no more restrictions on doctor confidentiality than existing laws, says privacy consultant Robert Gellman.

"Anything you tell your doctor can be given to the police, city or state health departments, national security agencies, researchers, or dozens of other institutions," he says. "When you talk to your doctor, you must make a tradeoff between protecting your privacy and getting the most effective health care."

AT THE BANK

All Offshore That's Going Offshore?

The Annoyance: I'm sick of U.S. banks tossing my private information around like so much confetti. I'm thinking about opening an offshore banking account. Is this legal? Will my money (and data) be protected?

The Fix: It's perfectly legal to open an account in a foreign bank. Many foreign jurisdictions have much stricter privacy laws than what you'll find stateside. But it's a lot more work, you'll have fewer ways to access your money, and it can be riskier.

Opening a foreign account typically takes two to three months, says Arnold Cornez, J.D., author of *The Offshore Money Book* (McGraw-Hill). You'll need to submit a lot of documentation, including proof of identity and letters of reference from banks and attorneys. You'll need to vet the banks, so you can separate the safe havens from the sharks, and at some point you may need to visit the bank in person to finalize the deal. Cornez says you can find agents that will handle the paperwork for $300 to $500, such as his own Global Group Limited (*http://www.global.bs/*).

Even then, your account will be somewhat limited. Getting a credit card on a foreign account can be nearly impossible, says Cornez, and most places of business won't accept checks based on a foreign currency. But you can get a debit card that works just as easily as it does in the U.S.

Another downside: if the bank fails, your assets won't be covered by the Federal Deposit Insurance Corporation. And don't view a foreign bank as a way to hide income from Uncle Sam or hungry creditors. If you have more than $10,000 in foreign accounts, you must file a form with the IRS and pay taxes on any interest the account earns. Any creditor collecting a judgment against you can also tap such an account—provided, of course, they find out about it.

Bottom line? If you do business overseas or simply travel a lot to your favorite floating bank haven, having a foreign bank account makes a lot of sense—and you can keep using it when you come back home. But if you're just looking to escape junk mail and marketing, a foreign account is probably more trouble than it's worth.

FINANCIAL PRIVACY? DON'T BANK ON IT.

By and large, your financial records are less secure than your video rental records. In 1999 Congress passed the Financial Services Modernization Act of 1999, better known as the Gramm-Leach-Bliley Act. GLBA's main aim was to break down the regulatory walls between banks, insurance companies, and brokerages, allowing them to merge into massive "financial supermarkets" that could sell products and share customer information on a massive scale.

GLBA also came with a few limited privacy protections. You can opt out of some marketing solicitations by telling the firm to not share your personal information with outside companies (see Chapter 2, "Foil Mailbox Miscreants"). If you don't opt out, the financial firm is free to sell your data to anyone. The firms must also send you a notice each year informing you of your privacy rights under GLBA, although as the Privacy Rights Clearinghouse has revealed, many firms do their best to make such notices look like junk mail.

However, under GLBA, consumers can't limit sharing among a company's many affiliates, or among companies that have a joint marketing agreement with the financial firm. So if a bank also owns an insurance company, or if it has inked a credit card marketing deal with an airline's frequent flyer program, you can't opt out. According to the California Consumer Federation, Citibank has at least 1600 affiliates, while Bank of America clocks in at more than 1400.

The Fair Credit Reporting Act (FCRA) lets you tell financial firms to not share information about your "creditworthiness" with affiliates—such as your credit score and whether you pay your bills on time. The downside is that you may end up paying a higher rate of interest on your credit cards. Information on how to opt out under the FCRA should be contained in the financial firm's annual notice and found on the firm's web site.

State laws may also offer more protection. As of June 2004, financial services firms doing business in California must get your permission before they can sell your data to third parties. You can also tell them to not share your information with any of their affiliates. Alaska, Connecticut, Illinois, Maryland, North Dakota and Vermont also offer stricter rules for protecting some forms of financial data. To find out about privacy laws where you live, check with consumer advocacy organizations such as your state chapter of Public Interest Research Group (*http://www.pirg.org*), or the office of your Secretary of State (*http://www.nass.org/sos/sos.html*).

Tell Insurers to Drop Your SSN

The Annoyance: My insurance company insists on printing my Social Security Number on my health card, which I must carry to my doctor's office every time I get a checkup. Isn't it stupid to carry your SSN around in your wallet, where any two-bit pickpocket can have access to it?

The Fix: It sure is. While it seems innocuous to use your SSN to identify you to insurers, it can be a huge problem if your wallet is lost or stolen with your health care card inside—making you a prime candidate for identity theft. Once someone else has your driver's license, your credit cards, and your SSN, you're a sitting duck.

Fortunately, some insurers such as Blue Cross and Blue Shield are voluntarily moving away from using SSNs to identify health plan members. And at least five states have banned the use of SSNs as insurance IDs.

If your SSN is on your insurance plan card, ask your insurer if they will give you a different number to identify you, or at least remove the number from your card. If they won't, take the card out of your wallet, write down your insurance plan number and take that with you to the doctor instead. You may have to train the personnel in your doctor's office to not automatically ask for your SSN every time you come in, however.

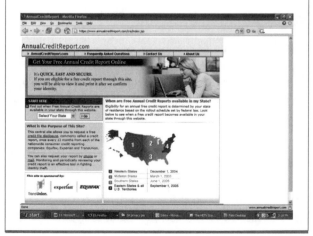

tip

Have you received a scary email from your bank warning you about problems with your account? Odds are it's from a phisher—a scam artist out to steal your account information and possibly your identity. Phisher emails can be extremely convincing looking, and may contain the same graphics used by your bank and valid links to your bank's web site. If you get any email that asks you for your account information or drives you to a web site where you must log in before continuing, stop and contact your bank to find out if that email is legit.

Safety in Boxes?

The Annoyance: I've got a lot of valuable documents I need to keep safe and private, but I can't afford to install a private vault, an alarm system, and a kennel full of Dobermans.

The Fix: You could stash the docs in a safe deposit box at your bank. That way, the documents are less likely to be stolen or destroyed in a fire or flood, and you get to say who can and can't open the box to get at them (with some exceptions, see below).

But while the contents of your box may be more private, they're not entirely safe. Unlike what you keep in a vault at home, the materials inside a safe deposit box may not be covered under your homeowner's insurance, says David McGuinn, president of Safe Deposit Specialists in Houston. If you use the box to store valuables such as jewelry or family heirlooms, you may need to get a separate "floater" on your homeowner's insurance covering those items.

Nor are items in boxes covered by the Federal Deposit Insurance Corporation, which protects the first $100,000 of your bank account assets. So if you stash cash inside them and a bomb goes off in the bank vault, you're out of pocket.

Note, too, that the privacy of a safe deposit box is far from absolute. They're subject to searches by law enforcement or court order. If the IRS decides you're using the box to hide assets, they can order it frozen so that you can't get inside it until they've completed their inquiry. And you can't get one

anonymously (at least, in the U.S.). The Patriot Act requires you to present photo identification before you can rent a box. McGuinn suggests you add the name of someone you trust to your box rental agreement, so that if something happens to you, they will be able to get at the box's contents without having to navigate a phalanx of attorneys and bureaucratic red tape.

FREE CREDIT REPORTS

The best defense against identity theft is to keep a close eye on your bank accounts and to know what's in your credit report. Starting in late 2004, the Big Three credit reporting agencies are required to send you a free annual credit report if you ask them for one. This service is being gradually rolled out region by region; full nationwide access should be available by September 2005. To find out how to obtain a free report in your area, visit *https://www.annualcreditreport.com*.

But make sure you visit the right site; there are a bevy of sites with names like "freecreditreport" designed to lure you into paying for a report or scamming you out of your personal information. According to a February 2005 report in the *St. Louis Post-Dispatch,* there were nearly 100 imposter sites with names closely resembling "annualcreditreport"; several were owned by the big credit reporting agencies. To avoid confusion (or worse), the World Privacy Forum is urging consumers to order their free reports by phone at (877) 322-8228.

PRIVACY IN PERIL: WHEN BANKS SELL TO CROOKS

You say you don't care if your bank sells your credit card number? Consider the case of Kenneth Taves. In November 1997, Taves purchased a list of 3.7 million credit card numbers from Charter Pacific Bank of Agoura Hills, California. At the time, Taves ran a service that handled billing for several web porn sites. He told the bank he planned to use the list to verify legitimate card numbers for site subscribers. Instead, he added bogus subscription charges to more than 900,000 account holders, many of whom didn't even own computers. Taves and his partners amassed nearly $46 million before they were finally caught. He pleaded guilty to fraud in January 2001 and was sentenced to 11 years.

While Taves's activity was fraudulent, it was (and still is) perfectly legal for a commercial entity to buy lists of credit card numbers. At the time of the purchase, Taves was on probation for check counterfeiting, but the bank performed no background checks. Most of the numbers on the list weren't even from customers of Charter Pacific—they belonged to customers of merchants who banked at Charter. The bank refunded customer's money and stopped the practice of selling credit card numbers; it was acquired by First Banks America Bank in May 2001.

Taves succeeded for as long as he did by charging relatively small amounts—typically under $20—which escaped most consumers' notice. Customers who did call Taves's companies to dispute the charges were sent into an endless voice mail loop.

Moral of the story? Examine your credit charges every month and challenge anything that looks suspicious, no matter how small. If the merchant is difficult to reach, notify the authorities—the fraud division of your local police and the FTC (*http://www.ftc.gov*) are good places to start. And tell your banks you don't want them to sell your records to anybody, by exercising your right to opt out. (See Chapter 2, "Foil Mailbox Miscreants.")

If you use a safe deposit box to store valuables, be sure to keep copies of any appraisals or proof of ownership in a separate location. It's also a good idea to photograph the items inside and store the photo elsewhere as well. If the box becomes inaccessible—say, a bomb goes off near your bank or the vault gets flooded—you'll need these documents to file a claim.

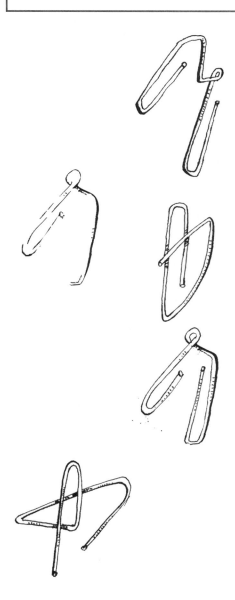

MISCELLANEOUS

Keep Those Cards at Home

The Annoyance: I just bought a new microwave oven. Inside the box was a product registration card saying that if I wanted warranty protection I'd need to fill out the card and mail it within 10 days. The card asked all sorts of nosy questions—like my annual income, marital status, ages of my children, and the types of credit cards I own. Do I have to give them any of this information?

The Fix: No. In fact, you don't have to fill out a registration card to qualify for warranty protection. In most cases all you need is a receipt indicating when and where you bought the product and how much you paid for it. These cards are really just marketing surveys in disguise. Most go directly to data mining companies, who use the info you provide to send you more junk mail, telemarketing pitches, and spam.

One exception to this rule is software. If you purchase software from a major vendor like Microsoft or Symantec, you may be compelled to register your copy online or it will stop working. Such procedures are used to combat software piracy (as well as compel users to renew their software subscriptions). If you must register, give the bare information necessary to activate your software, and be sure to opt out of any offers to add you to their mailing lists (unless you really want more junk in your life).

Get Debt Collectors Off Your Back

The Annoyance: For six months I've been getting calls from a collection agency for a debt owed by John J. Johnson. As I've explained to them many times, my name is John Q. Johnson, and I live in an entirely different city than John J. Yet the calls keep coming. What can I do to stop this harassment?

The Fix: Write the collection agency a letter asking them to stop dunning you, and explain why. Under the Fair Debt Collection Practices Act, after an agency receives such a request it can only contact you to say that the matter has been dropped, that it's planning to sue you, or to send proof of your debt, such as a copy of an unpaid bill. This written notice doesn't relieve you of an obligation to pay legitimate debts, it just stops the agency from nagging you about them.

The FDCPA has a number of other provisions to shield your privacy:

- If you have an attorney, you can tell the collector to contact him or her, not you.

- The agent may contact other people you know, but only to ask them how to reach you.

- Your friends and family are under no obligation to tell the agent anything, and in most cases the agent can't contact them more than once.

- Agents may not inform anyone other than you or your attorney about why they are calling.

- Agents can't call you at work if you tell them not to.

- An agent cannot threaten, harass, or curse at you, or threaten to sue you or take your property unless he or she is planning to do so—provided the agent has a legal right to do it.

If you feel a collection agency has violated the law, you can report it to the Federal Trade Commission's Consumer Sentinel (*http://www.consumer.gov/sentinel/*). For more information, see the FTC's FAQ on fair debt collection practices (*http://www.ftc.gov/bcp/conline/pubs/credit/fdc.htm*).

While you're at it, order a copy of your credit report to make sure that the other John Johnson's records aren't mixed up with yours. A June 2004 study by the Public Research Interest Group found that more than half of all credit reports contained personal information that was misspelled, outdated, or belonged to someone else.

Hello, My Name Is Brad, and I'll Be Your Thief This Evening

The Annoyance: I hand my credit card to a waiter, he disappears for a few minutes, then comes back with a slip for me to sign. A few months later mystery charges start showing up on my bank statement. Is there a connection?

The Fix: That waiter might have done more than stick his thumb in your soup; he may have also put his hand in your pocket. In a scam known as *skimming*, credit cards are swiped twice—once in the normal card scanner, and once in a pager-sized device that captures your account information. Skimming can happen anywhere cards are accepted, but it seems to be most widely reported in restaurants, most likely because the swipe usually occurs out of sight of the card holder.

In February 2004, San Jose police busted two credit fraud rings operating in Bay Area restaurants. College-age waiters were paid $10 for every card they skimmed. That information was used to create counterfeit or clone cards, which the ringleaders used to buy swag to then sell over the Internet.

Skimming accounts for an estimated $1 billion worth of losses each year, though the biggest danger for individuals is identity fraud. The only solution is to keep a close eye on your credit accounts and challenge any unusual charges. If you dispute charges within the time period specified by your bank (usually 60 days), you'll only be liable for $50 of it. These days most banks will absorb the entire charge if fraud is involved.

You might also want to keep a close eye on your waiter, or consider taking your credit card to the cashier yourself.

Get Ready for Your Close-Up

The Annoyance: I've never considered myself telegenic until I walked down a busy street and noticed a video camera perched above the sidewalk every 10 feet or so. Where I live it's too hot to walk around wearing a ski mask, so how do I handle this constant videotaping?

The Fix: Well, you could break into a song and dance routine. That's what the New York City Surveillance Camera Players do to publicize the pervasiveness of hidden cameras. (Another troupe has formed in San Francisco—you can find them at *http://www.survile.org*.) Bill Brown, who founded the SCP back in 1996, says the first thing people need to do is

---

PRIVACY IN PERIL: ORDER A PIZZA, PAY A FINE

Even your pepperoni isn't private anymore. In April 2004, the Missouri Office of State Courts Administrator hired Dallas-based ACS Inc. to track down citizens who haven't paid their fines. ACS does this by combing through consumer databases—in particular, pizza delivery records. (Apparently Missourians don't give their correct address to court officials, but they do give it to the pizza guy.)

The Missouri courts aren't the only ones exploring the Dominos Effect. The Ponemon Institute's Larry Ponemon says Federal law enforcement agencies are also looking at pizza deliveries as a way to catch terrorists, who apparently like to order pies and pay by credit card. So the next time you go for that lamb-and-feta-cheese special, don't put it on the plastic—unless you want to share a few slices with the Feds.

---

figure out where the cameras are. He conducts periodic tours of camera sites in different New York neighborhoods. You'll also find maps showing camera locations in Boston, Chicago, New York, Washington, DC, and other cities on his site at *http://www.notbored.org/maps-usa.html* (see Figure 5-4.) But besides trying to avoid streets where cameras are placed (virtually impossible in some cities) or becoming a street performer, there's not much ordinary citizens can do except lobby for laws that restrict the use of camera footage.

What's the big deal? While cameras are theoretically placed in public spaces to deter crime, many are also used for more covert purposes—such as recording the images and license plate numbers of political protestors. Over the last two years police have videotaped protests in Denver, San Francisco, Milwaukee, and Washington, DC, according to EPIC's Protestor Privacy Page (*http://www.epic.org/privacy/protest*). Cameras are also abused for more personal reasons (see "Privacy in Peril: Entertaining the Troopers"). For more information on pervasive (and invasive) surveillance, see Privacy International's site (*http://www.privacy.org/pi/activities/cctv*) and EPIC's Observing Surveillance site (*http://observingsurveillance.us*).

Map of the MPD surveillance cameras

The D.C. police department has 16 cameras at 15 sites that offer 360-degree views and magnify up to 17 times. Here are the locations of the cameras and their views:

1. Old Post Office Pavilion [1100 Pennsylvania Ave. NW] Primarily for views of Penn. Ave. NW, from 14th St. to the Capitol.

2. Smithsonian Institution Castle [1000 Jefferson Dr. SW] Views of the entire Mall in both directions.

3. L'Enfant Plaza [480 L'Enfant Plaza SW] Views of southbound I-395, the Pentagon and Reagan National Airport.

4. U.S. Department of Labor [2nd St. & Constitution Ave. NW] Views of the Capitol, the intersection of Constitution and Penn. Aves. NW, and 3rd St. north to the Dept. of Labor.

5. Voice of America [3rd St. & Independence Ave. SW] Views of Independence Ave. from the Capitol to 14th St. and 3rd St. north to the Dept. of Labor.

6. Dupont Circle [1350 Connecticut Ave. NW] Views of Dupont Circle area.

7. Park Tower [1001 N. 19th St. Arlington] Views of Key

8. Union Station [520 N. Capitol St. NW] Views of the plaza in front of the station.

9. Hotel Washington [15th St. & Pennsylvania Ave. NW] Views of 15th St. and Penn. Ave. NW between 12th St. and the White House.

10. Banana Republic [M St. & Wisconsin Ave. NW] Views of Wisconsin Ave. at M St. NW.

11. National Gallery of Art East Wing [3rd St. & Constitution Ave. NW] Camera installed only for special events at the request of the building management.

12. Columbia Plaza [24th St. & Virginia Ave. NW] Views of the Whitehurst Freeway, Roosevelt Bridge and Memorial Bridge.

13. Hilton Hotel [1919 Connecticut Ave. NW] Views of hotel surroundings and Conn. Ave. down to Dupont Circle.

14. World Bank (I) [19th St. & Pennsylvania Ave. NW] Views of surroundings of World Bank buildings and Penn. Ave. between 22nd & 17th Streets.

[map adapted from a Washington Post diagram]

Figure 5-4. Want to be seen in DC? This map will show you where to mug for the police cameras. Though the map shows only 16 locations, there are likely to be hundreds more private security cameras aimed at unsuspecting pedestrians.

PRIVACY IN PERIL: YOUR PRIVY'S NOT SO PRIVATE

As if junk mail, telemarketing, and spam weren't enough of an assault on your personal space, Islip, New York-based Healthquest Technologies has patented the Wizmark (*http://www.wizmark.com/electronic. htm*), a 3.5-inch waterproof screen mounted inside a urinal that displays electronic advertising. The screen is activated by... well, you can guess how it's activated. On the bright side, there's no better opportunity to express exactly how you feel about such ads.

PRIVACY IN PERIL: ENTERTAINING THE TROOPERS

In September 2003, state troopers in Tuscaloosa, Alabama found a creative use for one of the city's traffic cams. A video camera normally trained on an intersection near the University of Alabama campus was instead used to zoom in on bar-goers in the wee hours of the morning. According to eyewitnesses at *The Crimson White,* the school newspaper that first reported the story, the camera spent a lot of time zeroing in on the fleshier parts of young female pedestrians. An unnamed officer in the Trooper's headquarters responsible for the misuse of the camera was apparently unaware the cam was also broadcasting on local cable channel 45. That evening, the same traffic cam factored in three arrests—including a 22-year-old woman detained for flashing her breasts at the camera. After a public outcry, the city of Tuscaloosa disabled the troopers' ability to control the camera.

PRIVACY BY THE NUMBERS

500,000,000,000
Number of RFID tags predicted to be in use by 2010

172
**Colleges and universities that gave student records to
the FBI without a court order in 2002.**

5
**Flights Massachusetts Senator Ted Kennedy was kept
off as a result of the No Fly list**

25 million
Cars on road in 2004 with event data recorders

1 in 3
**Health care organizations that suffered a data
security breach in 2004**

5,000+
Complaints regarding HIPPA violations as of April 2004

$0
**Civil penalties imposed on HIPPA violators
as of April 2004**

7200
**Estimated number of public video surveillance cameras
in Manhattan**

*Sources: MIT Auto-ID Center, ACLU, National Highway Traffic
Safety Administration, Phoenix Health Systems/HIMSS,
Health Privacy Project, New York City Surveillance Camera
Players.*

6

Privacy and Uncle Sam

Nobody knows more about you than your Uncle Sam. From cradle to grave you spill information like bread crumbs, which gets scooped up by one governmental entity after another.

Computers have greatly expanded your Uncle's power to store and track every salient detail of your life. They make it easier for the Census Bureau to manage huge volumes of information (leading to more intrusive questionnaires), and for the IRS to pick candidates for tax audits (leading to Hell on earth). They also can provide your friends, neighbors, and other snoops a browser's-eye view of your family dramas, financial dilemmas, faulty driving, and much more. Let us not forget Uncle Sam's stepchildren—the many states, counties, cities, boroughs, and their panoply of agencies, small and large, that likewise trail you like a bloodhound hunting a possum. Unfortunately, government bureaucracies are notorious for being on the trailing edge of technology, especially when it comes to keeping your information safe and secure. Whether through carelessness or maliciousness, data tends to leak out in damaging and embarrassing ways.

There's also a darker side. You don't have to be a raving paranoid to acknowledge the government's power to take over your life. Laws passed in the wake of the 9/11 terrorist attacks have greatly expanded the government's ability to snoop on its citizens, with minimal oversight. Cutting-edge technologies such as DNA databases, biometric scanners, and RFID tracking could allow your Uncle to keep tabs on you 24/7.

With relatives like this, who needs enemies?

In some cases, you can limit what the government can do with your data. In other cases, your only recourse is to become informed and active in the fight to protect your rights. As with liberty, the price of privacy is eternal vigilance.

PUBLIC AGENCIES AND YOU

Private Lives, Public Information

The Annoyance: I thought I led a fairly private life. Then I got into a dispute with a business partner, who decided to tweak me by sending me a dossier he'd compiled about me—the names and birthdates of my children, some quiet property investments I'd made, and the details of my very messy divorce. Is this legal?

The Fix: It is. Not only is all of that public information, but in most states it would be illegal to conceal this information from the general public. Birth and death, marriage and divorce, home and business ownership, nearly every major rite of passage is considered part of the public record in most states. Until fairly recently, this information was hard to get at. Most of these records were kept in dusty credenzas in the bowels of county courthouses; anyone who wanted a look had to ask to see your paper file, and if they wanted to take the record home they had to make photocopies or scribble down the information by hand. Now, thanks to the wonder of the Web, many of these records are available easily—and often for a modest fee—online (see Table 6-1).

Public records serve a useful purpose. It's helpful to know who owns the house you're thinking of buying, or whether your ex-spouse is hiding assets, or if a convicted sex offender has moved into your neighborhood. But computers allow you to do things that the original authors of public records statutes surely never dreamed of, such as instantly looking up

Table 6-1. Public records versus private matters. What's private information and what's not? Laws vary by state and county, but many of your most vital pieces of data are available to anyone who bothers to look it up.

Public	Private
The property you own	The videos you rent
Your lousy driving record	Your lousy driver's license photo
Property taxes you owe	Personal income tax you've paid
The candidates you gave money to [a]	The candidates you voted for
Your messy divorce	Your messed-up back
Names and birthdates of your children	Names and birthdates of your adopted children [b]
Pets you've licensed	Books you've borrowed
Your criminal record	Your high school transcripts

[a] For contributions totaling more than $200.
[b] Alaska, Oregon, Kansas, Alabama, and New Hampshire allow adoptees to obtain birth certificates, according to Bastard Nation (*http://www.bastards.org*).

every piece of property owned by a particular person, or finding every legal dispute involving a particular business. In the age of the Internet, everyone is a gumshoe.

Some local governments are taking steps to limit online access to this information. Last July, Douglas County in Kansas removed the ability to search across property records by an individual's name, citing citizen complaints about potential privacy violations. Officials in Nassau County, New York, did something similar in 2002. You might try approaching local county officials and see if they'd consider restricting the ability to search for records online.

Private data brokers also mine public records databases and sell the information they find there. You may be able to convince some data brokers to stop selling information about you they've culled from public databases (see Chapter 3, "Fend off Cyber Stalkers"), but this won't remove the data from the public record or prevent state or county governments from sharing it with the world. (The Privacy Rights Clearinghouse publishes a partial list of information brokers at *http://www.privacyrights.org/ar/infobrokers.htm*).

(like periodicals), may only be forwarded three times. Once the temporary change expires, you'll need to directly contact those magazines and people you owe bills to and give them your new, permanent address.

Another way to reduce the junk is to use the Direct Marketing Association's Mail Preference Service (*http://www.dmaconsumers.org/cgi/offmailinglist*). This will eventually reduce but not entirely eliminate the crap you receive.

Your best recourse is to understand what information is available about you and try to limit the potential for harm (see Chapter 4, "Be Your Own Gumshoe"). If, for example, the public record includes transcripts from a family court case or some other potentially embarrassing legal proceeding, you might be able to petition the court to seal the record. At the very least, you won't be surprised when the details show up in your inbox.

Keep the USPS From Selling Your Address

The Annoyance: I recently moved across country. To make sure that all my magazine subscriptions and personal mail find me when I arrived, I filled out a US Postal Service Change of Address form. Now I'm getting even more junk mail than before. Am I being paranoid, or is there a connection?

The Fix: Connect away. Fill out the Postal Service's National Change of Address (NCOA) form and you're just begging for junk mail. According to the USPS privacy policy, if you file a permanent change of address (Form 3575), anybody who has your old address is entitled to obtain your new one. The Postal Service uses about 20 private contractors to process 40 million changes of address each year. Those contractors then sell your address to thousands of direct mail companies, who proceed to fill your mailbox with dead trees.

One partial solution is to mark your change of address as temporary; you use the same form, you just indicate a date when you want mail forwarding to stop (see Figure 6-1). Mail will be forwarded for up to 12 months, but your new address won't be added to the NCOA rolls that are shared with marketers. Most of the junk mail won't be forwarded, while some types of mail

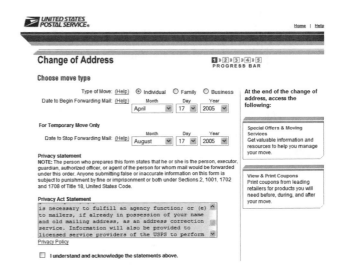

Figure 6-1. Moving? You can file a change of address at USPS.gov, but be sure to use the Temporary Move option—unless you want your junk mail to follow you.

PRIVACY IN PERIL: SMILE WHEN YOU BUY THAT STAMP

According to heavily redacted documents obtained by EPIC under the Freedom of Information Act, Automated Postal Center kiosks that sell postage and let you mail packages come with a little something extra inside: a camera that snaps a portrait of every customer, then stores it on an internal hard disk for 30 days. If you attempt to compromise the photo by, say, holding up a piece of paper (or an envelope) the machine won't complete your transaction. According to the documents, USPS says the cameras are required by the Federal Aviation Administration for security reasons. Go figure.

TEN WAYS UNCLE SAM INVADES YOUR PRIVACY

Nothing can crush your privacy faster than the big feet of Uncle Sam (and his state and local cousins). In some cases these violations affect only a handful of people, many of whom probably warrant closer scrutiny. But the government is also collecting and sharing data on millions of law-abiding citizens—and doing a poor job of protecting it from hackers, rogue employees, and other no-goodniks.

Publish your information on the Web. As governments continue to move public records online, more and more details of your private life are available to anyone with an Internet connection. For example, the Feds publish national databases of births, deaths, and Federal inmates; depending on where you live, your city or county may provide everything from the property you own to your political affiliations and traffic tickets—all available with just a few mouse clicks.

Obtain commercial data about you. Federal agencies are culling information about millions of Americans from privately held commercial databases in an effort to identify potential terrorists (and Lord only knows what else). Universities, grocery chains, and other organizations have voluntarily shared customer information without notifying their customers. Federal agencies have also purchased millions of records from data aggregators such as ChoicePoint and Seisint.

Create massive, insecure databases. Not only is Uncle Sam gathering massive amounts of information about you, he's making it easy pickings for hackers and data thieves. In 2003, the House Committee on Government Reform gave the Federal government a "D" for computer security, with eight departments (including the Department of Homeland Security) receiving an "F." See the full report card below

Abuse and misuse information. Rogue employees with access to sensitive data can be a lethal combination. Until 1997, it was legal for IRS employees to snoop on anyone's tax records. (Since then, the Government Accountability Office has documented thousands of unauthorized access attempts, though only a handful of IRS employees have been disciplined.) In 2001, a DEA agent sold information from various crime databases to private investigators, and then disappeared on the day of his trial.

(continued on next page)

FEDERAL COMPUTER SECURITY REPORT CARD

December 9, 2003

GOVERNMENTWIDE GRADE 2003: D

	2003	2002		2003	2002
NUCLEAR REGULATORY COMMISSION	A	C	GENERAL SERVICES ADMINISTRATION	D	D
NATIONAL SCIENCE FOUNDATION	A-	D-	DEPARTMENT OF THE TREASURY*	D	F
SOCIAL SECURITY ADMINISTRATION	B+	B-	OFFICE OF PERSONNEL MANAGEMENT	D-	F
DEPARTMENT OF LABOR	B	C+	NATIONAL AERONAUTICS AND SPACE ADMINISTRATION	D-	D+
DEPARTMENT OF EDUCATION	C+	D	DEPARTMENT OF ENERGY	F	F
DEPARTMENT OF VETERANS AFFAIRS*	C	F	DEPARTMENT OF JUSTICE	F	F
ENVIRONMENTAL PROTECTION AGENCY	C	D-	DEPARTMENT OF HEALTH AND HUMAN SERVICES	F	D-
DEPARTMENT OF COMMERCE	C-	D+	DEPARTMENT OF THE INTERIOR	F	F
SMALL BUSINESS ADMINISTRATION	C-	F	DEPARTMENT OF AGRICULTURE	F	F
AGENCY FOR INTERNATIONAL DEVELOPMENT	C-	F	DEPARTMENT OF HOUSING AND URBAN DEVELOPMENT	F	F
DEPARTMENT OF TRANSPORTATION	D+	F	DEPARTMENT OF STATE	F	F
DEPARTMENT OF DEFENSE*	D	F	DEPARTMENT OF HOMELAND SECURITY	F	--

TEN WAYS UNCLE SAM INVADES YOUR PRIVACY

Ask your employer or neighbors to snoop on you. Federal and local governments have initiated a series of "watch" programs encouraging individuals and employers to report possible terrorist behavior to the authorities (see "Privacy in Peril: A Nation of Spies?"). Your realtor, the UPS driver, the utility worker fixing the power line outside your house—all of them could be watching you, at the behest of Uncle Sam.

Put you on a watch list. According to the Government Accounting Office, the Federal government maintains more than a dozen "watch-lists" of suspected terrorists—from the Department of Homeland Security's 20,000-name "no-fly" list to the FBI's Most Wanted. Such lists are often full of useless information (the no-fly list includes names like "Ahmed the Tall") and rife with cases of mistaken identity—like the ones that kept Massachusetts Senator Ted Kennedy and Alaska Congressman Don Young from flying last summer.

Demand your grocery bills, bank statements, and library records. Under provisions of the Patriot Act, the FBI can demand business records for anyone deemed "relevant" to an anti-terror investigation (see "Is Privacy 'Patriotic?'"). Organizations that receive such requests are forbidden to notify the people being investigated. Documents obtained by EPIC and the ACLU reveal a list of such requests six pages long. The Department of Justice blacked out all the information on these documents, so the identities and exact number of recipients are unknown.

Monitor your electronic communications. Since the late 1990s, the FBI has used an electronic data-gathering system known as Carnivore to collect data from Internet service providers. (In January 2005, the FBI announced it was no longer using Carnivore, saying that it was able to achieve the same level of surveillance using commercial software.) The NSA's long-rumored Echelon program to monitor satellite communications worldwide became public knowledge in 1998.

Install a "spy" on your computer. In June 1999, FBI agents surreptitiously entered the office of alleged mobster Nicodemo S. Scarfo and planted key-logging software on his computer, to capture the passwords Scarfo typed when encrypting documents—a tactic that was later approved by a Federal court. The FBI has also admitted to a program called "Magic Lantern," which can plant such keyboard bugging devices remotely via the Internet.

Employ high-tech eavesdropping devices. The Feds have ways of spying on you that go way beyond wiretaps, cell phone scanners, and hidden microphones. They can use thermal imagers that detect body heat through the walls of your home (though a warrant is usually required) or read what's on your computer screen via the glow of your monitor against the wall.

Take Leave of Your Census

The Annoyance: I got a U.S. census form in the mail that asked me a bunch of highly intrusive questions—from my national ancestry and level of education, to how much money I make and whether I have flush toilets in my home. Do I have to answer these questions? And if I do, how safe are my answers?

The Fix: Gotta answer? Yep. Safe? More or less. The census was originally created to gather information about the U.S. population for the purpose of creating new Congressional districts, which of course, are based on population. Over the years, however, it's expanded to serve a wide range of other uses, such as calculating how to distribute funds for government programs like Medicaid or where to build future roads and schools. The data is also used extensively by businesses—for example, Starbucks uses census data to determine where to plant its next coffee franchise. Not surprisingly, the amount of information the Census Bureau gathers has grown dramatically. And instead of gathering this data once every 10 years, the Bureau now collects data from different households every month.

In 2000, U.S. citizens received either a short form survey (7 questions) or a long form (53 questions). Starting in 2005, the Bureau will distribute the long form under a new name (the American Community Survey) to 250,000 U.S. households each month (see Figure 6-2). The short form will continue to be mailed to every household every 10 years and will be used solely to determine Congressional representation.

The problem? Census data has occasionally been abused. It played a pivotal role in the identification and internment of Japanese Americans during World War II. More recently, the Department of Homeland Security (DHS) requested information from the 2000 Census regarding the makeup of Arab populations in the U.S. Bureau spokesman Stephen Buckner says the DHS's purpose was benign (the agency wanted to know what languages to use on signs at certain airports), and that this data was already publicly available on the bureau's web site. Still, it prompted the Census Bureau to change its policies; Bureau staff must now get the thumbs up from a higher-up before they release potentially sensitive information.

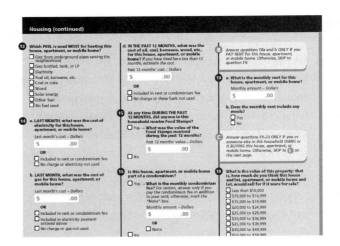

Figure 6-2. Do you heat your home with kerosene? Are you a high school dropout? Do you have trouble dressing yourself? These are some of the questions on the new U.S. Census long form. Approximately one in four households will receive this form in the mail over the next 10 years.

By law, census information is supposed to remain confidential; the Census Bureau does not reveal the names of anyone who fills out a form. Yet marketers combine census data with data gathered from other sources to identify you—a practice known as re-identification, which is perfectly legal. Carnegie Mellon computer scientist Latanya Sweeney has found that 87 percent of the U.S. population can be uniquely identified using just three bits of information (date of birth, gender, and ZIP code). At the very least, private firms can take small units of census data and extrapolate a great amount of detail about your income and interests, if not your actual identity. (For more information on census data and privacy, see EPIC's page at *http://www.epic.org/privacy/census/*.)

Unfortunately, filling out either the community survey or the standard short form is not optional. If you don't return the ACS form you'll get a follow-up phone call, and one in three non-responding households will find a Census Bureau employee on their doorstep. Even leaving some items blank can subject you to a $100 fine, though Bucker says the bureau doesn't usually press the issue. Despite the penalty, one out of three households never mailed back the 2000 census (Buckner says the new ACS has response rates above 97 percent). If the survey questions truly bug you, a hundred bucks is a cheap way to tell the Census Bureau to shove off.

Taking License with Your License

The Annoyance: I've heard that my DMV records—including photos—can be obtained by anyone for practically nothing. Is this legal?

The Fix: Not anymore. The Drivers Protection Privacy Act, a part of the Violent Crime Control and Law Enforcement Act of 1994, made it illegal for DMVs to provide public access to its records, though law enforcement, insurance firms, subpoena servers, and businesses doing ID checks may still access these records in most states. (Whether a business's request is truly legitimate—or anyone at the DMV bothers to check—is another question.) The law was inspired by the 1989 murder of Rebecca Schaeffer, an actress killed by a stalker who obtained her home address through her California DMV records. Later amendments to the law allowed states to sell driver data to marketers, provided they obtain your permission first. Some states, such as Arkansas and Wyoming, are stricter, limiting access to your DMV records to you, government entities, or anyone who has your written permission. (For a directory of state DMV web sites, see *http://www.dmv-department-of-motor-vehicles.com/*.)

Still, privacy advocate Robert Gellman notes such laws may be cold comfort for anyone who's been driving for more than ten years. Because so many states sold motor vehicle records prior to the law's passage, odds are good your information was purchased by marketers years ago.

The Taxman Cometh

The Annoyance: Yikes! I'm about to be audited by the Internal Revenue Service! Is there still time for me to shave my head, change my name, and move to Bolivia?

The Fix: A tax audit can be an incredibly invasive experience, but leaving the country or going underground probably isn't the best strategy for dealing with it. If you're unlucky enough to be audited, there are some things you can do to protect your privacy, says Frederick W. Daily, author of several books on taxpayer rights, including *Stand Up to the IRS* and *Tax Savvy for Small Business* (both from Nolo Press):

- **Hold the audit at a neutral site.** The IRS cannot demand to enter your home or the nonpublic areas of your place of business without a court order, says Daily. (Their aim, of course, is to see if your house or personal possessions jibe with the income you've claimed.) For example, if the IRS is auditing your restaurant, they can sit at a dinner table, but they don't have the right to rummage through your back office.

- **Don't volunteer information.** If you're being audited for the tax year 2002, don't start talking about your income in 2000 or 2003. Tax agents are trained to ferret out information about other years, which could lead to further audits. The exception: if something on the return being audited requires information from a previous tax year—for example, if you need to calculate depreciation for older equipment or property—you might have to delve into the past. Don't linger there.

- **Get representation.** You're entitled to have your accountant or a tax attorney present during an audit, or even have them represent you in absentia. If dealing with the Taxman makes you nervous (and it should), this approach might keep you from revealing too much.

- **Speak to an Advocate.** If the auditor seems especially adversarial or unfair, don't hesitate to contact the IRS's Taxpayer Advocate Service at (877) 777-4778. You may not be able to secure another auditor, but it won't count against you for trying. "The IRS is very concerned about appearing tough but fair," says Daily.

For more information, visit the IRS's Taxpayer Rights page at *http://www.irs.gov/advocate/article/0,,id=98206,00.html.*

It's sad, but oh so true: if you're self-employed, you're more likely to be audited. One way to lower your audit profile is to change your tax status to a partnership, Limited Liability Corporation, or Sub S Corporation, says Fred Daily. Such entities don't have to itemize their deductions on a Schedule C, which usually produces a lower score when IRS computers start trolling for audit candidates. But Daily warns that filing as a corporation can be more costly and complicated than filing as a self-employed person, so only take this step if your self-employment income—and your fear of a tax audit—are substantial.

PRIVACY IN PERIL: LAPTOP LOSSES

A March 2002 audit by the U.S. Treasury Department found that of the 6,600 computers the IRS loaned to private citizens working under the Volunteer Income Tax Assistance (VITA) and Tax Counseling for the Elderly (TCE) programs, about a third went missing. The computers were used by volunteers to help people fill out and file their tax forms electronically. After the audit, not only could the IRS not account for 2,332 of the machines, but the agency couldn't determine whether the personal tax information stored on those computers was ever removed.

The IRS is hardly the only Federal agency to lose its laptops. The Customs service reported losing some 2000 systems, while the Department of Justice put out an APB on about 400 wandering notebooks. Was there classified or sensitive material on any of the MIA machines? Your guess is as good as theirs.

POLITICAL PRIVACY

Vote Yes on Privacy

The Annoyance: I just moved across country, and one of the first things I did was register to vote in my new state. A few weeks later I started receiving phone calls, junk mail, and visits from local party officials. Did somebody take a peek at my voter registration records?

The Fix: They did a lot more than peek. Your voter registration information is part of the public record, though what's in it and who can access it depends on the state where you live. At a minimum, voter rolls contain your name, address, date of birth, and the elections you've voted in (though not whom you voted for). But many states also collect additional information, such as your party affiliation, gender, race, and all or part of your Social Security Number (see Table 6-2).

By Federal law, all 50 states and the District of Columbia must share your voter registration records with political candidates and their parties. The parties then plug this information into massive databases, combine it with other data, and use it to raise money, get out votes, and otherwise harangue you at election time.

Politicos aren't the only ones who have access to your voter data. According to a May 2004 study by the California Voter Foundation (*http://www.calvoter.org/*), 43 states use voter registration lists to find prospective jurors. (In Arkansas, Missouri, and Montana, voter rolls are the *only* source for filling the jury box). Some 22 states allow your registration records to be used for commercial purposes, such as soliciting contributions to the Sierra Club or the National Rifle Association. Most states will withhold or black out the more sensitive information (like your date of birth or SSN) before sharing your records, but not all of them do.

Table 6-2. What's on your voter card?

Info type	States that ask	States that require	States that withhold data from third parties
Name, address, signature	49*	49	0
Date of birth	49	49	11
Phone number	46	18	5
Gender	34	20	0
All or part of Social Security Number	30	13	29
Party Affiliation.	27	27	0
Place of birth	14	11	2
Driver's license number	11	4*	6
Race	9	3	0

ᵃ Data for Wyoming and North Dakota was unavailable.
ᵇ Will be mandatory for all states by 2006.
Source: California Voter Foundation, May 2004

Worse, the study found that 38 state voter registration forms ask for information that isn't required by state law, and only 13 forms contain notices that this information is optional. For example, although 46 states ask for a phone number, only 18 legally require it. Some 30 states ask for your Social Security Number, but only 8 states demand the whole number and only 5 require the last four digits. (Eventually, however, all states will require part of your SSN or your driver's license number, in order to comply with the Help America Vote Act of 2002.) So when you register to vote, your first line of defense is to only hand over information that's legally required. A good option is to use the "Motor Voter" form created under the National Voter Registration Act of 1993. This form limits the amount of information states can collect, leaving out fields like place of birth or school district that standard state forms may include (see Figure 6-3). Only three states (New Hampshire, Wisconsin, and Wyoming) won't accept the NVRA form in place of their own. You can download the form, along with 30-plus pages of notes detailing the requirements for each state, at *http://www.fec.gov/votregis/pdf/nvra.pdf*.

Figure 6-3. Drive-by voting...

> # tip
>
> Want to take your name off the public voter rolls (but still vote)? You may have that option, depending on where you live and your personal circumstances. According to the California Voter Foundation, 27 states give certain individuals the right to remove their name and/or address from voter registration records provided to third parties. Generally, this right is reserved for people in sensitive public positions, such as law enforcement officers and judges, those who can prove they've been the victim of domestic violence, or people at risk from stalkers. The department that handles such requests varies from state to state, but start your search by contacting your local county election board.

Voters for Sale

The Annoyance: I want to participate in the electoral process, but I don't want to give up my personal information to perfect strangers for the privilege. Just who can look up my voter registration record?

The Fix: Any citizen can visit your local board of elections and look up your paper record. And as of November 2002, 11 states let you look up anyone's voter registration info online for free, according to the California Voter Foundation study. While this makes it a snap to confirm you are indeed registered and find the correct polling place, it could also make it easier for strangers to look you up.

Most states require you to enter a PIN, part of your Social Security Number, or your date of birth before you can look at the records; others require only a name or street address. Seven states display only the polling place of the voter you look up, but four (both Carolinas, Delaware, and Georgia) display the voter's street address and sometimes a lot more. In North Carolina, for example, you can look up anyone's record by their name and view their gender, race, party affiliation, and whether they've voted recently. If you have their date of birth, you can also obtain their street address. The only way to remove your name from the state's online rolls is if you've got a court order stating you're the victim of domestic abuse or stalking, according to Don Wright, general counsel for the North Carolina State Board of Elections.

If you're willing to fork over some dough, you can get a lot more voter information. Sign up with Aristotle International's Voter Lists Online (*http://www.voterlistsonline.com*), and you can buy highly-specific lists of registered voters at $25 per 1000 names from nearly any state in the union. For example, you can buy the names and addresses of all 1.5 million registered Republicans in the state of North Carolina for about $38,000. When I narrowed that list to white homeowners

who make more than $50,000 a year and voted at least once in the last four years, Aristotle located 16,485 records (cost: $412.13). Among other things, Aristotle can cull information by state, county, or precinct; party affiliation; yearly income; race and religion; voting frequency; parental status; and political donations (see Figure 6-4).

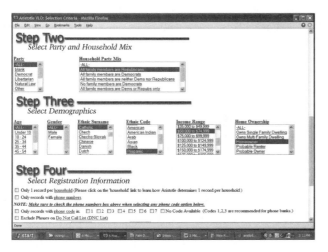

Figure 6-4. Aristotle's Voter Lists Online is your gateway to unearthing all sorts of data about voters based on location, party, income, race, religion, and more.

State laws vary widely on who can access this data and what they can use it for, but Aristotle doesn't make a huge effort to verify your claims. When I signed up, I got an email from an Aristotle representative asking how I was planning to use the information. The answer "research for a book" was good enough. Three states (Florida, Kentucky, and Virginia) don't provide information via Aristotle's site but let you order it by phone. Only Arizona forbids the sale of voter registration information online. (When contacted, Aristotle declined to comment.)

Although Aristotle is the best known service, it's just one of several that mine voter registration information and sell it to virtually anyone, says Kim Alexander, president and founder of the California Voter Foundation. "It's quite a cottage industry with very little oversight," she says. "There are laws on the books preventing re-use of voter data, but they're not being very carefully enforced."

Retail Politics

The Annoyance: Can people see how much I've donated to a political cause or candidate?

The Fix: Depends on how much you gave. If you contribute $200 or more to a single candidate, party, or political organization in any election cycle, the lucky recipient must give the Federal Election Commission your name, employer, the state you live in, the amount you gave, and who you gave it to. (Some organizations report all contributions, regardless of their amount.) Then the FEC (*http://www.fecinfo.com*) and sites like opensecrets.org, PoliticalMoneyLine.com, and CampaignMoney.com make that information available online to anyone who wants it.

For example, a quick search of the top individual donors on opensecrets.org reveals that Joseph and Sue Ellen Canizaro of New Orleans gave nearly $270,000 to Republican candidates in the 2004 election cycle, while the Democrats received around $258,000 from Jeffrey and Francesca Cooper of Edwardsville, Illinois. But that's pocket change compared to total contributions to political organizations (known as "527" groups, because their activities are governed under Section 527 of the Internal Revenue Code) made by liberal George Soros ($24 million) or conservative Bob Perry ($4.5 million). Wondering about your neighbors' or coworkers' political persuasions? You can get a list of donors by ZIP code, employer, occupation, and much more.

This isn't necessarily a bad thing—it's beneficial to society to know who's buying our politicians, and for how much. But right now there's a small loophole you can use to protect a dollop of your privacy. Although the FEC keeps a cumulative record of all your contributions, it doesn't provide electronic records for donations under $200 per candidate or group, says Larry Noble, executive director for the Center for Responsive Politics, which runs opensecrets.org. (Although he adds that the FEC could change its policy at any time.) If you want to keep your political leanings more private, you could spread your bets by making a series of small donations over time or donate small amounts to a range of like-minded organizations. Instead of writing a check for $2000, write 10 checks to various orgs for $199 each; though some of these donations may show up online, it's less likely. You could also funnel money to a nonpartisan group that's not required to report to the FEC—such as the United States Chamber of

Commerce—that devotes considerable resources to political causes. And, of course, you can volunteer your time in unlimited quantities, a form of contribution that isn't recorded by the FEC. (For a citizen's guide to FEC rules, see *http://www.fec.gov/pdf/citizen_guide_pub.pdf*).

Report an Unfair Market

It's illegal for anyone to use political donor databases for marketing purposes—so if someone sees you've given $95K to the RNC and tries to sell you a yacht, you can report them. If you feel your information was used illegally, file a complaint with the FEC at *http://www.fec.gov/pages/brochures/complain.shtml*.

LOCAL LAW ENFORCEMENT

Your Papers, Please

The Annoyance: There I was, just standing on the street minding my own business, when a cop stopped and demanded my identification. Am I required to give it to him?

The Fix: Technically no, though you may be required to state your name or risk spending time in jail. In Hiibel v. Nevada (2004), the U.S. Supreme Court upheld a Nevada court ruling that police may request identity in cases where officers have a reasonable suspicion of wrongdoing. According to Privacy International, 21 states have laws that allow police officers to conduct a "*Terry stop*," named for a landmark 1968 Terry v. Ohio decision that allowed police to frisk individuals if they have a reasonable suspicion the person is involved in criminal activity or poses a threat to them. In a Terry stop, an officer can ask for your identity if he or she can explain to a judge later what you were suspected of doing wrong. (Critics of the Terry decision claim it has been used as a pretext for police harassment, particularly of minorities—as in the classic traffic stop for "driving while black.") However,

the Supreme Court ruled in Hiibel that you're not required to flash an ID, just to give your correct name. Otherwise, you generally have the right to remain silent—at least until the Supreme Court decides to revisit the Miranda decision.

But if you're behind the wheel of a car or other vehicle, you're required to provide proof that you're licensed to operate said vehicle, as well as proof of ownership and insurance. Refusing to provide these documents could quickly land you in the slammer.

Anyone who's watched a cop show on TV can probably recite the Miranda warning by heart. ("You have the right to remain silent; anything you say can and will be used against you in a court of law..."). What you probably don't know is that Miranda only comes into play after you've been detained. (You'll know you've been detained when you ask if you can leave and the cops say no.) So if you spill the beans to a cop prior to being arrested, this information can be used against you later; the lack of a Miranda warning is no defense. If you can help the police investigate a crime, by all means do it—but not at the expense of your Constitutional rights.

NATIONAL ID: YOUR LICENSE TO LIVE?

Among other things, the National Intelligence Reform Act passed in December 2004, and the "Real ID Act" approved by the House in March 2005, mandate the creation of a national standard for driver's licenses. Many privacy advocates believe this is a big step toward a mandatory national identification card—what privacy guru Robert Ellis Smith has dubbed a "license to live."

Showing a state-issued ID is already required for boarding an airplane and buying alcohol or cigarettes; depending on where you are, it may also be required for voting, buying firearms, cashing a check, checking into a hotel, and opening a P.O. Box. These common practices may make driver's licenses the de facto ID for many other everyday events.

The NIRA also requires licenses to be "machine readable," which could lead to the use of Radio Frequency identification chips in licenses (see Chapter 5, "All RFID, All the Time"). An RFID chip could broadcast the information on your license to *any* scanner, making it relatively easy for others to track your movements. (For an idea of what people can learn from your license right now, see Figure 6-3.) Under these new laws, licenses would still be issued by individual states, but would contain similar data and be searchable via a nationwide database. A coalition of more than 40 liberal and conservative groups unsuccessfully opposed the driver's license provisions of the NIRA, arguing that it would do little to prevent terror but would greatly increase the ability of government to track the movements of law-abiding citizens. The laws would also make it easier for the government to deny someone a license—and by implication, deny that person the ability to fly, vote, buy booze, or enjoy other privileges of citizenship. And, of course, you wouldn't be able to drive.

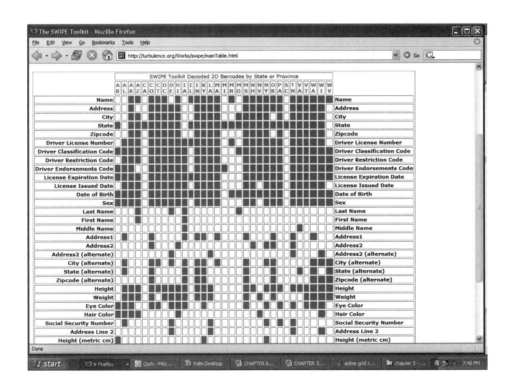

Table 6-3. Book 'em Danno. In many states, even the innocent must jump through hoops to clear their records.

State	Automaticaly destroys arrrest records after acquittal	Must petition court to seal or destroy record	Records remain, but you can deny arrests	Can request some criminal convictions be sealed
Alaska		✗		
Arizona		✗		
California		✗		
Colorado	✗	✗		
Connecticut	✗			
Delaware		✗		
District of Columbia		✗		
Florida		✗		
Hawaii		✗		
Illinois		✗		
Indiana		✗		
Louisiana	✗			
Massachusetts			✗	✗
Missouri	✗			
Nevada		✗		✗
New Jersey				✗
New York	✗			
Ohio				✗
Oregon				✗
Rhode Island	✗			
South Carolina	✗			
Tennessee	✗			
Utah		✗		✗
Virginia				
Washington		✗		
West Virginia	✗			

Source: *Compilation of State and Federal Privacy Laws.* Reprinted by permission of *Privacy Journal, http://www.privacyjournal.net*

You're Under Arrest—Forever

The Annoyance: I was arrested for a crime but the case never made it to court. Yet my local county courthouse still has a record of my arrest. Can this come back to haunt me if I apply for a job? How can I get my record cleared?

The Fix: At press time, there was no Federal law regarding arrest records, so what you can and can't get expunged depends entirely on the state where you got pinched. Some 34 states have laws on the books regarding arrest records, and they all differ in certain regards (see Table 6-3). If you've been arrested by the Feds and gone to trial, even if you've been acquitted, the court documents will be available for 7 cents a page via the Public Access to Court Electronic Records (PACER) service (*http://pacer.psc.uscourts.gov*).

Some states, such as Louisiana and South Carolina, automatically seal or destroy arrest records if you've been acquitted or the charges were dropped. In other states, such as Alaska or Washington, you must petition the court to destroy or seal your arrest records, even if you've never been convicted. Maryland and Massachusetts won't expunge the records but if you've been acquitted of a crime, you can legally say "no" if a potential employer asks if you've ever been arrested. Some state laws merely prohibit employers from gaining access to your arrest record, while others have no guidelines regarding arrest records and privacy. For a guide to privacy laws nationwide, order *Compilation of State and Privacy Laws* published annually by the Privacy Journal ($35, *http://www.privacyjournal.net/work1.htm*). This handy guide contains summaries and the relevant section numbers of the laws in each state. You can also find links to the laws of all 50 states at Cornell University Law School's Legal Information Institute site (*http://www.law.cornell.edu/statutes.html*), organized by state or topic.

Escaping the Long Arm of the Law

The Annoyance: When I was young and stupid I had a few run-ins with Johnny Law. Now that I'm old and respectable, I'd like to bury my past. Can I hide my youthful indiscretions or are they permanent blots on my record?

The Fix: As with arrest records, a mish-mash of state laws controls your ability to erase your criminal past. Nearly all states allow you to seal records of arrests and convictions that occurred while you were still a minor. In general, however, it's a lot harder to quash records of crimes you've been found guilty of as an adult. There are even commercial firms that make this data available for a fee (see Figure 6-5).

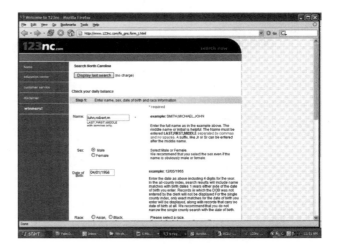

Figure 6-5. Many states make it possible for anyone to look up your criminal record online, either directly or through a private company such as 123nc.com, above. For $15, you can purchase criminal records on anyone in North Carolina, whether they've committed a traffic violation or murder.

But it's not impossible, especially if the crimes are fairly minor and you don't have an extensive criminal history. First-time offenders in Ohio and Oregon, for example, can petition the court after their release and ask that the conviction be expunged or "deemed not to have occurred." Or you may simply have to wait a while. Massachusetts and Nevada will expunge felonies from your record 15 years after your release, assuming you kept your nose clean in the interim. (For more information on expunging criminal records, see EPIC's page at *http://www.epic.org/privacy/expungement/*.)

If your state doesn't allow you to expunge or seal your criminal records, you could ask for a pardon from the governor. In most cases, you must have served your sentence in full, demonstrated that you're rehabilitated, and supply substantial amounts of personal information as well as testimonials from others. If you've committed a Federal offense, your pardon will have to come from the President. Good luck.

Pull Over and Show Me Your DNA

The Annoyance: The police took a swab of my DNA for use in a criminal investigation. What happens to this information? Is my genetic code permanently on file? Can I refuse to provide a sample or demand it be destroyed immediately after the investigation is concluded?

The Fix: For more than 15 years, law enforcement agencies have been gathering DNA samples to identify criminals and exonerate the wrongfully convicted. Cops can get their hands on your genetic code a number of ways. According to Smith Alling Lane (*http://www.dnaresource.com*), which runs a site devoted to DNA forensics policy, all 50 states take a DNA swab when you're convicted of violent crimes such as rape and murder; more than half may take samples if you've committed certain misdemeanors, and four states (California, Louisiana, Texas, and Virginia) collect your genes if you're merely *arrested* for certain felonies (see Table 6-4).

Table 6-4. Your DNA code versus the penal code.

Police collect your DNA if...	Number of states[a]
You've been convicted of a sex crime or murder	50
You're already incarcerated	48
You've been convicted of any felony	38
You're a juvenile offender	32
You've been convicted of certain misdemeanors	26
You're on probation or parole	22
You've been arrested for a violent crime	4

[a] As of December 2004

Source: Smith Alling Lane (dnaresource.com)

They can also ask you to voluntarily surrender your genetic code to help in a criminal investigation. But collecting the DNA of innocent people is problematic. For one thing, it's not very effective, says Sam Walker, a professor of criminal justice at the University of Nebraska in Omaha. In a report published in September 2004, the University's Police Professionalism Initiative looked at 18 cases where the cops conducted a "DNA sweep" and found only one where genetic evidence helped to nab a suspect.

More importantly, DNA sweeps may violate fundamental privacy protections against unreasonable search and self-incrimination. If you refuse to provide a sample, you may automatically become a suspect in a case, or at least suffer embarrassment in front of friends, family, or co-workers. "When you do an intrusive search on someone who's not a suspect, you're violating their basic Fourth Amendment rights," says Walker.

PRIVACY IN PERIL: TAILING BY SATELLITE

Think the police are following your car? They could be—and without ever leaving the squad room. In January 2005, a U.S. District Court judge in New York ruled that the police could attach GPS tracking devices to vehicles without authorization from a court. The devices can then be used to map the subject's movements remotely via satellite. In a drug case involving an attorney and a local Hells Angels Motorcycle Club, Judge David Hurd ruled that the police could affix a tracking device to the attorney's car without a warrant, because people had "no reasonable expectation of privacy" while driving on a public road. The ruling is only binding for cases tried in the Northern District, which includes most of upstate New York, but privacy advocates fear other judges will use it as grounds for allowing increased government surveillance in their districts.

Once you give up a DNA sample, you may have no control over what happens to it. Some jurisdictions destroy the sample but retain a digital snapshot of it, which can be used to identify you in the future. Others maintain the actual genetic sample, which could stay on file for years. Most states put some legal restrictions on who can access your DNA, but they vary widely.

Nearly two dozen Louisiana men who volunteered DNA samples during a 10-month hunt for a serial killer have sued the state to get their samples back. So far the state has denied their request, despite the fact the killer was caught and convicted. In the mid-1990s, the state of Michigan lost a similar suit; innocent suspects in that state may now have their DNA samples destroyed after an investigation has been completed.

DNA does more than identify you. It can indicate a propensity for particular diseases—something an employer or insurer might pay to know—as well as who's related to whom (something you may not want to know). With advances in science, DNA samples could eventually reveal behavioral tendencies, ethnicity, addictive disorders, or other personal characteristics having nothing to do with law enforcement. Think twice before giving up your DNA voluntarily, and familiarize yourself with your state laws regarding genetic privacy. The American Society of Law, Medicine, and Ethics maintains a highly detailed guide to the DNA database laws of all 50 states (see Figure 6-6) including grounds and methods for expunging your DNA records (see *http://www.aslme.org/ dna_04/grid/statute_grid.html*). For more information on DNA privacy in general, see EPIC's Genetic Privacy page (*http://www.epic.org/privacy/genetic/*).

	Alabama	Alaska	Arizona	Arkansas
Adult Qualifying Offenses	Ala. Code § 36-18-24	Alaska Stat. § 44.41.035	Ariz. Rev. Stat. § 13-610	Ark. Code Ann. § 12-12-1
Are All Felonies Included as Qualifying Offenses?	Yes	Yes	Yes	Yes
Are Misdemeanors Included as Qualifying Offenses?	Yes	Yes	Yes*	Yes
Misdemeanor Sex Crimes	Sexual misconduct Sexual abuse (2°) Indecent exposure Enticing child to enter place for immoral purposes	Sexual assault (4°) Sexual abuse of minor (4°) Indecent exposure (2°) Promoting prostitution of minors (3°)	Sexual assault of spouse (judge can downgrade to misdemeanor) Indecent exposure (3rd violation) Public sexual indecency (3rd violation) [Offense for which one must register as a sex offender]	Public sexual indecenc Indecent exposure Sodomy Sexual assault (4°) Failure to report computer ch
Misdemeanor Violent Crimes	Criminally negligent homicide Assault (3°) Menacing Reckless endangerment Criminal coercion Unlawful imprisonment (1°) Unlawful imprisonment (2°) Domestic violence (3°)	Assault (4°) Reckless endangerment Stalking (2°) Custodial interference (2°)	Unlawful imprisonment of minor	Repeat offense of a misdem "involving violence"
Misdemeanor Property Crimes	***	***	***	***
Miscellaneous Misdemeanors / Notes	***	***	*Those convicted of a misdemeanor can petition the court for expungement of the sample from the database	***
Inclusion of Juveniles	Ala. Code § 36-18-24	Alaska Stat. § 44.41.035	Ariz. Rev. Stat. § 13-610	Ark. Code Ann. § 9-27-3
Are Juveniles Adjudicated Delinquent (Or Its Equivalent) Included in the Database?	Unclear. The statute applies to "persons convicted" of a qualifying offense. However, other statutes (§ 12-15-102 and § 15-20-27) provide for DNA to	Yes. The statute applies to juveniles tried as adults, and juveniles 16 yrs. or older adjudicated delinquent.	Yes. The statute applies to juveniles adjudicated delinquent.	Yes. The statute applies to ju adjudicated delinquent for sp sexual and violent offens

Figure 6-6. What happens to your genetic code once the cops get their hands on it? The American Society of Law, Medicine, and Ethics maintains a handy guide to state laws regarding DNA databases.

SPOOKS AND SNOOPS

G-Man Spam

The Annoyance: I recently got an email purportedly from the FBI saying that my IP address "had been logged" and that I'd been caught illegally sharing files. Is this some idiot's idea of a joke?

The Fix: Yes, it's a hoax. But it's much worse than a joke, because some copies of this message contained a variant of the Sober worm. If you've gotten one of these, the FBI urges you to forward it to the Internet Fraud Complaint Center (*http://www.ifccfbi.gov/index.asp*) and to delete the original. Of course, this doesn't mean the FBI isn't watching you—the feds are actively investigating file swappers and purveyors and consumers of child pornography, along with terrorists—but if they were, they wouldn't send you an email warning you about it.

Are the Feds Tapping Your Phone?

The Annoyance: Call me paranoid, but I swear the FBI is tapping my phone. How can I find out? Can I kill the tap by switching to a voice over IP phone (VoIP)?

The Fix: It's possible your line is bugged, but unless you're a drug kingpin or a terrorist mastermind, it's not very likely. If a private entity is tapping your phone—say your spouse or a business competitor hired someone to spy on you—you can ask the phone company to examine your line for illegal listening devices. But if the cops or the Feds have you wired, there's no legal way to find out. Unlike in the movies, they don't need to break into your home and install a bug in your phone—they can tap the line at the phone company's central office, and your carrier isn't allowed to tell you about it. (See Chapter 2, "Is Your Phone Tapped?")

There are different types of taps with varying levels of invasiveness and legal requirements. A *pen register* records numbers or electronic addresses transmitted by the device being tapped—essentially, who the suspect has called or emailed—but not the content of the conversation. A *trap and trace* device captures the same information for incoming communications. (If you have one you usually have the other, so these are usually referred to as a *pen trap*.) An actual wiretap allows investigators to listen in and record conversations,

provided they're relevant to the investigation. Any of these intercepts must be approved by court order, although the requirements for full wiretaps are tougher. Even so, in 2003, not a single wiretap request was refused by a judge.

Law enforcement "intercepts"—which include phone wiretaps, hidden microphones, and monitoring of electronic communications—increased from 1,358 in 2002 to 1,442 in 2003, according to the annual report published by the Administrative Office of the U.S. Courts (*http://www. uscourts.gov/wiretap03/contents.html*). The Center for Democracy and Technology (*http://www.cdt.org/wiretap/ tapstraps.php*) estimates that about ten times as many pen traps are approved each year.

There's a second type of wiretap that's easier to obtain and much more secretive. Under the Foreign Intelligence Surveillance Act (FISA), the government may eavesdrop on agents of foreign powers and suspected terrorists without obtaining a warrant or demonstrating probable cause. These wiretap applications are approved by a secret court made up of 11 Federal judges. In 2003, the FISA Court approved 1,724 wiretaps (out of 1,727 requests), up from 1,228 in 2002.

Can you use VoIP to keep the Feds from listening in? Maybe, but not for long. In August 2004, the FCC ruled that VoIP service providers must allow wiretaps on their networks. Some vendors have already configured their voice networks to allow law enforcement access; others were due to follow sometime in 2005.

PRIVACY IN PERIL: A NATION OF SPIES?

When two Secret Service agents knocked on the apartment door of A. J. Brown, a 19-year-old freshman at Durham Technical Community College in North Carolina, she thought they were door-to-door salesmen. But when they started asking pointed questions about an anti-Bush poster hanging on her wall, she realized that their October 2001 visit was no sales call. Because they had no search warrant, Brown refused to let them inside, though she spent about 40 minutes at the door answering questions.

The agents told her they'd received a tip that she had a poster on her wall depicting the President with a noose around his neck. (In fact, the poster depicted then-Governor Bush as a hangman, to protest the execution of 152 inmates during his term as governor of Texas.) Someone, whom the Secret Service refused to identify, had seen the poster and alerted them to it.

An isolated incident? Not exactly. In January 2002, the U.S. Department of Justice announced the formation of the Terrorism Information and Prevention System (TIPS), which was intended to create a network of spies using utility workers, cable repairmen, mail carriers, and others whose professions brought them inside people's homes. The plan was met with an immediate storm of protest, and Congress quickly killed it.

But TIPS lives on in smaller, regional programs that don't have direct ties to the Federal government (and thus operate largely outside the scope of Congressional oversight). According to the ACLU's August 2004 report *The Surveillance-Industrial Complex*, several TIPS-like programs are operating in different parts of the nation with names like "Coastal Beacon" (for fishermen in Maine), "Highway Watch" (interstate truckers), and "Community Anti-Terror Training Institute" (CAT-Eyes), a kind of uber neighborhood watch program for East Coast communities. From realtors in Cincinnati to utility workers in Florida, ordinary citizens are being trained to report "suspicious" activity to authorities, though exactly what constitutes suspicious activity, and what happens to these reports, is largely unknown.

A related but even larger problem is when corporations voluntarily share data with Federal agencies without telling their customers. Because the Feds don't really need to know when you've used your bank's drive-thru teller or bought a burger at McDonald's, the ACLU has started a letter-writing campaign to ask the biggest corporations in the country to take a "No Spy Pledge." You'll find sample letters, as well as a copy of the ACLU surveillance report, at *http://www.aclu.org/privatize*.

IS PRIVACY "PATRIOTIC"?

No single act of legislation has stirred more privacy concerns than the Patriot Act of 2001. Passed six weeks after the attacks of 9/11 with virtually no Congressional review, the Act has proven extremely contentious—lauded by some as an essential tool in the fight against terrorism, reviled by others as an assault on the Bill of Rights.

The Patriot Act of 2001 took the looser restrictions of FISA and applied them to people who are only tangentially related to a terrorist investigation (see Table 6-5). It expanded the ability of the government to conduct secret searches and wiretaps on ordinary citizens, and allowed prosecutors to use this evidence in criminal cases. In some circumstances, the Act bypasses judicial oversight entirely, leaving it to the Feds to decide who's an appropriate target. (That's particularly troubling in light of the Department of Justice's admission in September 2000 that it had provided 75 pieces of false information in various FISA requests since the law was enacted in 1978.)

It has been nearly impossible for American citizens to learn the scope and extent of how the Act has been applied. Requests for information filed under the Freedom of Information Act have largely been rebuffed by the Department of Justice. At press time, 375 communities in 43 states had passed resolutions opposing the Patriot Act. Thinking of moving? The ACLU has a handy map at *http://www.aclu.org/resolutions*.

Many of the Act's most controversial provisions are scheduled to expire (or "sunset") at the end of 2005. As this book was being prepared, a battle was brewing in Congress over whether to renew those provisions or even expand them. Table 6-5 summarizes the key sections of the Patriot Act and how they could erode your personal privacy. It's not a pretty picture.

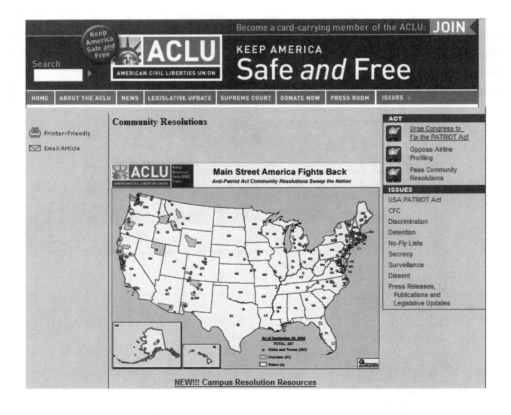

Table 6-5. The Patriot Act and your privacy.

Section of the Act	What's affected	What the Act does	Caveats
215	"Business records" maintained by your bank, doctor, ISP, library, school—just about any entity that has data on you.	Allows FBI to demand personal records for "terror-related" investigations. The FISA Court cannot deny such requests. Anyone receiving a demand can't tell you about it, so you can't challenge its legality.	U.S. citizens can't be investigated solely because of First Amendment activities (in other words, to suppress political dissent). Sunsets at the end of 2005.
505	"Business records" maintained by your bank, doctor, ISP, library, school—just about any entity that has data on you.	Allows FBI to deliver "National Security Letters" demanding your records without any judicial oversight. As with Section 215, it can apply to anyone the Feds deem relevant to a terror investigation, and the subject cannot be notified of (or challenge) the demand.	A Federal judge struck down this provision in September 2004; the government is expected to file an appeal in 2005.
206	Phone and electronic communications.	Authorizes use of "roving wiretaps" so that Feds can bug any communications device used by a suspect (and anyone else) in any location.	Sunsets in 2005.
218	Searches of home and personal property.	Expands secret searches without probable cause under FISA. Information can be shared between intelligence and criminal investigators—allowing evidence obtained without a warrant to be used in criminal cases.	Some requests have been denied by the FISA Court. Sunsets in 2005.
213	Searches of home and personal property.	Expands the FBI's ability to conduct secret "sneak and peek" searches without a warrant. The Feds can delay notifying the subject of a search indefinitely, if a court agrees.	In July 2003, the House voted to de-fund this provision of the Act, but this was later undone by the Senate. There is no sunset clause.
220	Your email, electronic records, and web surfing habits.	Allows FBI to obtain a single search warrant from a friendly judge and apply it to all jurisdictions in the U.S., and applies to criminal as well as terrorism investigations.	Sunsets in 2005.

Sources: ACLU, Center for Democracy and Technology, Electronic Frontier Foundation, Slate.com

What's in Your Files?

The Annoyance: Back in the day, I used to give Uncle Sam hell. I'm sure I've got an FBI file a mile long. How can I find out what the Feds know about me?

The Fix: There's virtually nothing you can do to keep the Feds from spying on you, but you can usually get a general idea of what information they've collected. In 1966 Congress passed the Freedom of Information Act, which allows any citizen to obtain any information gathered about them by the executive branch and the agencies that serve it. (The Act has been updated several times since.) The FOIA, however, doesn't apply to the courts, Congress, or any agency that acts as a consultant to the President (such as the Office of the Vice President). An agency may deny your request or limit the type of information it shares, if the information is classified or otherwise covered under one of the Act's nine exemptions.

The rules for filing a FOIA request can be complicated. George Washington University's National Security Archive offers an easy-to-follow guide and sample letters at *http://www2.gwu.edu/~nsarchiv/nsa/foia.html*. Here are some quick tips on filing a FOIA request:

- **Pick the right agency.** Unfortunately, you can't just send one blanket request to an address in Washington, DC and expect to get anything useful in return. You must query each agency individually, so pick the ones that are relevant to your situation. For example, if you believe you're been the victim of domestic surveillance, you'll have better luck with the FBI (see Figure 6-7) than the CIA, since the latter doesn't maintain clandestine operations in this country (as far as we know, anyway). Each bureaucracy has its own FOIA rules and forms, which you can usually find on the agency web site. The FBI's FOIA site can be found at *http://foia.fbi.gov/*; for links to other Federal agency sites, visit FirstGov at *http://www.firstgov.gov*.

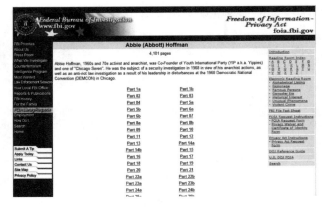

Figure 6-7. Think the FBI has been spying on you? You're in good company. The agency maintains a web site "reading room" detailing the records it has maintained on many famous folk, from Einstein to Elvis—all made available through someone's Freedom of Information Act request.

- **Don't forget the Privacy Act.** This 1974 law gives you the right to request records, correct or expunge inaccurate ones, and to sue if the agency refuses you access. But it's more limited than the FOIA in the types of records you can access—for example, under the Privacy Act you can only ask for records that relate to you personally. So you may want to cite both Acts when you make your request.

- **Be as specific as possible.** Give names, places, dates, and any aliases you may have used. Depending on the request you may also need to submit a notarized signature, your Social Security Number, date of birth, histories of where you've lived and where you've traveled, and other personal information. Just remember: if they didn't have this information before, they'll have it now.

- **Bring your wallet.** Under the FOIA, the first two hours an agency spends researching your request, as well as the first 100 pages of copies, are free. Beyond that, it's allowed to charge for research and copies. If you suspect your records are voluminous but your budget isn't, you can specify the maximum amount of money you'd like to pay, and the agency will search until it hits that limit. You can also ask the agency to waive fees if making the information public would serve a scholarly, historic, or current public interest.

- **Apply online.** Many agencies provide a web-based form that you can submit electronically, saving you time and hassles. But be sure to print out a copy or save the form to your hard disk—you may need it later if your request is delayed or denied.

- **Prepare to wait.** Federal agencies have up to 20 business days to respond to your request and tell you if it's been accepted or denied under the law's many exceptions. But with such a huge backlog of requests—and more than 3.2 million new ones in 2003—finding out what's actually in your file will usually take much longer. According to the Department of Justice's 2003 annual report, response times ranged from a median of 22 days (for the Department of Commerce) to 312 days (Department of State).

IF THE FEDS COME A-KNOCKIN'...

In July 2004, members of the FBI Joint Terrorism Task Force paid a visit to three young political activists in Missouri, to inquire about upcoming protests at that summer's political conventions. When the young men refused to cooperate, they were put under surveillance and ordered to appear before a grand jury. According to a *New York Times* report, more than 40 political activists across the country received similar visits.

Such visits are part of a pattern of deliberate political intimidation, says Denise Lieberman, Legal Director of the ACLU of Eastern Missouri, who represented the young men.

Fortunately, when law enforcement shows up your doorstep, you have more rights than when they stop you on the street or in your car. Here's what to do if the coppers or G-men ring your bell.

Step outside and shut the door. Don't invite them in. If there's anything in plain view that might constitute evidence of a crime, they can search your premises, no warrant required.

Ask for ID. How do you know they're really cops or FBI agents? Write down all their badge information. Most agents carry business cards, so ask for them.

Ask to see a warrant. A search warrant will specify what they're looking for, which will limit where they can look. (For example, if they're looking for a stolen TV, they can't rifle your medicine cabinet for illegal drugs—or, at least, use the evidence against you). An arrest warrant must specify who is being arrested. Make sure it's really you they want before they slap the cuffs on.

Don't give silent consent. If there's no warrant and you don't want them to search your home, say so. You must affirmatively state that you do not consent to a search. Simply allowing agents into your home may constitute consent, unless you tell them no first (which is why you want to step outside).

Don't volunteer information. Once you find out what the agents want, you can decide if you want to talk. You're not legally obliged to say anything. But if you want to talk, don't do it there. Smile politely and say you'd be happy to schedule an appointment for you *and your attorney* to speak with them at their offices.

Record the event. If you've got a handheld recorder, use it to record your interaction. If not, take notes about what happened after the agents have left. This information will come in handy later if it turns out you're being unfairly targeted.

Stay cool, calm, and collected. Getting huffy about your rights won't help. The more adversarial you are, the more likely you'll end up with an unhappy result, says Lieberman. Don't try to stop them from performing a search, even if you believe it's illegal. Better to let a judge throw out the evidence later than to have the cops throw you in jail for obstruction.

Find an attorney. Your local bar association (*http://www. abanet.org/legalservices/lris/directory.html*) can put you in touch with a good criminal attorney. If you think you're being targeted for political beliefs or activities, contact your local chapter of the ACLU (*http://www.aclu.org/*).

Of course, you can ignore all of this advice and simply cooperate. If you're not the target of the investigation, that's probably the simplest route you can take. But don't give up your rights without a good reason—or we may all soon find we don't have them any more.

PRIVACY BY THE NUMBERS

$175,000
Fee USPS charges marketers to access the automated
change-of-address system

57
Number of questions on the U.S. Census
long form in 2000

3,169
Criminal and secret FISA wiretaps requested in 2003

3
Wiretap requests denied by the courts in 2003

4.1 million
Conversations intercepted under U.S. wiretaps in 2003

375
Number of U.S. communities passing resolutions
condemning the Patriot Act as of March 2005

2, 074,934
Profiles on file in FBI's DNA database as
of November 2004

1
States defining DNA samples as your personal property

*Sources: USPS, U.S. Bureau of the Census, Center for
Democracy and Technology, ACLU, FBI, National Conference
of State Legislatures*

Privacy in the Future

Last August, to dramatize its Total Surveillance Society campaign, the ACLU created a clever, flash-based animation that portrays a future where privacy has been obliterated and data brokers run amok.

In the scene, you hear a man calling a pizza delivery service to order two double-meat pies delivered to his home (see Figure 7-1). You then look over the shoulder of a perky Pizza Palace employee who proceeds to click through a series of screens detailing the customer's medical records, financial history, library loans, travel plans, and recent retail purchases. Because he's got high blood pressure, his insurance company insists on a $20 surcharge for ordering a meat pizza (although the submarine sprout combo is available at a discount).

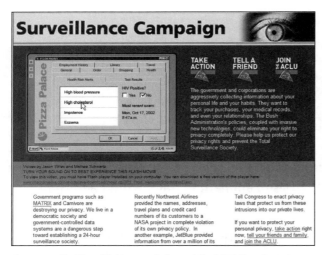

Figure 7-1. Would you like Viagra with that pie? The ACLU's "Pizza" animation imagines a world where your most highly personal information is available to virtually anyone, even the folks at the local pizza parlor.

He lives in a high-crime neighborhood, so she adds $15 to the delivery charge. She sees that his credit cards are maxed out (probably because he charged those airline tickets to Hawaii) and that he wears a 42-inch waist, which entitles him to $3 off a subscription to Total Men's Fitness magazine. At the end, the exasperated man orders the sub sprout combo and agrees to schlep down to the parlor himself. (You'll find the animation at *http://www.aclu.org/pizza/*.)Though a comic exaggeration, this scenario is more feasible than you might imagine. By and large, the technology to acquire and share this type of data exists, while laws protecting most of this data are scarce.

But the future doesn't have to look like this. There are many organizations working on ways to slam spam, foil phishers, keep your identity safe from online thieves, and curb Corporate America's and Uncle Sam's seemingly insatiable appetite for information. Here are some of the more promising approaches toward a more private future.

SLAMMING SPAM

Besides buttinski bosses, nosy marketers, and not-so-benevolent bureaucracies, the root of many privacy ills comes down to email—or, more accurately, spam. For the last five years, unsolicited email has been the delivery mechanism of choice for virus and worm authors. Tens of millions of PCs have been infected worldwide, spawning an epidemic in networks of zombie PCs and other malware infestations.

Meanwhile, the fastest growing privacy threat is phisher scams, a form of spam that looks remarkably like legitimate email from real organizations but is designed to steal your personal information (see Chapter 3, "Don't Bank on It"). A typical phisher email looks like it comes from your bank and usually directs you to a web site, where you're prompted to enter your name and account information. Once you do, it's game over—you've just handed your information to an international crime ring, who will sell it to others, use it to make purchases in your name, or create false identities that can be used by other criminals (see "The Identity Black Market"). And unlike being mugged or losing your wallet, it can be months or even years before you realize what has happened to you.

Around 75 percent of all email is spam, according to estimates by MessageLabs and The Spamhaus Project (*http://www.spamhaus.org*). At the current rate of growth, that could increase to 95 percent by mid-2006.

So stopping spam—or at least slowing the flood to a trickle—is key to protecting your privacy. That's why spam filters are one of the essential tools I recommend in Chapter 3. But down the road, more spam will be stopped before it reaches your inbox, thanks to new authentication systems (e.g., Sender Policy Framework and Yahoo DomainKeys) and reputation systems (e.g., IronPort's SenderBase), which are just starting to ramp up.

ASSURING AUTHENTICATION

Long before commercial spam filters were available, ISP administrators and other uber-geeks created so-called "blacklists" of Internet Protocol (IP) addresses used to send spam. Individuals, ISPs and corporations would then set their email servers to reject any messages coming from these addresses. Once the spam merchants discovered their mail was being automatically rejected, they resorted to devious methods: spoofing, or imitating, legitimate email addresses by faking the return address in the message's "From" field; rerouting email through so-called *open relays* that forward messages while obscuring where they originally came from; and hijacking other machines, so the spam looks like it came from somewhere else. In the dark underbelly of the Net, malware authors do a brisk trade in renting out their networks of zombie PCs—better known as *botnets*—to spammers.

So the first step in solving the spam problem is verifying that the message that says it came from "mom@yourisp.com" really did come from dear old mom and not some vile spammer living in a doublewide in Del Ray Beach, Florida. The process is called authentication—essentially Caller ID for your email. There are various ways to accomplish this, but the technologies with the most momentum behind them are Sender Policy Framework (SPF) and Yahoo DomainKeys.

With SPF, Internet service providers and corporations publish their IP addresses on their domain name servers. When mail arrives at your ISP, its servers check the message's actual IP address against the address given in the "From" field. If the two don't match, your ISP can block the message or send it on to you with a warning. Besides identifying phisher emails, this can solve a problem that has flummoxed nearly every spam filter I've tested: junk email that pretends to be sent from your own email address. (For more on SPF, visit *http://spf.pobox.com/*).

DomainKeys is similar to SPF but it sends an encrypted digital signature along with each piece of mail. Mail servers at the recipient's ISP unlock the encrypted signature to verify the identity of the sender. (For more on DomainKeys, see *http://antispam.yahoo.com/domainkeys*.)

The problem is that today most corporations and ISPs don't use either technology yet. According to a November 2004 survey by security firm CipherTrust, roughly 50 of the Fortune 1000 publish their IP addresses via SPF. Yahoo invented DomainKeys and uses the technology for all its web mail, but it's virtually the only company that did at press time. In February 2005, Qurb released a spam filter for Outlook and Outlook Express that uses SPF to verify email domains; in my experience, Qurb could only identify senders for about 1 out of 10 messages. But that number will surely grow over time (see Figure 7-2).

Figure 7-2. Qurb 3.0's spam filter tells you whether that email really is from who it says it's from—provided the legit sender makes its IP addresses available.

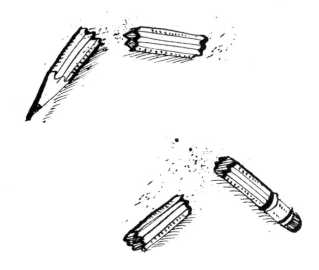

REGARDING REPUTATION

Of course, there's nothing to keep spammers—particularly quasi-legit ones distributing ads for things like cut-rate mortgages and pasta pots—from using sender authentication schemes. In fact, they've already started doing it. So the second piece of the puzzle is a reputation system that lets your ISP or email software know what kind of mail the sender is spewing out.

The largest email reputation system is run by IronPort, which publishes some of its data at a free site called SenderBase (*http://www.senderbase.org*). IronPort analyzes millions of messages every day, then generates a reputation score for each sender, similar to a person's credit score (see Figure 7-3). The score factors in parameters such as the sender's geographical location, how long the address has been active, whether it can receive mail (most spammers won't), and if ISPs have received abuse complaints about the sender. This lets IronPort differentiate between high-volume but legit senders like AOL or Comcast and sites that spring up overnight and begin spewing millions of messages per hour—a likely sign they're a spam house.

Figure 7-3. Reputation systems like IronPort's SenderBase give you the scoop on who's spamming who.

Email administrators can check SenderBase and manually set their servers to accept or reject messages based on the sender's reputation. IronPort also sells network appliances that let ISPs and corporations automatically access its reputation system, check a sender's score, and throttle down the volume of email they receive from suspect IP addresses. Legit mail will eventually get through (albeit slowly), but spammers generally give up and go elsewhere.

However, longtime anti-spam activist and privacy consultant Ray Everett Church says ideas like SPF and DomainKeys are a good beginning, but only a beginning. "SPF and DomainKeys don't tell you anything about the content of the message or its permission basis," he says. "They don't give you the kind of information you need to make a better decision about whether you want that piece of email." And while reputation systems may help block the sleaziest of spammers, Church believes they're a smokescreen that will ultimately allow commercial e-marketers to flood your inbox with ads.

A longer-term solution? Rewriting the simple mail transfer protocol (SMTP) that governs Internet email so that each message comes with information regarding its authenticity, the type of email it is (transactional, commercial, or personal), and whether the sender has been given permission to send it to you. In October 2004, Church, John Levine, and Vincent Schiavone published a draft memo outlining these concepts with the Internet Engineering Task Force—one of several proposed plans for overhauling the 30-year-old email protocols. But overhauling a system that shuttles 20 billion messages a day is not going to happen soon, if it happens at all.

FOILING PHISHERS

In a perfect world, phisher spam would be turned away at your ISP's mail server and never despoil your inbox. But in the real world, phisher scams and other fraudulent email will occasionally get around even the savviest spam filters. And with pharming, DNS poisoning, and other more insidious threats on the rise (see Chapter 3, "Don't Buy the Pharm"), even savvy users who'd never fall for a phisher email can get nailed. So banks and other financial institutions are trying to make it harder for someone to spoof your identity when you log on, as well as make it harder for scammers to create bogus sites that look like your bank's.

Banks and ISPs are hoping that "two-factor authentication" will do the trick. This scheme combines something you know (such as a password) with something you have (a card or other device). If you've ever withdrawn money using an ATM card and a PIN, you've used two-factor authentication.

Hardware security tokens such as smart cards and computer dongles have been around for 20 years, but they've mostly been issued to employees at security-conscious corporations. By 2007, research firm Gartner, Inc. predicts up to 75 percent of financial institutions will employ some form of additional authentication, whether it's via software, hardware tokens, or an "out-of-band" authentication device such as a cell phone or pager.

In September 2004, America Online and RSA Security introduced the AOL PassCode service, which employs a keychain fob that produces a new six-digit code every minute. Users log onto their accounts using both a password and the dynamically generated number. The PassCode service costs $2 to $5 a month, depending on the number of screen names on each account, plus $10 for the fob. E-Trade, Yahoo, and Sony Online Entertainment are eyeing similar technology.

Another scheme put forth by RSA Security involves your cell phone. When you log into your bank account, the web site sends a text message containing a numeric code to your phone. You must enter this code, along with your password, in order to gain entry. So far, banks in Europe and New Zealand have implemented this plan, but no U.S. banks have publicly employed it.

Palo Alto, California-based PassMark offers bank customers an easy-to-understand defense against phishers. After you enter your username, you're shown an image (say, a picture of your dog) and asked to enter a pass phrase (e.g., "bad dog,

no biscuit") before you can log on. Such PassMarks can also be put in email, so you know the message really came from your bank (see Figure 7-4).

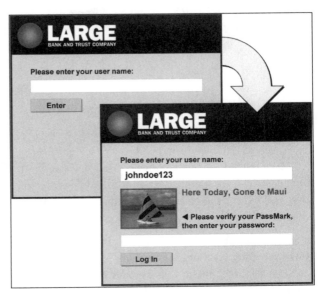

Figure 7-4. With PassMark's authentication scheme, bank customers must enter their username and a pass phrase before they can log in; the image confirms it's really their bank they're talking to.

BOT'S ALL, FOLKS

2004 might well be remembered as the year of the zombie. During the first six months of 2004, Symantec's early warning system detected an average of 30,000 new zombies *every day*. During the last six months of the year, however, the daily average dropped to only 5,000, according to Symantec's March 2005 Internet Security Threat Report.

Why the sudden plunge? One reason is that large regional and backbone service providers have gotten more proactive in identifying botnets and shutting them down, says Alfred Huger, senior director of engineering for Symantec's security response team. Another reason: Windows XP Service Pack 2, which turns on Windows' built-in firewall by default.

"The day SP2 came out, we saw a marked decrease in the number of bots showing up in our system," says Huger. "It's difficult to attribute it to anything else but SP2."

But there's a third, less sunny reason for the drop in bots: the hackers have changed tactics. Systems like Symantec's watch for port scanning, where a zombie PC actively scans ranges of IP addresses looking for unprotected machines. But attackers are increasingly abandoning this scheme for other methods, such as hiding a Trojan horse inside a free downloadable program they can use to hijack your PC, or via "drive-by hacking" where your computer can be infected merely by visiting a web site or viewing a pop-up ad. These new tactics make the number of zombies in the wild much harder to ascertain and defeat.

There's one thing that won't change in the foreseeable future. The best way to fight zombies is to install anti-virus, firewall, and anti-spy apps, and keep them up to date. It's a lousy job, but somebody has to do it—and that somebody is you.

The idea here is that while a phisher scammer could easily create a bogus email message or web site that looks exactly like your banks' home page, they'd find it pretty hard to duplicate your dog (or whatever image you choose). As a second precaution, PassMark assigns a unique ID to every device you use to access your account, then makes sure the device and the account info match up before you can log on.

RATING RISKS

The problem with these authentication schemes is that they solve yesterday's problem, says security guru Bruce Schneier, CTO and founder of Counterpane Internet Security. For example, two-factor authentication does nothing to prevent so-called "Man in the Middle" (MIM) attacks or Trojan horse exploits.

In an MIM attack, the scammer lures you to a fake web site where you enter your log-on information. He then logs onto your bank himself, enters your account info, and transmits information back to you via the phony site—so you can complete your transactions and never know you weren't at your bank's actual site. He can then log back into your account at any time and have his way with it.

A Trojan horse attack uses a zombie PC to accomplish the same deed. The attacker is alerted when you attempt to log onto your bank. He waits until you've finished logging on, then "walks" into the bank with you, where he can do anything he wants with your money.

"Banks are paying far more attention to authentication than they should be," argues Schneier. "They need to worry about transactions, not individuals."

Naftali Bennett agrees. "Simple two-factor authentication represents a sledgehammer approach," says Bennett, CEO of Cyota, which provides Internet security services for 9 of the 12 largest U.S. banks. "We believe authentication should be based on the risk of a given activity."

Cyota's scheme involves highly sophisticated analysis software and a relatively low-tech communications device—the telephone. Cyota's "e-vision" software analyzes every online transaction, examining factors such as the type of transaction and where it originated, then assigns a fraud risk score to each. This is similar to how credit card companies analyze purchase patterns and alert you if, say, your card is used to make purchases in different cities on the same day.

So if you're logging on from home to check your account balance, your risk score would be essentially zero. If someone logs onto your account from an IP address in Ghana and tries to transfer $10,000 to an account in the Caymans, the risk score would shoot through the roof. Depending on the score, the bank can approve the transaction, decline it, or call the customer and ask questions to determine whether everything's legit. At press time, the e-vision system was in trials at three major banks.

Cyota also fights phishers using another clever tactic it calls "dilution." When Cyota's early warning system detects a phishing attack against one of its client banks, its software automatically logs onto the phisher's site and begins feeding it bogus account information. Cyota's bots use a variety of Internet addresses, operating systems, and browsers—they even "type" slowly—to fool scammers into thinking they're a human being. By using multiple bots on each phisher site, they tie up the site's bandwidth so the bank's real customers are unable to log on. The bogus information dilutes the quality of the data the scammer collects, which in turn ruins the scammers' reputation on the identity black market.

Schneier proposes a radical solution banks and consumers might find difficult to swallow: make it harder for people to get credit cards. "Over the decades, the barriers to getting a credit card have become extraordinarily low," he says. "There's nothing you can do technologically to solve the threat. In two years, phishing will be quaint, and the criminals will have moved on to something else. The only thing you can do is to make fraudulent transactions less likely to happen."

INSULATING IDENTITY

Today's Internet consists mostly of computers, web sites, and email systems. Tomorrow's Net will be crammed full of devices from cell phones to toasters, all of them with the ability to share information about you. The possibilities are both extremely cool and a little creepy.

UCLA computer scientist Len Kleinrock sees a future where Net-connected "smart spaces" can instantly identify you, using RFID chips in the walls, floors, and even under your skin.

"When you walk into a room, the room will know you walked into it," says Kleinrock, whose seminal research on computer networks provided the theoretical basis for the Internet. "It will call up your profile and know your privileges and preferences. You'll be able to ask the room questions, and it will display the answers on a screen or as a hologram."

That's the cool part. The creepy part is when the room tries to sell you a time-share, pulls up your outstanding warrants and calls the cops, or simply records everything you say and do there.

So researchers are working on schemes to minimize the flow of personal data across the Net. At the Internet2's Shibboleth Project, computer scientists have created Internet middleware that negotiates transactions between individuals and web sites using the bare minimum of data needed. So if you want to access a school's online library, its web site could use Shibboleth to verify that you're a student without needing to know your name or address. If you're applying for a loan, your bank could find out your identity and your credit score, but not what school you attended or the name of your employer.

"It's based on the usual way we exchange information with strangers," says Ken Klingenstein, director of Internet2's Middleware Initiative. "Say we're on the phone and you tell me that you're an albino hermaphrodite. I might say, 'hey, I'm an albino hermaphrodite too!' When you reveal some information, I'm inclined to reveal more. It's called 'progressive disclosure.' We're trying to find ways to do that electronically."

THE IDENTITY BLACK MARKET

Quick, what's your identity worth? If it's stolen, it can cost you thousands of dollars to undo the damage. But to an ID thief, your identity is worth only $15 to $30—maybe $60 or $70 if you've got a platinum account. That's the going rate on the Net's thriving identity black market.

In chat rooms and underground web sites, cyber criminals barter stolen credit card accounts like baseball trading cards. On these "carder" sites you can download do-it-yourself phisher email kits, rent bot networks, hire spammers, buy and sell stolen card numbers, and locate networks of unwitting accomplices to transfer the money oversees. In October 2004, the U.S. Secret Service's Operation Firewall closed down three carder sites named CarderPlanet, Darkprofits, and Shadowcrew (see Figure 7-5), indicting 19 suspects in seven countries who are charged with stealing more than 1.7 million identities.

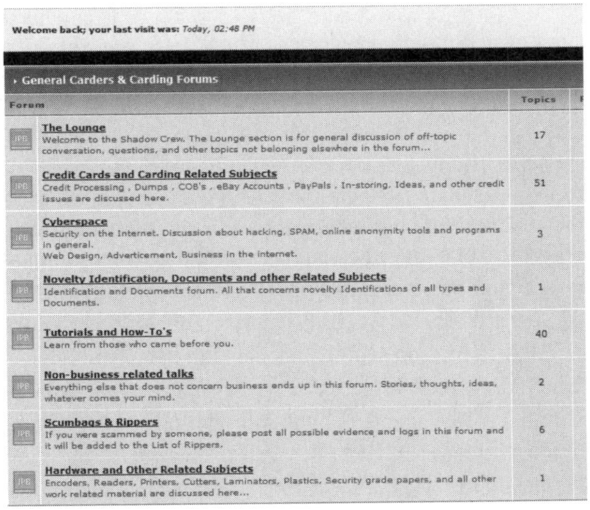

Operation Firewall was the first public bust of a carder network, but it hardly made a dent in the market. One of the sites started back up a few months later under a slightly different name (by press time it had been shut down again). And the real deals get done via private invitations to Internet Relay Chat rooms, which can form instantly and then disappear. But while the Feds were watching the carders, the carders were watching back. One of them hacked into T-Mobile's cell phone servers, gaining access to the files of Secret Service agent Peter Cavicchia, one of the investigators involved in Operation Firewall, who used a T-Mobile Sidekick—a cell phone-

Figure 7-5. Carder site Shadow-Crew.net (now closed) was a bustling marketplace for identity thieves, spammers, phishers, and other denizens of the dark side.

cum-camera-cum-email device. (The hacker also broke into accounts for Paris Hilton, Demi Moore, and other celebrities, then posted their personal address books and photos on the Web.) Cavicchia's e-mail account contained highly-confidential documents including subpoenas, agency memos, and a mutual assistance agreement with Russian law enforcement. He has since resigned from the service. The hacker, 22-year-old Nicholas Jacobsen, pleaded guilty to a single charge of intentionally accessing a protected computer in February 2005; at press time he was awaiting sentencing.

So far, Shibboleth has been employed largely by universities. For example, students at Penn State use it to log onto the school-supplied Napster music service. The system verifies that users are enrolled and eligible to use the service, but doesn't identify them by name.

Klingenstein admits a huge amount of work still needs to be done before systems like Shibboleth become a standard way to negotiate online transactions. A big chunk of that work will be convincing corporations and government agencies that hoarding information can hurt them in the long run.

"The best way for companies to reduce their liability for privacy exposures is to avoid collecting the information in the first place," he says. "They don't necessarily need to know who you are, they just need to know that you have an attribute that's relevant to the service they're offering."

Peter Wayner, programmer and author of *Translucent Databases* (Flyzone Press), has proposed another way web sites could confirm your identity, but without storing information about you that could be sold to marketers, stolen by hackers, or confiscated by the FBI.

Wayner's solution is to build databases using a Secure Hash Algorithm, a one-way encryption scheme that turns information like your name or email address into a randomly generated string of characters. Unlike some encryption schemes, with SHA there's no way to go back and figure out what information was encrypted. When you log in to your Amazon account, an SHA converts that information into the same character string each time; Amazon knows you're the same customer, but they can't unscramble the string to get at your name—and neither can anyone who hacks into Amazon's database. The site can then use your encrypted identity to customize the web site to your liking, send you email offers, or unlock your credit card and shipping information when you purchase something.

Wayner claims the same technology can be used to secure databases for libraries, travel agencies, gambling sites, stock exchanges—virtually any place private transactions are at a premium. Today, however, translucent databases are largely used to secure password files, though Wayner says he knows of one company that uses it to protect its mailing lists from being stolen by clients.

THE CLOCK IS TICKING ON NET ANONYMITY

Researchers at the University of California at San Diego have figured out how to identify specific computers on the Internet from thousands of miles away. In March 2005, computer scientists Tadayoshi Kohno, Andre Broido, and kc claffy published a paper in which they describe how specific machines can be identified by recording microscopic deviations in the device's internal clock. They discovered that every computer, from desktops to handhelds, generates a consistent digital fingerprint, no matter what operating system it uses, how it accesses the Net, or where it's located. This effect can be measured without the owner of the machine being aware of it.

Regardless of what steps you may take to anonymize your surfing, an ISP or web site could identify the exact machine that accessed a particular IP address at a specific time (though they wouldn't necessarily know whose fingers were on the keyboard). At press time the trio was slated to present its findings to a meeting of the Institute of Electrical and Electronics Engineers in May 2005. If their results prove to be genuine, digital fingerprints could become a standard part of electronic surveillance and provide evidence in legal disputes.

WHITHER WASHINGTON?

The climate for personal privacy in Washington, D.C. hasn't been this chilly since the days when J. Edgar Hoover wore pumps. However, there are recent signs the Feds are at least acknowledging the increased threat to privacy, even if they're not doing much to stop it.

In February 2005, the Department of Homeland Security announced the formation of a Data Privacy and Integrity Advisory Committee to consult on "issues that affect privacy, data integrity, and data interoperability in DHS programs." But the 20-member board has drawn criticism for being composed largely of corporate executives, including D. Reed Freeman, chief privacy officer for Claria (makers of the controversial Gator adware application). Many longtime privacy advocates were shut out.

Committee member Jim Harper, director of information policy studies for the Cato Institute and editor of Privacilla (*http://www.privacilla.org*), believes the panel will spur the DHS to think harder about privacy issues. And, he adds, "it will give me and others a microphone and an opportunity to quit loudly if DHS disregards privacy."

In March 2005, the DHS issued a report on its ill-fated Computer Assisted Passenger Pre-screening System II (CAPPS II) in which the agency's Inspector General acknowledged a host of shoddy privacy practices. Among the highlights: the Transportation Safety Agency (TSA) failed to obtain confidentiality agreements with some companies with whom it shared data, and/or failed to enforce such agreements; it allowed passenger records to be transferred between companies unencrypted and without password protection; and the agency publicly denied having actual passenger data in its possession, when in fact it did. However, the report concluded that the agency had not broken any Federal laws.

(The report includes this wonderful slice of bureaucratese: "In 2003 and 2004, TSA officials made inaccurate statements regarding these transfers that undermined public trust in the agency. These misstatements were apparently not meant to mischaracterize known facts. Instead, they were premised on an incomplete understanding of the underlying facts at the time the statements were made." In other words, they lied, but they didn't know they were lying, and even if they did know they were lying, it wasn't their fault.)

THE CAN SPIES ACT?

As this book goes to press Congress is mulling yet another cyber-security bill with a cutesy acronym, this one aimed at spyware. The Securely Protect Yourself Against Cyber Trespass Act (or "SPY ACT") (*H.R. 29*) would make it illegal for spyware companies to hijack your browser, disable your security software, collect personal information, or install software on your computer without your consent. Unfortunately, the bill would do nothing to prevent companies like Claria from obtaining consent via an epic-length end-user license agreement (see Chapter 3, "EULA Be Sorry You Did"). At press time the bill had passed committee but had yet to be voted on by the full House; a similar bill passed the House last year by a vote of 399 to 1.

A competing House bill, the I-SPY Prevention Act of 2005 (*H.R. 744*), would make it a Federal crime to install software or steal personal information from a protected computer without its owner's authorization. The bill also authorizes funds for enforcement and establishes criminal sentences of 2 to 5 years. At press time the bill was still in committee.

The Anti-Phishing Act of 2005 (*S.489*) would make it a crime to send a phishing email or set up a phishing web site, regardless of whether anyone suffered harm from them, but provides no funds to pay for enforcement. It too was in committee at press time.

Bottom line: if passed, these laws will likely have as great an impact on spyware and phisher scams as the CAN SPAM bill did on junk email—allowing Congress to claim it took action, but leaving users in the same leaky boat.

The good news is that the TSA has asked privacy consultants, including security guru Bruce Schneier, to serve on an oversight committee for its Secure Flight proposal, the successor to CAPPS II. The bad news is that a March 2005 report by the Government Accountability Office reveals that the TSA has yet to articulate how it's going to safeguard passenger privacy with Secure Flight, despite plans to launch the service in late summer 2005.

Thanks to the recent, egregious data leaks at ChoicePoint, Acxiom, LexisNexis, and Bank of America, Congress will almost certainly pass some kind of law regarding identity theft. Likely legislation could range from requiring data brokers (see Figure 7-6) to notify consumers when their information has been stolen (what the data brokers are pushing) to making it harder for them to sell sensitive information like Social Security numbers (what the brokers are definitely opposing).

Figure 7-6. Quick—are you a Boomtown Single, a City Startup, or a Middleburg Manager? These are some of the faux categories dreamed up by data vendors like Claritas, who slice and dice demographic data, then sell it for a profit.

The Electronic Privacy Information Center (EPIC), which has been contacted by Congressional offices on both sides of the aisle seeking guidance on ID theft issues, is pushing to expand the Fair Credit Reporting Act to include data brokers like ChoicePoint and Acxiom. Putting data mining firms under the umbrella of the FCRA would provide consumers access to their data, notice about how it's being used, and the ability to correct inaccurate information—which becomes especially vital when that data is used by government agencies to identify possible terrorists.

UNCLE SAM'S SECRET OBSESSION

Despite the Bush Administration's dismal record of protecting personal privacy, there's one area where it zealously guards sensitive information—its own documents. According to the Federation of American Scientists Project on Government Secrecy, the number of documents classified as "secret" by the Bush Administration has jumped 75 percent—from 9 million in 2001 to 16 million in 2004. This administration has granted the Environmental Protection Agency, the Department of Agriculture, and the Health and Human Services department the ability to mark documents as "secret." According to FAS project director Steven Aftergood, thousands of *unclassified* documents have been purged from government web sites and the National Archives in the last three years.

Directives issued by then-Attorney General John Ashcroft in late 2001 instructed Federal agencies to resist Freedom of Information Act requests whenever they could find legal grounds to do so. The result has been an enormous backlog of FOIA requests (see Chapter 6, "What's In in Your Files?") and increasing discomfort on both sides of the political spectrum.

Earlier this year, Senators Pat Leahy (D-Vermont) and John Cornyn (R-Texas) introduced bills to make it easier to file a FOIA request, limit the number of exemptions Federal agencies can claim under the Act, and expedite processing of requests. But given current political realities, any move to loosen the Bush Administration's tight grip on information is a long shot.

Writing for Slate (*http://slate.msn.com/id/2114963/*), Aftergood summed up the situation eloquently: "Information is the oxygen of democracy," he wrote. "Day by day, the Bush administration is cutting off the supply.

PRIVACY POWER

Fundamentally, the problem with privacy boils down to the fact that in the USA you have few (if any) legal rights to your own data. Time and again, courts have ruled that corporations and governments may do what they wish with your information, barring any laws to the contrary. This is in stark contrast to European Union privacy directives, which work on the assumption that data about an individual belongs to that individual, and anyone who wants to use it must ask nicely first.

"The biggest privacy threats are political, not technical," says Bruce Schneier. "They're the fact that you don't own your own data. It's not like it is in Europe, where data collected for one purpose can only be used for that purpose. You have no rights to the data ChoicePoint has about you—no rights to make it accurate or say 'I don't want that data available about me, take it down'."

Yet passing an EU-style privacy law is unlikely and could actually lead to harmful consequences, warns Peter Swire, a professor at Ohio State University's Moritz College of Law and former Chief Counselor for Privacy in the Clinton Administration.

"A lot of European laws are aspirational—they state what they hope people will do," says Swire. "When we pass laws in the U.S., we actually expect people to enforce them. So any overarching Federal law has to be written with great care, so we don't drown our lives in opt-in forms or put limits on data that should be shared. It could apply a level of bureaucracy most Americans wouldn't want."

For more than 20 years, privacy advocate Robert Gellman has argued for the creation of an independent, non-regulatory privacy commission, similar to the early U.S. Commission on Civil Rights, which could act as a privacy watchdog.

"In its early days, the Civil Rights Commission was an opinion leader," he says. "They held hearings and focused the public's attention. An independent privacy commission could comment on what other agencies are doing, could say the President's or Congress's latest proposals are seriously deficient from a privacy perspective. And it could be a great resource for legislators who often know nothing about privacy."

"Giving such an agency regulatory powers would be an enormous challenge," adds Gellman. "I also don't think it's possible to regulate privacy in this country. But I think a lot could be accomplished in a non-regulatory manner."

One reason European countries have such strong privacy protections is that they've seen totalitarian governments up close, says Bill Scannell, a media strategist and creator of the Boycott Delta web site (*http://www.boycottdelta.org/*), which he built to oppose CAPPS II. Scannell says people in this country are naïve about what can happen when a government has too much power and too much information.

"People love to say they care about privacy, but then they're willing to provide a DNA sample in return for a coupon for a free Snickers bar," says Scannell. "Where's the privacy lobby in this country? There isn't one. Part of that is because we've never experienced true totalitarianism. But we are certainly headed in that direction, unless we make some serious policy decisions regarding all of this surveillance technology."

In a post-9/11 world, I believe we need both security and privacy, and that one doesn't necessarily cancel out the other. But we have to start by asserting our own rights to our own data and guarding both of them zealously, before our privacy—and our rights—both disappear.

Index

Symbols

@Backup, 17

A

AACRAO, 109
access, computer, 14
accounts, limited user, 12
ACLU surveillance report, 151
Acme, 122
Acme Rent-a-Car, 116
ACNielsen Homescan, 96
Active Scan software, 55
Acxiom, 6, 39
   data leaks, 166
   hackers and, 9
Ad-Aware, 42
Administrative Office of the
        U.S. Courts, 25, 150
adware/spyware blockers, 38
Aftab, Parry, 77, 92
Aftergood, Steven, 166
AIDS, being tested for, 119
airline baggage, 112
   banned items, 113
   theft, 113
airport security, 114
air travel, 111
Akonix L7 Enforcer, 79
Aladdin Internet Cleanup, 43
Albertsons' pharmacy, 122
Albrecht, Katherine, 96, 98
Alexander, Kim, 143
Amazon, personalization cookie, 60
Americans with Disabilities Act, 5, 84

American Association of Collegiate
        Registrars and Admissions
        Officers, 107
American Association of Physicians and
        Surgeons, 119
American Booksellers Association, 105
American Library Association
   library privacy policies and
        procedures, 106
   web site, 105
American Management Association
        (AMA), 81
American Management Association
        survey, 76
American Power Conversion, 19
American Society of Law, Medicine, and
        Ethics, 149
The Anarchist's Cookbook, 106
Annenberg Public Policy Center
        web site, 59
AnonX, 64
Anonymity Checker web site, 76
Anonymizer web site, 76
anonymous
   call reject, 27
   domain name registration, 70
   email service, 80
   proxy servers, 76, 80
   speech options, 72
Anti-Phishing Act of 2005, 165
antivirus software, 38, 56
   Marx, Andreas, 56
AnyWho, 40
Any Password, 17
AOL
   Guardian, filtering, 66
   PassCode service, 161
   privacy settings, 69

Applied Digital Solutions' VeriChip, 102
Aristotle International's Voter Lists
        Online, 142
arrest records, 84, 147
Ashcroft, John, 166
Association of American Physicians and
        Surgeons, 121
AT&T Wireless "Find Friends" service, 23
ATX Technologies, 8, 116
Australia, privacy protections, 87
Australia and workplace privacy, 87
authentication, 159
   systems, 158
   two-factor, 160
Automated Copyright Notice System,
        109
automobile surveillance, 118

B

Baas, Daniel, 9
background checks, 4, 75, 82
   performing your own, 83
backup files, 16
Bagle worm, 57
banks and privacy, 124–127
   foreign bank accounts, 124
Bank of America data leaks, 166
Bennett, Naftali, 162
Biometric Password Manager, 19
blacklists of IP addresses, 159
black box, 8, 118
blocklists, 48
blogging
   moblogs (mobile web logs), 24
   privacy, and libel, 71
   privacy and, 89

Bluebugging, 24
Bluejacking, 24
Bluesnarfing, 24
Bluetooth viruses, 24
Bluetracking, 24
BMW, 116
Bork, Robert, 103
Boycott Delta web site, 167
Boycott Gillette web site, 104
Brown, A. J., 151
browser
    cookies, 34
    default, setting, 43
    privacy settings, 36
    settings, 34
browsing history, 2
Buckner, Stephen, 138
Burlington Northern Santa Fe
        Corporation, 5
Bush Administration, 166

C

Cabir cell phone virus, 24
cable service, 101
California
    Consumer Federation, 125
    Department of Social Services, 139
    In-Home Supportive Services
        program, 139
    privacy protections, 88
    Voter Foundation, 141, 142
Caller ID, 27
    blocking, 27
CampaignMoney.com, 143
Campaign for Reader Privacy's online
        petition, 107
Canizaro, Sue Ellen, 143
CAN SPAM Act of 2003, 23, 49, 62
capture and logging software, 75
CarderPlanet, 163
CareerBuilder.com, 85
Carmack, Howard (Buffalo Spammer),
        49
car rentals, 116
Catalina Marketing Corp., 97
catalogs, 29
Cato Institute, 165
Cavicchia, Peter, 163
Cellular Telecommunications and
        Internet Association
        (CTIA), 23

cell phones
    E911 capable, 8
    eavesdropping, 25
    Enhanced 911 (E911), 23
    moblogs (mobile web logs), 24
    spam, 23
    Video Voyeurism Prevention Act of
        2004, 24
    viruses, 24
    wiretaps, 26
Census Bureau, 138
Center for Business Ethics, The, 76
Center for Democracy and Technology,
        95, 150
challenge/response spam blocking, 48
channels, WiFi, 22
charities, donating old computers, 20
Charter Pacific Bank, 127
ChartOne, 121
checks, information on, 14
ChoicePoint, 6
    data leaks, 166
    hackers and, 9
Church, Ray Everett, 160
Cingular "Find Friends" service, 23
CipherTrust, 159
Citibank, 125
Civil Rights Commission, 167
Claria, 165
Coalition Against Unsolicited
        Commercial Email
        (CAUCE), 45
collection agencies, 128
CollegeNet, 109
college applications, 108
college records, 107
Collins, Judith, 88
commercial databases, 7
company policies on web surfing, 76
Compilation of State and Privacy Laws,
        147
computers
    controlling access to, 14
    impounding, 2
    insecure, 3
    locking, 12
    viewing activity, 2
Computer Assisted Passenger Pre-
        screening System II
        (CAPPS II), 7, 165

Computer Professionals for Social
        Responsibility site, 101
confidentiality laws, 123
Connected's DataProtector service, 17
Constitutional rights, 144
Consumers Against Supermarket Privacy
        Invasion and Numbering
        (CASPIAN), 96
Consumer Privacy Guide, 95
Content Protect, filtering, 66
contests, 14
Controlling the Assault of Non-
        Solicited Pornography and
        Marketing (CAN SPAM), 49
cookies
    managers, 38
    managing, 34, 39
Cool Web Search spyware, 43
Cooper, Jeffrey and Francesca, 143
copyrighted material, swapping, 109
Cornell University Law School's Legal
        Information Institute, 147
Cornez, Arnold, 124
Cornyn, John, 166
Counterexploitation web site, 41
Counterpane Internet Security, 162
CounterSpy, 43
Court Access site, 135
credit cards
    Secure Socket Layer encryption, 58
    skimming, 129
credit card numbers
    buying lists of, 127
    disposable, 59
    on receipts, 96
credit reporting agencies, 30
    contact information, 31
credit reporting laws, 4
credit reports, 14
    checking, 31
    errors, 7
    free, 126
criminal records, expunging, 147
The Crimson White, 130
cyber-security bills, 165
CyberScrub, 21
    Privacy Suite, 16
    Privacy Suite Professional 4.0, 35
CyberSitter, filtering, 66
cyberstalkers, 40
Cyota, 162

D

Daily, Frederick W., 139, 140
Darik's Boot and Nuke, 21
Darkprofits, 163
data brokers, 40, 134
data leaks, 166
data mining companies, 6, 9
Data Privacy and Integrity Advisory
    Committee, 165
data theft, 24
DEA agent, 136
deleted files, 2, 16
deleting files permanently, 16
Department of Agriculture, 166
Department of Education's Family Policy
    Compliance Office, 111
Department of Health and Human
    Services' Office of Civil
    Rights, 123
Department of Homeland Security
    (DHS), 6, 136, 138, 165
Department of Justice, 123
DeWine, Mike, 89
Direct Marketing Association's Mail
    Preference Service, 26, 29
discount cards, 96
Dixon, Pam, 85
DMV (Department of Motor Vehicles),
    101
    records, 139
DNA
    criminal investigations, 148
    database laws, 149
doctors and privacy, 119–123
    doctor/patient confidentiality, 123
Domains by Proxy web site, 70
domain registration information, block-
    ing, 71
domestic surveillance, 154
domestic violence, 103
donating old computers, 20
donating to political cause or
    candidate, 143
Download Manager, 35
Do Not Call List, 26
driver's licenses, 8
    DMV records and, 139
    identity theft (see identity theft)
    legal case involving, 123
    putting number on checks, 14

sharing information, 14
stores requesting information, 96
swiping, 100
swiping barcode, 100
voter registration and, 141
Drivers Protection Privacy Act, 139
DrivingRecord.com web site, 83
Drug Policy Alliance, 110
    web site, 81
drug testing, 81
drug tests, 75, 81
    random, 110
dumpster divers, foiling, 30
DVR, PC-based, 18

E

E911 capable cell phones, 8
Earthlink, 17
    spyware scanner, 42
    toolbar (phish detector), 38
eavesdropping, 25
Edelman, Ben, 42
Edmunds.com, 117
EDRs (Event Data Recorders), 8, 118
Electronic Frontier Foundation (EFF), 95
    web site, 64
electronic passes, 8
Electronic Privacy Information
    Center, 95
email
    addresses, disposable, 45
    attachments, 55
    encrypting, 78, 80
    free web mail and ads, 52
    plain text versus HTML-formatted
        mail, 46
    reputation systems, 158, 160
    scanning, 75
    workplace privacy, 78
    worms, 2
employees
    bill of rights, 90
    employers spying on, 4
    identity theft, 88
    snitching, 75
Employee Polygraph Protection Act, 86
employers
    access to medical records, 91
    illegally collecting data, 5
    spying on employees, 4

Encrypting File System (EFS) tool, 15
encryption, 15
    Microsoft Office, 19
    software, 38
    WiFi, 22
Enhanced 911 (E911), 23
Enigma Anti-Telemarketing software, 27
Environmental Protection Agency, 166
EPIC (Electronic Privacy Information
    Center), 7, 25, 166
    Genetic Privacy page, 149
    web page, 138
    web site, 76
Equifax, 30
    contact information, 31
Erowid web site, 82
essential privacy practices, 14
European countries and privacy, 167
Event Data Recorders (EDRs), 8, 118
Executive Software's Undelete, 16
Expedia, 6
Experian, 30
    contact information, 31
expunging criminal records, 147
EZ Pass, 115

F

F-Secure, 24
FaceTime Communications, 79
Fair and Accurate Credit Transactions
    Act (FACTA), 31, 96
Fair Credit Reporting Act (FCRA), 7, 10,
    84, 166
    financial privacy, 125
    protections, 58
    revised, 82
Fair Debt Collection Practices Act, 128
Fair Information Practice Principles, 7
false positive drug test, 81
Family Educational Rights and Privacy
    Act, 10
Family Educational Rights and Privacy
    Act (FERPA), 107
Family Policy Compliance Office, 111
FasTrak, 115
FAT, 13
FAT32, 13
faxes, 123
    junk, 28

FBI
    Consumer Sentinel site, 27
    FOIA site, 154
    Joint Terrorism Task Force, 155
    phone tapping, 150
FCC, 23
    VoIP vendors and, 25
FEC rules, citizen's guide to, 144
Federal Deposit Insurance Corporation, 126
Federal Election Commission, 143
federal surveillance, 97
Federal Trade Commission's Consumer Sentinel, 128
Federal Trade Commission's Do Not Call List, 26
Federation of American Scientists Project on Government Secrecy, 166
Feders Computer Security Report Card, 136
files
    attachments, 3
    backup, 16
    deleted, 16
    hiding, 15
    private, 13
    sharing, 13
        copyrighted materials, 109
        selective, 21
FileVault, 15
file swapping, 63, 64
    avoiding prosecution, 64
    FBI Cybercrime unit, 63
    legal options, 64
    subpeona search, 64
    Subpoena Defense web site, 64
filtering
    AOL Guardian, 66
    Content Protect, 66
    CyberSitter, 66
    Incredimail, 67
    instant messaging, 68
    Internet Explorer, 65
    Kidmail, 67
    Net Nanny, 66
    Peacefire web site, 66
    using firewall to block specific information, 67
    ZoneAlarm Security Suite, 66

financial institutions and authentication, 161
financial records, 125
Financial Services Modernization Act of 1999, 125
"Find Friends" service, 23
fines, tracking people owing, 129
Firefox, 44
    forms management, 36
    history settings, 34
firewalls, 38, 161
    blocking information going out, 67
FirstGov for Consumers, 95
Florida, Catalina Marketing Corp., 97
flying, 111
    pat-down, 114
    physical searches at airports, 114
folders
    private, 13
    selective sharing, 21
foreign-born students, 108
foreign bank accounts, 124
Foreign Intelligence Surveillance Act (FISA), 25, 150
forms management, 36
Forrester Consulting and Proofpoint survey, 79
FotoLog, 24
Fourth Amendment protections against unlawful search and seizure, 92
Freedom of Information Act, 152, 166
Freedom to Read Protection Act, 107
Freeman, D. Reed, 165
Free Clinic Foundation of America's site, 119
Friery, Tena, 83

G

Garrido, Charmaine, 81
Gartner research group, 3
Gateway Learning privacy policy, 61
Gator Advertising Information Network, 42
Gator adware application, 165
Gator Information Center, 42
Gellman, Robert, 121, 123, 124, 167
George Washington University's National Security Archive, 154

Gibson, Steve, 37
Gillette, 104
Givens, Beth, 4
Global Liberty Internet Campaign, 72
Global Will Registry service, 68
Gmail
    mail accounts and ads, 53
Gnutella, 64
Google, 40
Government Accountability Office, 136, 166
government documents
    secret, 166
GPS (Global Positioning Systems), 8
    tracking devices, 148
    transponder, 116
Gramm-Leach-Bliley Act, 10, 125
Griffin, Rod, 101
grocery stores, 97

H

hackers, 3
    Acxiom, 9
    ChoicePoint, 9
hacker safe logo, 62
hard drives
    reformatting, 20
    snooping, 75
Harper, Jim, 165
Harris, Don, 87
Harris Technical Services, 118
Hasbrouck, Edward, 114, 115
Healthquest Technologies, 130
Health and Human Services department, 166
health cards and Social Security Number, 125
health insurance, 119
Health Insurance Portability and Accountability Act (HIPAA), 91, 119, 120
Health Insurance Portability and Privacy Act., 10
Health Privacy Project, 91, 95, 120, 121
Hells Angels Motorcycle Club, 148
Help America Vote Act of 2002, 141
Henry J. Kaiser Family Foundation's State Health Facts web site, 119
Hibbert, Chris, 101

hiding files, 15
hijacking browsers, 165
history settings, 34
HIV, being tested for, 119
home address, 14
Hoofnagle, Chris, 8, 25
Hoover, J. Edgar, 165
hospital stays, 121
Hotmail accounts and ads, 53
HR Privacy Solutions, 87
HR Privacy Solutions web site, 85
Hurd, David, 148
Hushmail
    encrypted email, 78
    encryption, 38
Hush Messenger encrypted instant
        messaging, 80

I

I-PASS, 115
I-SPY Prevention Act of 2005, 165
identity theft, 4, 30–32, 62
    black market, 163
    free credit reports, 126
    Global Will Registry service, 68
    insulating, 162
    in the workplace, 88
    recovering from, 32
    requesting new SSN, 103
    statistics, 32
Identity Theft Crime Lab, 88
Identity Theft Resource Center, 32
Identity Theft Resource Center web
        site, 68
impairment testing versus drug
        screening, 81
IMpasse encrypted instant messaging,
        80
IM Auditor, 79
Incredimail, filtering, 67
information sharing, 5, 14
Information Technology Association of
        America's RFID page, 98
Innovis, 30
    contact information, 31
insecure machines, 3
instant messaging
    encrypting, 79
    filtering, 68

monitoring, 79
    workplace privacy, 79
Intelius, 40
    web site, 83
Internet
    at work, 74
    moblogs (mobile web logs), 24
    savvy, 14
Internet2's Shibboleth Project, 163
Internet Content Ratings Association,
        65
Internet Corporation for Assigned
        Names and Numbers
        (ICANN) web site, 70
Internet Engineering Task Force, 160
Internet Explorer
    Content Advisor filtering, 65
    deleting files in cache, 35
    forms management, 36
    history settings, 34
    U.S. Computer Emergency Readiness
        Team cautions against, 44
Internet Fraud Complaint Center, 150
Internet Security Barrier, 43
invasion of privacy, US government, 136
IP addresses, blacklists of, 159
IronPort's SenderBase, 158, 160
IRS (Internal Revenue Service), 139
    employees, 136
    Taxpayer Rights page, 140

J

Jacobsen, Nicholas, 163
Jiiva AutoScrubber, 16, 43
job hunting at work, 80
Junkbusters, 27, 95
    Declarations Form, 30
junk mail, 29

K

Kahn, Dan, 117
Kaspersky Labs, 24
keylogger, 3
keylogging programs, 78
Kidmail, filtering, 67
Kleinrock, Len, 162
KnowX, 40

L

Lane, Frederick S., III, 79, 90
Lane, Smith Alling, 148
laws
    of all 50 states, 147
    state truncation, 96
law enforcement, local, 144–149
Leahy, Pat, 166
legal rights, 14
Levine, John, 160
LexisNexis
    data leaks, 166
libel and blogging, 71
libraries and schools, 104–111
Library, Bookseller, and Personal Records
        Privacy Act, 107
library computers, 104, 105
library privacy policies and procedures,
        106
library records, 105
    fines on late books, 106
Lieberman, Denise, 155
lie detector test, 86
Lilly, Eli, 122
Limited Liability Corporation, 140
limited user account, 12
locking computers, 12
logons, password-protected, 12
loyalty programs, 96
Lycos WhoWhere, 40
Lyons, Philip Scott, 8, 97

M

Mac firewall settings, 54
Mac OS X
    encryption, 15
    FileVault, 15
    file sharing, 13
    sharing files and folders, 22
Mac spyware security, 43
magazines, 29
mail
    junk, 29
    selective, 30
MailFrontier Desktop, 38
Mail Frontier Desktop, spam
        filtering and, 47
MAKE magazine, 101
Maltby, Lewis, 74, 89

malware, 3, 54
Mamakos, Louis, 25
Man in the Middle (MIM) attacks, 162
Marx, Andreas, 56
McGuinn, David, 126
McNealy, Scott, 1
Media Access Control (MAC)
    address, 22
Medical Information Bureau, 122
medical records, 94, 119, 121
    accidently sharing, 123
    doctor/patient confidentiality, 123
    employer access to, 91
    Health Insurance Portability and
        Privacy Act., 10
    transferring, 123
Mercedes Benz, telematics, 116
MessageLabs, 158
Michigan State University, 4
Microsoft Network, 17
Microsoft Office
    encryption, 19
Microsoft Windows AntiSpyware, 43
Miller vs. U.S., 5
MIMESweeper email scanner, 75
Miranda warning, 144
moblogs (mobile web logs), 24
monitoring employee web surfing, 74
Monster.com, 85
Motion Picture Association of America
    (MPAA), 63
movie rentals, 103
multiple users, 12

N

Napster, 109
National Business Ethics Survey, 75
National Change of Address (NCOA)
    form, 135
National Conference of State
    Legislatures (NCSL), 81
National Intelligence Reform Act, 145
National Rifle Association, 141
National Transportation Safety
    Board, 8, 118
National Voter Registration Act of
    1993, 141
National Workrights Institute
    web site, 74
Nelson, David C., 111

NetNanny web monitor, 38
netReplay software, 78
Netscape
    cookies, managing, 34
    deleting files in cache, 35
    forms management, 36
    history, deleting, 36
    mail accounts and ads, 52
networks, wireless (see wireless
        networks, hacking)
Network Solutions, Inc. (NSI), 70
Net Nanny, filtering, 66
Net Stumbler, 21
Nissarian, Barmack, 108
no-fly lists, 111
    No Fly/Watchlist Complaint
        Form, 112
Noble, Larry, 143
North Carolina State Board of
    Elections, 142
Norton AntiVirus 2005, 38
Norton Internet Security, 43
Norton SystemWorks 2005, 21
No Child Left Behind Act, 111
No Electronic Theft Act, 63
NTFS, 13

O

O'Carroll, Derek, 80
"one-party" rules, 26
online
    directories, 14
    purchases, 2
    storage space, 17
OnStar, 8, 116
opensecrets.org, 143
Operation Firewall, 163
opt in versus opt out, 62
Orbitz, 6
Osco, 122

P

P2P virus, 64
Pam Dixon's Job Search Privacy site, 85
Passenger Name Records, 114, 115
PassMark, 161
passports, 8
passwords
    general rules, 17
    Microsoft Office, 19

password-protected logon, 12
password protecting screensaver, 12
pat-down, 114
patient directories, 121
Patriot Act, 137, 152, 153
    reading about, 107
PayPal accounts, 59
PC-based DVR, 18
PC Pitstop, 3
Peacefire web site, 66
pen register, 150
PeopleData, opting out, 41
permanently deleting files, 16
Perry, Bob, 143
personal data
    business inquiries, 94
    insulating, 162
    movie rentals, 103
personal information, sharing, 14
personal privacy, 167
    in Washington, D.C, 165
personal searches, 75
personnel records, 86
    secured, 84
PestPatrol spyware scanner, 42
PGP 8.1, 78
PGP Personal Desktop, 78
pharmaceutical companies, 121, 122
pharmaceutical profiling, 97
phisher
    email, 3, 48
    scams, 126, 158
        foiling, 160
    (see also Anti-Phishing Act of 2005)
phish detectors, 38
phone
    and address directories, unlisting, 39
    recording, 75
    tapping, 150
phonebooks, 14
phone number, 94
PhotoBlocker, 117
Photo Fog, 117
Photo Stopper, 117
physical searches at airports, 114
PKZIP, 16
Pointsec Mobile Technologies, 20
police, 144–149
    attaching GPS tracking devices to
        vehicles without authori-
        zation from a court, 8, 148

police (*continued*)
  clearing arrest records, 146, 147
  demanding identification, 144
  DNA for criminal investigation, 148
  national IDs, 145
  sealing arrest records, 147
policies, privacy at work, 74
PoliticalMoneyLine.com, 143
political cause or candidate, donating
      to, 143
Politics, Center for Responsive, 143
Ponemon, Larry, 94, 97, 129
Ponemon Institute's Privacy Trust
      Surveys, 97
pop-up blockers, 38, 41
pornography, 77
postage stamps, 135
Post Office box, 14
preference settings, 34
prescriptions, 121
Pretty Good Privacy (PGP)
      encryption, 78
Princeton Review, 109
priority ring, 27
Privacilla, 165
privacy
  at risk, 1–10
    viewing computer activity, 2
  banks and, 124–127
  doctors and, 119–123
  European countries and, 167
  guards, 38
  libraries and schools, 104–111
  personal, 167
  personal, in Washington, D.C, 165
  policies, 59, 61
  practices, 14
  retail and, 94–103
  state-by-state guide to retail privacy
      laws, 94
  state and federal laws, 146
  traveling and, 111–117
  web sites, 95
  workplace, 73–92
Privacy Act of 1974, 10
privacy disclosure, 123
Privacy Guard, 21
Privacy Guardian for Windows, 35

Privacy International, 95
Privacy Journal, 95, 147
Privacy Rights Clearinghouse
      (PRC), 4, 82, 95, 134
  Albertsons' pharmacy, 122
  fact sheet, 32
  protecting SSN, 101
  state-by-state guide to retail privacy
      laws, 94
  web site, 29
private
  files and folders, 13
  information versus public
      records, 134
  mail drop, 14
  sector privacy rights, 91
Proctor & Gamble, 104
products with RFID chips, 98
product warranty protection, 128
Protecting Intellectual Rights Against
      Theft and Expropriation
      (PIRATE) Act of 2004
      (S.2237), 63
Prozac, 122
Public Access to Court Electronic
      Records (PACER)
      service, 147
public computers, 104
Public Interest Research Group, 125
Public Proxy Servers web site, 76
public records
  laws, 6
  versus private information, 134
Public Record Finder web site, 52
Public Research Interest Group, 128
  web site, 83
public voter rolls, 142
purchase histories, analyzing, 7

Q

Qurb (spam filter), 38, 159
  spam filtering and, 47

R

racial profiling, 97, 112
Real ID Act, 145
receipts, 96

Recreational Software Advisory Council
      (RASCi), 65
reformatting hard drive, 20
The Register, 77
Registered Traveler program, 113
rental cars, 116
ReplayTV, 18
reputation systems, 158, 160
restricting access to public records, 134
résumés, 85
retail privacy, 94, 94–103
RFID (Radio Frequency Identification),
      8, 98
  common uses, 99
  EZ Pass, 115
  transmitter, 102
RFID Journal, 98
RIAA
  Privacy Resolutions PC page, 63
  Radar web site, 64
  Recording Industry Association of
      America, 63
  Remix CD, 64
Ridge, Tom, 7
Rivera, Robert, 97
Roberti, Mark, 98
Robertson, April, 121
Rolls Royce, telematics, 116
Rowe, Mark, 77
RSA Security, 161

S

SafeSurf IE plug-in, 65
Safeway Club Card, 8
safe deposit boxes, 126, 127
Safe Deposit Specialists, 126
Safe Teens web site, 68
Sanders, Bernie, 107
Save-On, 122
scammers, 27
Scannell, Bill, 167
Scarfo, Nicodemo S., 137
Schaeffer, Rebecca, 139
Schiavone, Vincent, 160
Schneier, Bruce, 162, 166, 167
schools and libraries, 104–111
school disciplinary records, 110
screensavers, password protecting, 12

Search Systems web site, 52
Secretary of State, 125
secret government documents, 166
Securely Protect Yourself Against Cyber
        Trespass Act (or "SPY
        ACT"), 165
SecureZIP, 17
Secure Flight, 166
Secure Socket Layer (SSL)
        encryption, 61
security suites, 38
Sender Policy Framework, 158
Sender Policy Framework (SPF), 159
sensitive data on old computers, 20
Shadowcrew, 163
sharing information, 14
Sheridan, Gavin, 71
Shibboleth, 163
ShieldsUP web site, 53
Shoot The Messenger applet, 44
shoulder surfing, 105
Sierra Club, 141
Silverman, Scott, 102
simple mail transfer protocol (SMTP),
        160
Singer, Brooke, 101
skimming, 129
Smith, Robert Ellis, 145
SMTP (simple mail transfer protocol),
        160
sniffer, web monitoring, 78
snooping, 13
Snopes Urban Legends web site, 52
Sober worm, 150
Social Security Administration's
        site, 101
Social Security Number, 101
    health cards and, 125
    political privacy and, 141
    requesting new, 103
    résumés, 85
    sharing information, 14, 101
    stores requesting information, 96
    voter registration and, 141
    ZoneAlarm and, 67
Society for Human Resource
        Management, 92
The Society for Human Resource
        Management, 4
Soden, Michael, 77
software warranty protection, 128

SonicBlue, 18
Soros, George, 143
spam, 45
    cell phones, 23
    filtering, 47
    legitimate, 61
    phisher scams, 158
    stopping, 158
    suing spammers, 49
spamBlocker spam blocking, 48
The Spamhaus Project, 158
SpamSieve, 43
Spam Arrest, spam blocking, 48
spam filters, 38
speed-radar traffic camera, 117
speeding, 116
SpoofStick toolbar, anti-phisher, 50
Spybot Search and Destroy, 42
spying, employers spying on
        employees, 4
spyware, 3, 41, 165
SSID (Service Set Identifier), 22
stamps, postage, 135
Stanfield, Shelby, 108
state-issued IDs, 145
state and federal privacy laws, 146
state laws, 147
state truncation laws, 96
STOPZilla pop-up blocker, 38
Stop RFID site, 100
stores and privacy, 94–103
students and extracurricular
        activities, 110
Student and Exchange Visitor
        Information System
        (SEVIS), 108
student directories, 108
Styn, Ronald L., 117
Subpoena Defense web site, 64
Sub S Corporation, 140
Sunbelt Software's CounterSpy, 38
SurfControl software, 75
surveillance, 154
    cams, 75, 92
    equipment, 25
The Surveillance-Industrial
        Complex, 151
surveys, 14
swapping copyrighted material, 109
Sweeney, Latanya, 138
sweepstakes, 14

SWIPE, 100, 101
swipe cards, 100
Swire, Peter, 167
Switchboard.com, 40
Symantec, 3, 21
Symantec's early warning system, 161

T

tagging individual products, 98
Taves, Kenneth, 127
tax audit, 139
Tax Counseling for the Elderly (TCE),
        140
Technical Job Search web site, 86
Tech Law Advisor blog, 63
telemarketers, 26
    ways to avoid, 27
telematics
    manufacturers, 116
    systems, 8
Telephone Consumer Protection Act of
        1991, 10, 28
temp folders, deleting, 35
TerraServer, 40
Terrorism Information and Prevention
        System (TIPS), 151
terrorists, 114
Texas Public Information Act, 108
TextAmerica, 24
The Tin Drum, 103
TiVos, 18
toiletcams, 92
toll-free numbers, 28
toll booths, 115
Tombros, Nicholas, 49
traffic cameras, 117
Transportation Safety Agency (TSA), 165
Transportation Security Administration,
        111
    Office of Civil Rights, 114
    Registered Traveler fact sheet, 113
    Registered Traveler program, 113
TransUnion, 30
    contact information, 31
traveling and privacy, 111–117
    automobile surveillance, 118
    bag inspection, 112, 113
    car rental, 116
    GPS-based directional systems, 116
    no-fly lists, 111

traveling and privacy (*continued*)
    passenger name record (PNR), 115
    pat downs, 114
    Registered Traveler program, 113
    traffic cameras, 117
Travelocity, 6
Trojan Horse
    defined, 54
    exploits, 162
    programs used in cybercrimes, 55
TSA (Security Administration), x
two-factor authentication, 160

U

U.S. census, 138
U.S. Department of Education, 111
U.S. Department of Health and Human
    Services' Office of Civil
    Rights, 120
U.S. Department of Health and Human
    Services Office for Civil
    Rights web site, 91
U.S. Department of Justice, 151
U.S. Immigration and Customs
    Enforcement, 108
U.S. Postal Service, 135
U.S. privacy laws, 14
U.S. Public Interest Research Group
    study, 7
U.S. Search, 40
U.S. Secret Service's Operation Firewall,
    163
U.S. Treasury Department, 140
Undelete, 16
Unique Management Services, 106
United States Chamber of
    Commerce, 143
Universal Music Group, 109
University of Nebraska Police
    Professionalism Initiative,
    148
unlawful questions, handling, 84
unsubscribing, 62
USA Patriot Act (see Patriot Act)
USA Today, 3
users
    limited user accounts, 12
    multiple, 12
US Search web site, 83

V

VeriChip, 102
videotaping public areas, 129
Video Voyeurism Prevention Act of
    2004, 24
Violent Crime Control and Law
    Enforcement Act of 1994,
    139
virus, defined, 54
viruses, 2, 24
    antivirus software, 56
    Bagle worm, 57
    Cabir virus, 24
    cell phones, 24
    file attachments, 55
    infecting others, 57
    instant messaging, 80
    overview, 54
    P2P, 64
    scanners, 57
    Trojans, 54
    worms, 54
    zombies, 53
Virus Information Library web site, 64
Vivendi Universal Entertainment, 109
voice mail, 27
voice over IP phone (VoIP), 150
Volunteer Income Tax Assistance (VITA),
    140
voter registration information, 142–144
voter registration records, 141
voter rolls, 142

W

Wal-Mart, 5, 104
Walgreens, 122
Walker, Sam, 148
Walls, John, 23
Wall Street Journal, 6
wardriving, 21
warranty protection of products, 128
watch-lists, 137
WebRoot's Spy Sweeper, 38
Websense software, 75
web bugs in email, 52
Web Bug Detector software, 52
Web monitoring, 75
web monitors, 38
web site privacy, 95

web surfing using company
    equipment, 77
whitelists, 48
Whitepages.com, 40
Whois database, 70
WhoWhere, Lycos, 40
WiFi
    encryption, 22
    hacking, 21
    securing networks, 22
    sharing files and folders, 22
WiFi Protected Access (WPA), 22
WinBackUp, 16
Windows
    hiding files, 15
Windows Firewall, 54
Windows Media Center PC, 18
Windows Messenger Service spam, 44
Windows XP
    encryption, 15
    sharing files and folders, 21
Windows XP Home
    protecting individual files, 15
Windows XP Service Pack 2, 56, 161
WinGuides' Privacy Guardian 3.0, 16
Wired Teens web site, 68
Wireless Encryption Protocol (WEP), 22
wireless networks, hacking, 21
wiretaps, 26
    authorized, 25
wire tapping, 150
Wizmark, 130
Workplace Fairness web site, 91
workplace privacy, 73–92
    Australia, 87
    background checks, 82
    blogging, 89
    drug testing, 81
    email, 78
    Employee Bill of Rights, 90
    employee ID theft, 88
    employer searching offices, 92
    employer snooping on PC, 77
    Fair Credit Reporting Act, 84
    federal rights, 91
    HR files, 87
    instant messaging, 79
    invasive questions, 84
    IT spies, 79
    job hunting, 80
    lie detector test, 86

medical records, 91
monitoring calls for quality
assurance, 89
monitoring employee web activity,
74
personnel files, 86
pornography, 77
recreational web surfing, 76
surveillance cameras, 92
ten ways bosses can spy on you, 75
Work Number, The (web site), 87
World Privacy Forum, 126
World Privacy Forum report, 85
worm, defined, 54
Wright, Don, 142

Y

Yahoo, 17
mail accounts and ads, 53
Yahoo DomainKeys, 158, 159
Yahoo people search, 40

Z

zip code, 94
Zix Corp, 120
ZoEmail, temporary email addresses, 45
zombies, 53, 161
zombie PCs, 3
ZoneAlarm Pro, 54
ZoneAlarm Security Suite, 38
filtering, 66

Colophon

Our look is the result of reader comments, our own experimentation, and feedback from distribution channels. Distinctive covers complement our distinctive approach to technical topics, breathing personality and life into potentially dry subjects.

Philip Dangler was the production editor and proofreader for *Computer Privacy Annoyances.* Derek Di Matteo was the copyeditor. Philip Dangler did the typesetting and page makeup. Phyllis McKee, Mary Brady, and Claire Cloutier provided quality control. Julie Hawks wrote the index.

The cover design is based on a series design by Volume Design, Inc. Ellie Volckhausen designed the cover with Adobe InDesign CS. Karen Montgomery produced the cover layout with Adobe InDesign CS using Gravur Condensed and Adobe's Sabon font.

Patti Capaldi designed the interior layout using Adobe InDesign CS. The text and heading fonts are Rotis Sans Serif, Lineto Gravur, and Myriad Pro; the code font is The Sans Mono Condensed. Joe Wizda converted the text to Adobe InDesign CS. The screenshots and technical illustrations that appear in the book were produced by Robert Romano amd Jessamyn Read using Macromedia Freehand MX and Adobe Photoshop 7. The cartoon illustrations used on the cover and in the interior of this book are copyright © 2005 Hal Mayforth.

Better than e-books

Buy *Computer Privacy Annoyances* and access
the digital edition FREE on Safari for 45 days.

Go to www.oreilly.com/go/safarienabled
and type in coupon code KDI8-AZQG-ZRWK-XGG1-2K6H

Search
over 2000 top tech books

Download
whole chapters

Cut and Paste
code examples

Find
answers fast

Search Safari! The premier electronic reference
library for programmers and IT professionals

Kee~ ~ O'Reilly

FEB 0 3 2006

Download example

To find example files
www.oreilly.com/catal
and follow the "Exan

Register your O'Rei

Register your bool
Why register your bc
registered your O'Rei

- Win O'Reilly book
  coupons in our m

- Get special offers
  registered O'Reilly

- Get catalogs anno
  (US and UK only).

- Get email notifical
  of the O'Reilly bo

Join our email lists

Sign up to get topic-s
new books and confe
special offers, and O'
technology newslette

elists.oreilly.com

It's easy to customize
you'll get exactly the
you want.

Get the latest news

www.oreilly.com

- "Top 100 Sites on the web —PC Magazine

- CIO Magazine's Web Business 50 Awards

Our web site contains a library of comprehensive
product information (including book excerpts and
tables of contents), downloadable software, background articles, interviews with technology leaders,
links to relevant sites, book cover art, and more.

Work for O'Reilly

Check out our web site for current
employment opportunities:

jobs.oreilly.com

Contact us

O'Reilly Media, Inc.
1005 Gravenstein Hwy North
Sebastopol, CA 95472 USA
Tel: 707-827-7000 or 800-998-9938
     (6am to 5pm PST)

ns regarding
ucts:

ur latest catalog: **catalog@oreilly.**

nical questions
h@oreilly.com

y, government,
orporate@oreilly.com

roposals to our
anagers:

our international
on queries:

academic

utors outside
k out:
/distributors.html

new

O'REILLY®

Our books are available at most retail and online bookstores.
To order direct: 1-800-998-9938 • *order@oreilly.com* • *www.oreilly.com*
Online editions of most O'Reilly titles are available by subscription at *safari.oreilly.com*